Ax

Mrs. R. D. Nicklin
846 Liberty Street
Franklin, Pennsylvania

1st ed

S —
m

Pathway of Empire

To the hundreds of thousands of foreigners who have entered New York Harbor during the last half century Bartholdi's famous statue has been the symbol of a newer and richer life.

Pathway of Empire

BY EDWARD HUNGERFORD

WITH AN INTRODUCTION BY DIXON RYAN FOX,
PRESIDENT OF THE NEW YORK
STATE HISTORICAL ASSOCIATION

ILLUSTRATED

New York
ROBERT M. McBRIDE & COMPANY

PATHWAY OF EMPIRE
COPYRIGHT, 1935
BY EDWARD HUNGERFORD
PRINTED IN THE UNITED STATES
OF AMERICA
FIRST EDITION

For Anne

CONTENTS

		PAGE
	FOREWORD	xi
	PREFACE	xv

CHAPTER		
I.	BY WAY OF INTRODUCTION	3
II.	THE BIG CITY	17
III.	THE HUDSON FLOWS TO THE SEA	45
IV.	THE MOHAWK FLOWS TO THE HUDSON	79
V.	CENTRAL NEW YORK—EMPIRE OF BEAUTY	112
VI.	THE FINGER LAKES COUNTRY	132
VII.	THE GENESEE FLOWS GRANDLY TO THE NORTH	156
VIII.	SENTINEL STANDS THE WESTERN GATEWAY	188
IX.	SOUTHERN TIER	217
X.	NORTH COUNTRY	245
XI.	THE LADY OF THE SNOWS	267
XII.	THE LONG ISLAND	302

ILLUSTRATIONS

The Symbol of a Newer and Richer Life   *Frontispiece*

                                        PAGE

Lower Manhattan as Viewed from an Aeroplane   16

Central Park, the First of America's Great Public Recreation Centers   17

Forty-four Stories above the Street   32

The Lower East Side of Manhattan Island   33

Chinatown, a Favorite Spot for Tourists   33

The Plaza before the New York Public Library   40

Union Square East   41

The Sidewalks of New York   41

In Beauty and Dignity Few American Colleges Surpass Those of New York State   160

Some of New York's Waterfalls   161

ILLUSTRATIONS

	PAGE
A Few Picturesque Covered Bridges Still Survive	176
For Charming Bits of Architecture Look at New York's Village Churches	177
New York is Heavily Dotted with Points of Historical Interest	288
Nothing Suggests the Rich Tradition of New York State More Readily than Its Old Houses	289
The Protestant Episcopal Cathedral at Garden City	304
The Light at Montauk Point is Visible for Nineteen Miles	304
Jones Beach is the Largest and Most Attractive Beach in the World	305

FOREWORD

$\mathfrak{I}$N writing *The Pathway of Empire* I think Edward Hungerford has done more for New York State than if he had presented it with a million-dollar bridge or set up an industry employing many families. The rich state can build great engineering works, and geographical strategy will assure it industries. What it needs most for its own enjoyment is state sentiment, state pride. Community sentiment—the prevalent sense of pleasant and exclusive partnership in certain values and the common recognition of common responsibilities—cannot be suddenly and artificially created. No evangelistic zeal could develop that sentiment unless there was a solid base for it. To many of us there seems to be a sound basis for an affectionate pride in New York State, and yet, by and large, state sentiment in New York is only a faint shadow of what it might and should be. Some of the applause that will greet this book will come from those who love New York and, like all enthusiasts, eagerly hope that an increasing number can be brought to share their sentiment.

There are rather obvious reasons why this state has not commanded a special affection from the many hundreds of thousands who live within it, some of these reasons applying respectively to other states as well. Through the rapid word and the almost equally swift means of travel, we know as much of other regions as of our own. Partly from the same causes our personal concerns merge more and more in those of the government in Washington. In the light of these impersonal tendencies, with increasing national consciousness and loyalty, state spirit seems to many as anachronism. So it should be if and where the state is a mere geographical convenience of administration. But where there is an integral and individual history behind it, where its people have peculiar common interests, where, if not homogeneity, there may be discerned general elements of cultural color, life would be much poorer for the disappearance of this feeling.

Does Mr. Hungerford reveal a basis for state spirit? He pretends to no such thesis in his book, yet oftentimes results have no relation to intention. If we were to put the question a little differently it might be more easily answered: What is a Yorker? This word which was common enough down to the days of Fenimore Cooper has now passed out of usage. Has all it stood for passed out too? The answer is that Mr. Hungerford is a Yorker, and along with his picture of New York he has, by indirection and no doubt unconsciously, painted a portrait of the Yorker type.

A Yorker is very different from what is now known as a New Yorker, proud of his own urban insularity. Mr. Hungerford writes with understanding and affection of every part of the state. Obviously he is at home in every county of New York and would not be entirely at home anywhere else. Bathing in the glow of his enthusiasm we recall that we have known other men and women somewhat like him in this regard, though few with his breadth of knowledge of his homeland. There are Yorkers still, and the whole state can be encompassed in a man's heart.

Yet true as this may be, the book well indicates divisive factors in the state. Were its chapters spaced according to population, six out of the eleven would be given to the metropolis; instead, there is one. The fact is that New York City does not belong peculiarly to New York State. A man from Kingston or a man from Canandaigua walking up 5TH Avenue no more feels that he is on his own soil than one from New Haven or even one from Denver. The city belongs to the nation. Had the capital of the state remained in New York City, the situation would have been very different. But by the demand of dominant agricultural interests no great city is now the capital of its state, except Boston. Conversely Boston is the most state-minded of great cities. Only there is to be found a relationship between metropolis-capital and countryside remotely like that found generally in European countries. Our important cities are generally found at the edges of the states, because the states are generally bordered by waterways. Like Chicago, New York City is set in an extreme corner of the state, but much more than Chicago it has important interior competitors around which the state's life naturally revolves.

Politically, of course, the great city is interlocked with the upstate counties and must study rural opinion, but that, for the most part, concerns only the small class of professional politicians. The city's water supply is largely from the hills of its own state, but its myriad citizens do not drink in state consciousness with state water. The summer home and garden that contrast with the avenue apartment, are quite as likely to be in New England as upstate. But there is a large racial group of city dwellers, not deeply rooted in our past, who now take vacation in the Sullivan hills, the Catskills, Sharon Springs, Saratoga, and in certain parts of the Adirondacks, and by this acquaintance with charming rural scenery they may develop an affectionate regard not unimportant in the sentiment of the state.

It is about a hundred and fifteen years since men began to talk about the Empire State, and now, more than then, it is imperial in its diversity as well as in its wealth and prestige. As in landscape, so in economic and social interests the sections seem sharply different. Those who, like Mr. Hungerford, have long roamed the whole state find a fundamental cohesion that is easier to feel than to explain; perhaps its strongest ties come out of a long history. But there is no dreary monotony; in most sections of the state a ride of fifty miles takes one to very different outlooks, scenic and social.

Lacking precedent and model, but opulent in the resources of his memory and observation; speaking with special authority on transportation and industry, but broadly grounded in the humane traditions of the state; clear-headed and acute in judgment, yet warmed by an old affection for the land and its people, Mr. Hungerford has written a revelation of New York new to native and stranger alike. It is charmingly discursive, lingering where the author cares to linger, with no tyranny of precise apportionment. Animated, but not ebullient, in style—fresh without being "fresh"—the book carries the reader from chapter to chapter in the companionship of a delightful personality.

DIXON RYAN FOX

Union College,
August, 1935.

PREFACE

So many people have helped me in the preparation of this book that it is difficult to pick out by name even those who have been most helpful. However, I would be remiss if I did not refer at least to Dr. Dixon Ryan Fox of Union College, Schenectady; Dr. Livingston Farrand, President, Cornell University; Dr. Rush Rhees, former president of the University of Rochester; Mr. Edward S. Jarrett, Acting President, Rensselaer Polytechnic Institute at Troy; Mr. W. E. Beazell of Saratoga, Mr. F. B. Richards of Glens Falls, Mr. George H. Foote of Port Henry, Dr. Godfrey Dewey of Lake Placid, Dr. John B. Howe of Skaneateles, Mr. Samuel Hopkins Adams of Auburn, Messrs. E. R. Foreman and Paul Favour of Rochester, Mrs. John G. Wickser and Mr. Alexander Osborne of Buffalo, Mr. J. Arnold Rathbone and Mr. Jarvis Langdon of Elmira.

I should like to give a special credit and word of thanks to my aides who have worked with me so faithfully in the production of the book: Mr. Peter Nelson of Albany, Miss Veronica Kelly and Miss Elsie Scott of this city.

This book does not aim to be history. It merely endeavors in a very simple manner to give a picture of New York State of today, with as much historical background as is essential to a painting of the picture.

E. H.

Pathway
of
Empire

CHAPTER I

By Way of Introduction

STRETCHING from the Atlantic Ocean to the Great Lakes, from one of the busiest harbors in the world to the waters of the St. Lawrence, covered with glorious hills and mountains, yet containing the most amazing city the world has ever known—this is New York, well named the Empire State. It is a far-reaching commonwealth, within whose miles of area there lie many great cities, many towns, large and small, broad lakes and beautiful rivers, swift and powerful and navigable; an astounding variety of scenery of every sort—from the miles of broad, white sandy beach along the south edge of Long Island to the deep gorge and eternal cataract of Niagara. There is plenty of fertile country, broad fat farms whose luxurious growth proclaims their abundance, and in between these and the cities and the towns, great areas of wilderness.

There is at times a broad rift between metropolitan New York and upstate. This divergence of thought and of action is reflected in many ways. For instance, politically one of the great national parties usually controls the city of New York; its traditional rival is strongly entrenched in the rural regions upstate. Once in four years or less the opposing forces come to the scratch in the battle of the ballots.

Either the Democratic city of New York wins the fight, or else it is won north of the Harlem River by the Republican legions, whose votes come swarming down to that traditional boundary line. Between elections the fight goes on endlessly at Albany. Metropolitan New York, by the force of its numbers, its power, and its wealth, seeks sometimes to dominate the entire state. The rural districts resent this. Yet, sometimes, in their very resentment they, too, grow arrogant and a bit unfair as well. But that is almost always the way of politics.

The upstater who goes at the close of day to the Grand Central in the Big City and thence to the *Ohio State,* or any other of the many fast expresses that stand waiting within its trainshed to bear him to his native Utica or Rochester or Buffalo, drops much of his New York manner once he is off and away from Manhattan Island. He quickly becomes Utica or Rochester or Buffalo again. His frequent pilgrimages to the Big City, pious or otherwise, are eagerly anticipated, feverishly enjoyed. For the time being he is as much a metropolitan as the man who was born in the house in which he lives on the north side of Washington Square, and who admits to being over seventy. The New Yorker from upstate shares this man's clubs, his restaurants, his theaters, his pleasures of every sort, and takes good care to see that no one shall even suspect that he is "upstate." It is only when he returns to his native heath that again he becomes chauvinistic. Then he may even speak scornfully of the Big City. But the scorn is generally spoken with the tongue at least partly in the cheek.

Between the extremes of your somewhat typical resident of Manhattan Island or its environs who knows or cares of little beyond the North River or the Harlem and your thoroughgoing native of St. Lawrence County or Otsego or Steuben, there is seemingly a great gulf. And yet it is a gulf that upon occasion, or necessity, may be bridged, and quickly. When the need arises, the entire great state of New York, with its population of some twelve million souls, can act as a powerful unit. Some large political forces that lie without the state have found that out—sometimes to their own discomfiture.

Geographically it is a sprawling state; its political boundaries have left it uncouth in form. If one follows the natural pathways of travel across the state from the far east end, he will go from Montauk Point at the tip of Long Island—the hand of that arm that reaches into the salt waters of the Atlantic—to an orchard on the shore of Lake Erie, west of Dunkirk, and he will have gone more than six hundred miles by the odometer. One hundred miles of it will be up the backbone of Long Island. The next one hundred and fifty miles will be up the historic valley of the Hudson to the state's capital town, Albany. At Albany this traditional pathway makes a right-angled turn, from due north to due west. The Hudson disappears off toward the mountains of the north, and one now finds himself ascending the valley of the Mohawk. At Rome, a hundred miles from Albany, good-bys are said to the Mohawk, and thereafter until one comes within sight of the waters of that inland sea, Ontario, it is cross-country travel, breasting important north-running streams all the way to the important city of Buffalo (three hundred miles from Albany) and the Niagara frontier. From here to the Pennsylvania line at the edge of Lake Erie, the extreme westernmost point of the state of New York, there are about sixty more miles.

Here is the natural, the historic, the traditional pathway across the state. One gains respect for its importance when he discovers that between New York and Buffalo alone, within a belt not exceeding at any point twenty miles in width, are six out of the seven large metropolitan areas of the state, most of its great and dominating industries, eighty-four per cent of its population and more than this of its wealth. The answer to this rather astonishing showing is transportation. From earliest days here was the easiest pathway across the state, and consequently the natural one. None other along the entire seaboard is quite like it. This pathway stretched itself between the Atlantic at the safe and accessible harbor of Dutch New Amsterdam to the vast and little-known terrain that surrounded the fifteen-hundred-mile chain of easily navigable inland seas, known as the Great Lakes. From New Amsterdam (soon to become the British port of New York) to Albany was easy passage up a broad and navigable river. The Mohawk was not as broad and not nearly as navigable as the Hudson, but it served for small *bateaux* and at about the time that the British port of New York became the American city and port of New York, men already were at work easing the passage of these *bateaux* through the valley of the Mohawk by building crude locks of stone at Little Falls, its narrowest and most difficult portion.

From Rome—at first, Fort Stanwix—there was an easy carry over level land for comparatively sizable boats for a brief eight or ten miles and then the wide waters of Oneida Lake, leading into the Oswego River and down that river to the port of Oswego. Then you were on the waters of Ontario itself. The Niagara River formed a terrific barrier to navigation between Ontario and the upper lakes. But men strove to find the way to overcome that. And not long after the end of the second war with England, the first Welland Canal, reaching across a jutting point of lower Canada and connecting the waters of Lake Ontario with those of Erie, was in active and successful operation. Long before that time highway transportation had been well developed all the way across the state, from New York north over the historic and still much used Albany Post Road; from Albany west through the Mohawk Valley highways or else over the Cherry Valley and the Genesee turnpikes, which straddled the high hills to the south of that valley and so avoided at times flood and other disagreeable travel conditions. These main thoroughfares ran rather closely parallel to each other, all the way across the state from Albany to the Niagara frontier. On the one to the south sprang up the earlier towns of importance—Richfield Springs (with Cooperstown closely adjacent), Auburn, Geneva, Canandaigua, Avon, Batavia. It had its terminus at Buffalo, at the extreme foot of Lake Erie, where shipping could ascend the entire length of the upper four Great Lakes.

On the Mohawk Valley route grew Schenectady and Utica and Rome and eventually Syracuse and Rochester. It really terminated at Niagara Falls, although at Rochester one might take his choice of coaching routes, west over the Ridge Road to Niagara, or southwest to Batavia and the Genesee Turnpike through to Buffalo and beyond. In similar fashion, the Genesee Turnpike officially reached out of Utica.

These were then important roads. Largely because of their importance, sizable and growing towns and industries attached themselves to them. In the days of their renaissance, nearly a full century later, they again were important roads. Stony surfaces, and sometimes muddy, had been replaced by smooth hard concrete, ancient narrow bridges of timber or of stone had given way to broad ones of steel or of concrete, and hard grades had been eased or almost completely abolished. Such has been the triumph of the highway since man first began to drive his engined car up the broad highroad.

Lateral roads came to join these chief highways of early New York State. There was a road that met the Post Road near Albany after it had forced itself over the sharp slopes of the Berkshires from Pittsfield and other Bay State towns, and it presented no joy or comfort to the traveler that used it. Another reached from the state capital down to the head waters of the Susquehanna and then along the course of that lovely stream to the little towns in the so-called Southern Tier, over the hills to early Ithaca. An improved highway ran from Newburgh to Cococton on the Delaware, where it crossed into Pennsylvania. From Oneonta, close to the source of the Susquehanna at Cooperstown, a road straggled, almost literally, over the tops of the tall Catskills to the Hudson edge at Kingston, colonial town and the first capital of the state of New York. A rough pavement of huge cut stones, like a crude railroad track, was laid down for the entire 108 miles of its length, but even that did not help very much. And its building nearly bankrupted the small city of Kingston.

There were roads from Albany—always a natural traffic center—north to Saratoga and Whitehall, to Troy and Vermont, and even to Montreal. A historic post road led from Utica to the valley of the Black River and down it to that thriving manufacturing place,

Watertown, and the then important port of Sackets Harbor, a strategic military center at the foot of Ontario. A thin and poorly kept highway, built in the War of 1812 and to this day known as the Military Road, reached from Sackets Harbor to Ogdensburg on the St. Lawrence and to Plattsburg upon the edge of Lake Champlain, at almost the extreme northeastern corner of the state.

But all of these last were comparatively unimportant. The ones over which mighty traffic rode its way unceasingly were the Post Road up to Albany and the two parallel routes due west from the old town. And just because traffic rode them so steadily and so tirelessly—men, horses, wagons, coaches, the peopling of a giant hinterland so great as to be a vast nation in itself—there came increasing demands for relief. The roads were crowded, night and day, summer and winter, almost to the bursting point. They were bitter cold in winter, burning hot in summer, in turn, snow-filled, slippery, dusty, rutty, muddy. The man who dodged part of the ordeal by taking a packet sloop or early steamboat as far as Albany found that an unkind fate was apt to pursue him upon the highroad west of there.

In England and in France, before the time of the American Revolution, astonishing aptitude had been shown in fashioning artificial waterways, which they called canals. In these water-filled trenches, boats of a considerable freight capacity could operate as fast at least as freighting-wagons over rough and hilly roads. Boats could also be run upon these canals for passengers, giving them much more comfort, if not as much speed, as stage-coaches. Benjamin Franklin wrote: "Rivers are unmanageable things, especially in hilly countries. Canals are quiet and very manageable."

The war for independence over, eastern America began to follow the example of Europe in many things. One fine day a man up in the old state house at Albany suggested that a canal be dug all the way from the port of that very town, 365 miles (by actual route) west to the port of Buffalo. In this way the navigable Hudson, leading to the broad Atlantic would be connected by navigable waterway with the entire series of the upper Great Lakes and the rivers tributary.

The man suggested and the man persisted. His name was De Witt Clinton, and people laughed at the sheer idiocy of his suggestion. And when finally the canal began to be dug it was called Clinton's Folly. But not for long. It was the longest canal in all America, and it was the most successful, not alone in the increasing traffic that came to it but in the fact that it gave New York the most dominating position on the Atlantic seaboard.

The Erie Canal, as it became known officially, completely transformed the state of New York. Those fine, classical old towns, Richfield and Auburn and Canandaigua and Batavia, were submerged under the noisy progress of such busy canal places as Utica and Syracuse and Rochester, which started to assume their dominant rôles in the industrial growth of the state. The machine age had arrived and had begun to take its firm place in America by 1825, which was the year in which the Erie Canal finally was completed and, with a deal of pomp and ceremony, opened all the way from Albany to Buffalo. It was a success from the outset, and the cities and towns that were fortunate to be situated upon its banks shared its success.

The success of the canal made the promoters of the first railroads, which followed hard upon the heels of the early canals, covet the natural path across New York for their particular form of transport. For a long time it looked as if they might covet it in vain. They were private enterprise and the Erie Canal was public work. It had cost a great deal of money to construct, and the wonder of it all was that the men at Albany had had the courage to embark upon the enterprise. But having gone into it, they saw it through. And they were prepared to defend it, jealously, against any inroads of competition. Baltimore suffered from the success of the canal. The Erie deprived it of much of its fine traffic, nearly ruining the commerce on the National Road, which led west from its docks. Since the contours of Maryland made it practically impossible for Baltimore to build a canal of its own through Ohio, it seized upon the railroad as a possible means of regaining its prestige as a transportation center. It sent some of its leading citizens to England to see the remarkable new railways that had come into existence there at the end of the first quarter of the nineteenth century, and this was the example that it proposed to follow. Philadelphia and Pennsylvania also chose to favor railroads. The railroad fever in the United States became even more virulent than the canal fever, and New York was not to be exempt from it.

Within six years after the completion of the Erie Canal, a double-track railroad had been put down between Albany and Schenectady (seventeen miles) and even if this little Mohawk & Hudson Railroad was a crude affair indeed—with horses at first as a part of its motive power and cumbersome inclines with cables at either end of it—it proved itself a utility with a curious position to fulfill. It shortened, by a considerable number of miles, the canal distance between the two old Dutch communities. Moreover that particular stretch of the Erie was an extremely slow one to navigate. The canal rose, in many locks, from the level of the Hudson to that of the Mohawk, and to negotiate these locks took much time indeed. So through travelers to the west from Albany and points east of it saved much valuable time by leaving coach or steamboat at the Albany dock and taking the new railroad in a direct line across to the Schenectady dock, where they might embark upon an Erie packet-boat bound toward the setting sun.

Rochester was a will-o-the-wisp town that sprang up almost overnight, from a highly successful power development and a neatly patterned townsite at the lower falls of the Genesee, and grew with such astounding rapidity that it speedily was dubbed "The Young Lion of the West." The boom days of the first twenty years of its existence—it hardly came into being prior to 1820—were to be duplicated afterwards in towns such as Chicago and Kansas City and Minneapolis and Los Angeles. Monroe County, of which it was the shiretown, had a flat fertile soil well adapted to wheat culture, and Rochester early became known as the Flour City. Its great granite mills, perched upon the very edges of the high banks of the gorge of the Genesee, ground their grist unceasingly day and night and made great wealth for the town.

So Rochester, with no small traffic of its own to command, early became railroad-conscious and railroad-ambitious. To reach Buffalo from Rochester by the Erie Canal was a tedious business, a roundabout route with many time-taking locks. It was a hundred miles by a canal against seventy in a direct line and across level country. So it was that the first railroad enterprise in the western part of the state again sought to shorten the canal distance. The Tonawanda Railroad came into existence in just this way; and like the Mohawk & Hudson it was a success from the outset.

It will be noticed that neither of these young railroads directly paralleled the state's canal. This was in accordance with an unwritten law that the canal must not be closely paralleled by any railroad. The fact that winter in upstate New York is none too gentle a thing, and that the canal is generally closed by ice for nearly five months out of the twelve, was as nothing. When the first railroad aspired to follow directly the waterway—a David confronting Goliath, as it were—it sought, and under great public pressure obtained, a charter from the state; which document solemnly stated that it must not carry freight in the months when the Erie was open and free to do business. That railroad was the Utica & Schenectady, in effect a western continuation of the Mohawk & Hudson, and that absurd provision remained in its charter for a number of years after the road was opened for business. In fact it was not until 1853 that the railroad dared to parallel the *sacrosanct* canal for its entire length. It was finally the first New York Central, with its vast political power, that dared to do the thing.

Here, then, was the path of empire as it blazed and streaked its great trail three hundred miles from east to west across the state; river, highway, canal, railroad and—years later—the highway once again. Each has had its own large part in making impress upon the business life, the social life, all the progress of the richest and most powerful of American commonwealths. The prestige once gained by that broad band was not to be lost. In due time the Southern Tier, the counties at the south edge of the state along the New Jersey and Pennsylvania borders, were to feel the impetus and growth of their own railroad system, the New York & Erie, from the Hudson through to Lake Erie, first at Dunkirk and then at the swiftly growing port of Buffalo. That was 1851. The contour of the Southern Tier, high hills and deep dales, had proved entirely too difficult for any extensive system of canals. The railroad conquered those hills and dales without vast difficulty, and Binghamton and Elmira emerged from being crude little towns into charming and distinctive cities.

In the same way the North Country struggled in early years against the overwhelming prestige and power and wealth of the central tier counties. It presented few physical barriers to the construction of the railroad. Save for the Adirondack region, wherein rises the tallest peak in the state—Mount Marcy, rising 5,344 feet above sea level—the greater part of the area is comparatively level.

Boston, aroused by the swift growth of New York, Philadelphia and Baltimore in the first third of the last century, sought her own route to the inland country. To stretch a rail line across upper New York, from the northwestern corner of Vermont, past the foot of Lake Champlain and to the navigable St. Lawrence at Ogdensburg, just above the rapids, seemed a feasible thing to do. And so it came to pass that the first time the locomotive ever entered Northern New York it was from the east, rather than up from the south. Trains were running from St. Albans to Ogdensburg some time before they reached Watertown from the central belt of the state; a long time before they had entered Ogdensburg from Watertown.

So it was that Ogdensburg, at a comparatively early date, and although more than a hundred miles from Ontario, became a lake port of consequence, with several lines of steamers running from her wharves to Detroit and Chicago and the Lake Superior ports. Like Oswego, she gave fine promise of becoming an important waterside city; a promise that in neither case was ever quite to be fulfilled.

Northern New York was a terrain holding treasure trove. Its hard rock acres were a crusty shell for rich minerals just underneath. Iron, both magnetite and hematite of a high grade, was to be found in profusion along the west shore of Lake Champlain and in the counties of Jefferson and St. Lawrence. And in between all of these were the vast and ineffable forests that from the beginning were to be known more often simply as the North Woods rather than by the more imposing title of Adirondacks. And so the first industry in the North Country, even ahead of mining, became lumbering; first cutting into the seemingly endless acres of standing timber, then floating it or dragging it out, as seemed most feasible, and having as a sole—but very profitable—by-product the making of potash. Gradually there came refinements to this industry. Wood-working factories were established, turning out at first such simple things as kitchen utensils or axe handles and then, in due time, furniture and wagon wheels and even wagons and carriages themselves. And finally there was destined to come almost the greatest of forest products, paper. The first paper mill was set up in 1808 at Watertown, for years the center of that industry in America, and the Knowlton Brothers have been steadily at it ever since, without a change in name or management.

Swift-running rivers are a splendid incentive to manufacturing industry. Waterwheels turn rapidly and give stout and powerful muscle for the fabrication of many things. The Black is one of the swiftest running rivers of the North Country, and for years its course has been past dams and through flumes and the beat of wheel blades. Far to the north of it, the Oswegatchie and the Grasse and the Racquette have done the same, only in less degree.

And, as in the north the Black River and its fellows have turned literally hundreds of waterwheels—so in the west, the Genesee also was power; in Central New York, the Oriskany and the Sauquoit; and in the eastern part of the state the upper waters of the lordly

Hudson, and almost innumerable little streams beating their way down to the lower river from the steep slopes of its shores below Albany. Easy power. Cheap power. Abundant power. No wonder that the making of textiles, now a factory enterprise, swept out of New England and fell gladly upon the swiftly running streams of Columbia and Dutchess and Oneida and Jefferson Counties. Utica and the region aroundabout it became a weaving place for woolens; and Cohoes, with the great falls of the Mohawk, just as it enters the Hudson, one for cottons. Carpets were made in Amsterdam; and, in due time, rubber textiles and felt at Little Falls and Dolgeville. The spinning industry, with its hundreds and thousands of tireless spindles, at one time even reached as far north as Watertown. In fact there was a sizable cotton factory in Malone, close to the Canada line, as early as 1829.

There was flour production on a large scale in Rochester, on a slightly smaller scale in Buffalo and Oswego and Albany and Troy, and in an intimate local way in more than a hundred towns large and small elsewhere in the state. And eventually there was also iron production. From the beginning there had been iron-mongering establishments of one sort or another, but generally these had been little more than blacksmith shops. You still can see at Tuxedo in the Ramapo Valley the ruins of the forge of Revolutionary days in which was wrought the great chain put across the Hudson at West Point to prevent the British battleships from ascending that stream.

Troy became the chief iron-making city not only of the state, but of the whole land. If Troy had finally achieved the destiny that seemed to have been set for it, there might have been no Pittsburgh, no Youngstown, no Gary. Troy began rather simply with its forges, with such humble products as nails, knives and forks, farm implements, kitchen utensils, and eventually made building material for the buildings in a short and awful period in our architecture. Then came bigger things. A Scottish engineer—by name, Henry Burden —had come to the town and, in the language of the present-day

Rotarian, "put it on the map." Before Burden had gone very far, his great hearthstones and his forges and his rolls were making railroad rails and bridges, as well as trains.

This is not the time and place to tell in detail of the swift progress of New York as a great industrial state. From the outset she had taken an outstanding position in the wealth and variety of her forest and her agricultural products; in the ingenuity of her manufactures she refused to be surpassed. As the years went on she specialized in the fineness and the variety of her manufactured output—boots and shoes in Binghamton and (clothing as well) in Rochester; typewriters in Ilion, in Groton, and in Syracuse; carriages here and there and everywhere all over the state—there seemed to be no end to her industry.

Even the metropolitan city of New York and its adjoining neighbor, the old city of Brooklyn, were not averse to the stout support of manufacturing industry. The East River at an early day was lined with shipyards. They built clipper ships and ocean-going steamships, and big white-bodied steamboats, for river and Sound, wide-bellied ferryboats and a large variety of other craft as well. From the beginning New York specialized in musical instruments—the pianos that once went out from a single factory on Park Avenue were not surpassed by those of any other country in all the world.

In the course of time and in the progress of this book there will be told, in the stories of the several sections of the state, something more of this astonishing industrial development, as well as some of its retrogressions; how its economic factors became social factors of consequence, and how, in some cases, other social forces overcame them. Paralleling the industrial development of the state, I shall tell the story of its social development. Attention will be given to its rare and unusual beauty, that brings to it each year thousands and thousands of tourists from every corner of the Union; also to the way New York sweats and works, laughs and plays. So is set this giant stage. The drama of more than a hundred years is to be in the story.

The features of the state that especially appeal to me are the fine old houses and the lovely rivers. There will be plenty about both in these pages. Of the two, I think I prefer the rivers. Four of the major streams of the northeastern part of the United States begin within the state of New York—the Hudson, the Delaware, the Susquehanna and the Allegheny, which eventually becomes the Ohio and then, in due time, the Mississippi. For more than one hundred miles the northern edge of the state is laved by the mighty St. Lawrence. The Genesee begins just across the state line, in the hills of Pennsylvania. It is one of the few large rivers in the East that makes its way northward. The Mohawk, the Black, the Oswegatchie, the Grasse and the Racquette are each of them lovely rivers, whose courses are entirely within the confines of the state.

With the rivers, we shall begin with the greatest, the Hudson. Big River it is to us, even though the city of New York with a curious sort of provincialism long since named it the North River. However, this name does not apply far beyond the limits of the metropolitan city. To us it is the Big River and was the Big River when Henry Hudson first ascended it three centuries and a quarter ago. Yet, before we come to it, let us stop for a while at the Big City that sprawls itself at its mouth.

Lower Manhattan as viewed from an airplane. The entire island has an area of only twenty-two square miles, yet it is the largest commercial and industrial center in the world and houses nearly two million people.

A sanctuary of nature in the midst of the big city. Central Park, the first of America's great public recreation centers, has more than justified the landscape theories and the work of its creator, Frederick

CHAPTER II

The Big City

A BOOK of this sort has to have a beginning—and so it might be just as well to start this one with the Big City. But, beware; the Big City, big as it is, is not going to monopolize this volume. This is the story of the entire state of New York, not merely of New York City. Great as the city is, the state is greater. If you were to divorce the Big City (or even Long Island) from upstate, the residue still would be a great state, still larger, more populous, more industrious, more wealthy than most of the other states of the Union. But it would be a sad bill of divorcement, indeed. For New York City is not only the brave front door of New York State, but its chief nerve center as well.

One may speak of it in its grand superlatives, in such sweeping enterprises as the George Washington Bridge or the Holland Tube or the elevated express highroad along the west edge of Manhattan; in its towering skyscrapers, in such groupings of huge buildings as Radio City or the Grand Central Terminal, or of those vast and almost limitless congestions of humanity, the West Side, Williamsburgh, Brownsville, the Bronx—all of this part and parcel of what has come to be the mightiest community in the history of the world. Or you may seek to interpret the Big City in its individual humanities—the courteous policeman on the street, the newsdealer at the corner, the restaurant waiter, the family of means in the smart flat in the smug East 60's or the even smugger East 70's and East 80's, the poor families in apartments not so smart—it all comes to the same thing. Carve New York apart, piecemeal if you will, and you have upstate, piecemeal. It is, in the last analysis, a group of Rochesters or Uticas or Carthages or Malones. In a real sense, it is no bigger than the smallest organized community in the whole state—in many ways, not one whit more important. That's the Big City.

The New York that I first came to visit in the mid-'eighties and then to work in, twelve years later, were both somewhat different from the Big City of today. Something may have been gained in all those years, but not really very much.

The New York of the fall of 1884 was a vastly different-looking town than it is now. It was then a well-ordered, not overcrowded city. Young as I was, I remember it well. We stopped—my mother and father and I—at the Continental Hotel, at the northeast corner of Broadway and 20th Street. Diagonally opposite from the windows of our parlor was Lord & Taylor's store, then a curious iron-fronted structure, the tower of which still remains. Fifth Avenue, which still was exclusively residential, was but a stone's throw away. The horse-car railway had just been built on Broadway—after many years of contention and a nasty bit of scandal—but the buses still crowded the thoroughfares. Most of these buses, horse-drawn of course, were painted white, and they gave the street a gay and animated appearance.

Around our hotel was a nice residential neighborhood. One of the Roosevelts—his name was Theodore—had been born on 20th Street, less than half a block away, and his family still dwelt in the handsome brownstone-front house. In fact it still stands, nowadays a good deal of a local shrine. Gramercy Park was not far away, and the gods have been good enough to permit it also to remain, quite unchanged, although almost everything else roundabout has been swept away long since. Union Square was the Rialto, although I was a little too young to understand or to appreciate what that meant. Once—just once on that memorable trip from upstate to the Big City—was I taken to the theater; to the Casino, still very new, up upon the fringe of the then uptown business section, at 39th Street. The theater was of very ornate Moorish architecture, and its auditorium was upstairs, with a roof-garden high above everything else. We went up to the roof-garden after the opera (it was the popular *Little Duke*) and found it a very fanciful paradise, with tables where people ate and drank, a band of music and many gay, colored gaslights. It was the sort of a place a boy was not apt to forget.

Of course if the New Yorker of that day wanted really serious opera he went to the new yellow-brick Metropolitan, diagonally across Broadway from the Casino, or the sedate old Academy of Music, in the highly musical 14th Street.

There had not been one single skyscraper in 1884; twelve years later there were many, at least faintly deserving of the phrase. There were no more buses in Broadway, and there now were plenty of cable railroads; but these already were being supplanted by electric cars, whose power came from underground rails in the cable slots. Modern they were, very clean and rather wonderful. Electric power was supplanting the puffing little locomotives upon the elevated railroads, and they were talking a great deal about an underground railroad that would make its way up and down the backbone of Manhattan Island—a very difficult and expensive undertaking it was certain to be; but the swift progress that was being made in the use of electricity as a railroad motive power made such an elongated tunnel a practical possibility, even though an expensive one.

In 1896 the migration of the large department stores uptown had not yet begun. West 23rd Street still was in the fine flower of its glory. And so was the near-by 6th Avenue. While a merchant by the name of Wanamaker from Philadelphia had just taken over the handsome store, of Parisian type, which A. T. Stewart had built on Broadway from 9th Street to 10th, and was preparing to do big things with it, Macy's was to begin the movement uptown, with its huge new store facing Bennett's *Herald,* at 34th Street. But that was not to come until 1902, though the firm already was contemplating the move.

Theaters, too, were coming uptown. No longer were the Casino and the Metropolitan Opera House isolated at 39th Street. There were many in the neighborhood now to keep them company, but as yet there were no large newspaper offices in the district. The *Herald,* in its jewel box of a building, with the blinking owls and the men hammering the hours upon the clock, still was an uptown pioneer. The theater district ended at Longacre Square. North of that busy new *platz* the only amusement landmark was the still-new Carnegie Hall in 57th Street, unless you excepted the German *spielhäusern* and beer-gardens over Yorkville way. And there were one or two handsome theaters, of legitimate type, away up in Harlem, which did not then dream of the black avalanche that one day was to descend upon it.

That was the New York that I knew in the end of the Gay 'Nineties . . . funny old boarding-houses with landladies, either very fat or very thin . . . Huyler's and Hudnut's (in mid-Broadway) —the last with ice-cream soda at twenty cents that seemed ridiculously high-priced then . . . *Floradora* forever playing at the Casino; the glories of Weber and Fields . . . jolly rides summer evenings on the open cars of the Broadway line; up Lexington Avenue, across 116th Street, and back by the way of Columbus Avenue—all for a nickel. It was nice, taking a girl who lived somewhere in the neighborhood of Washington or Union or Madison squares, on that two-hour trolley ride, and then blowing her to a swell twenty-cent soda at the faintly scented Hudnut's, afterwards. Or, if one felt more affluent, seeking the roof-garden of the new Waldorf-Astoria and sitting there under real stars and ruminating upon a life that seemed to be all future, and very little past.

Brooklyn was more of a journey. One generally went down to Park Row or to Park Place on the 3rd or the 6th Avenue elevateds, mounted the eternal stairs that led to the bridge station and there took the cable cars over to the City of Churches, so soon to lose its identity in the new Greater New York, just as it had, itself, swallowed up the handsome old city of Williamsburgh, many years before. Does one ever think of the Amphion Theater, Williamsburgh, any more; or even of Hyde & Behmans and the Montauk, in Brooklyn city itself? Yet each of those houses had a great tradition. Theaters get that way. I saw the old Brooklyn Academy of Music in Montague Street burn down. It was an ugly old theater, yet one almost could weep when one thought of the hopes and the memories that went up in the flames, almost within one hour. And the newer and more magnificent Academy that came to replace it, a little farther uptown, is already growing old.

Prospect Park then, as now, was a place of rare beauty. In those days its entrance was guarded by a sentinel tower and reservoir, as well as by the MacMonnies Quadriga and arch. Nearly a quarter of a century ago they completely spoiled that vista by the erection of the first section of a grandiloquent new public library. Those few of us who protested were told that we stood in the way of civic improvement; that soon there would arise, close to the curb of Flatbush Avenue, one of the handsomest buildings in the greater city. Some one lost interest in the new library and civic improvement, and for twenty-five years the structure has stood an unfinished ruin, a monument to civic indifference.

The Big City of today seeks (diligently it would seem) to efface most of its landmarks of the past, or at least it did so until the days of the Big Depression. In Manhattan few of the yesterdays are still to be found. Fraunces Tavern, of course . . . and so, also, of course, St. Paul's . . . and Trinity burying-ground with its modern church, now ninety years old . . . the lovely old City Hall, so soon to face again its beloved Broadway (and not the back of the ugly Mullet Post Office which has confronted it for more than sixty years) . . . that club of clubs, the Players' at Gramercy Park . . . Carnegie Hall . . . the Metropolitan Opera House . . . the Murray Hill Hotel, still beloved of New Englanders. . . .

A page or two on hotels and restaurants:

It is hardly possible that a hotel will ever again burst upon the Big City with the glory and effulgence that the first Waldorf-Astoria brought with it. The second one has done pretty well—thanks to a liberal advertising policy and good management. But it had the patent misfortune of coming at a time when it was not really needed. The town already was chock-a-block with most excellent hotels; most of whom were consistently failing to pay a profit on the investment. When the genial Boldt opened the doors of the first W-A, there was a paucity of good hostels in New York—only a handful of them all told—the Holland House, the Imperial, the Hoffman and the old 5th Avenue, at Madison Square; the Windsor and the Buckingham, farther up 5th Avenue; the Savoy, the Plaza and the Netherlands, at 59th Street—possibly two or three others. But they were all good hotels, if not all sumptuous. And they knew good food and good wines as New York does not know them now, and probably never again will know them. Wild fowl and game of every sort, terrapin and other most unusual produce of the sea appeared regularly on their menus. The modern generation goes into Charley's or Tony's or Gus's (the latest popular favorite is hardly a favorite for more than four to six months, and then is quickly supplanted and gradually forgotten) and knows little of what it eats or drinks. It is fed hors d'œuvres, soup (with things in it), a dish or two borrowed from the *restaurateurs* of Paris; blazed at by a jazz band—and this is supposed to be the elegant eating of the chief city of America and the largest city in the world! The drinking is not much better. That was a pretty fell blow that Prohibition gave. The average wine of the average restaurant in the Big City is hardly worthy of the name; it is generally inferior French or German stuff. Despite the fact that right here in our upstate New York (to say nothing of the vaunted California) wine can be produced and is produced which is at least the equal of the average wine from Bordeaux or Burgundy or the valleys of the Moselle and the Rhine, there is as yet little or no restaurant drinking of American wines. Perhaps the reason for this is that as yet they are not very well known. More likely it is because Americans are not wine-drinkers. Try and laugh that off. It is actual truth, and there is no denying it. We may have the native wines but we have not the native taste—not yet, at any rate. We still are gin guzzlers and whiskey soaks. It is going to take a lot of education to cultivate a wine taste in this country.

It really seems a pity that the *grande dame* of all New York hotels, the elegant old Waldorf-Astoria, had to pick up her heavy skirts and hustle uptown with all the other business enterprises. The new costume is a becoming one, and with her face lifted, Waldorf-Astoria still is a charming lady, much sought after, quite worth while. But at 34th Street and 5th Avenue she stood in the chief location of the whole big town. The old Waldorf-Astoria never lost position. It became a little less smart in its latter years, but not less accessible. It was a real pity indeed that it had to be torn down and apart—every blessed vestige of it—and that there had to be erected in its place an unwanted and unprofitable skyscraper, the tallest building in the world, with its 102 stories and its mooring mast for dirigibles (at which there was not the slightest possibility that a dirigible ever would be moored).

Within recent years the tendency of the city to group itself into newly created business centers, such as the Grand Central Terminal and Radio City—to cite the most conspicuous examples—has become marked indeed. That these groupings have vastly increased the traffic and other street problems of the Big City is undeniable. If there are, in normal times, some sixty or seventy-five thousand workers in the Grand Central group—the entire population of an upstate Troy or Utica, but concentrated in less than one-twentieth of the area of each of these fairly compact old towns—imagine the effect upon New York's arteries of travel when evening comes and these workers are discharged upon the street! No other great city in the world has to face such a staggering problem, yet it is characteristic of the Big City that she shrugs her shoulders at it and then proceeds to create for herself another and more staggering problem, such as Radio City, or the theater district in and about Times Square.

For the town's tendency to group itself is not limited to business structures, the suit-and-cloak and other industries, or to theaters. It has long since also shown itself in huge residential groupings—on the West Side, at 23rd Street and 9th and 10th Avenues; and upon the East on the very bank of the East River, at 42nd Street, at Beekman Place, at Sutton Place, and still again, at the foot of 86th Street. Park Avenue, from 46th to 96th Street (two miles and a half) is hardly anything else but a succession of residential dwellings, even though trade all the while is making desperate efforts to force itself, unwanted, into the sacred thoroughfare, which not so long ago was little else than the right-of-way of the main lines of the New York Central and the New Haven railroads. Some day, some one is going to immortalize these vast housing projects. To me they always seem like enormous aggregations of cubicles, which if you could but remove their outer skin would seem to be something like the shelves of a gargantuan shoe-store, with intricate passageways between the shoe boxes and numberless swift devices with which to whisk their occupants up from the ground and back again.

We seem to have progressed a good deal in some of these matters; but sometimes I wonder how much we really have progressed in the creation of the modern apartment house. We are ahead of London, which has very few apartments, or, as they prefer to call them, "flats." We are ahead of Berlin in that there is no system of espionage at our outer door, and that door firmly locked at a fairly early hour. We are ahead of Paris in that we have elevators that are swift and safe and employee-operated, in which one may safely descend or ascend. We have open fireplaces for wood fires, but no mail chutes in our multiple houses; electric refrigerators, but little or no soundproofing; a good deal of front and impeccably uniformed doormen.

Also some of our apartments have penthouses. I understand that many of them are rather elegant affairs, and that all are not the dens of iniquity that the forces of drama would have us believe.

Most of the apartments of New York are not penthouses. A good many of them are fortunate, facing as they do narrow streets and still narrower courtyards, if they get even a modicum of the precious sunlight during the course of the day, but the folk who live in them seem to forget about sunlight (except on their summer vacations and perhaps riding atop the 5th Avenue buses). We New Yorkers are fast coming to be a gnomelike people. We may progress, but it generally is a pretty slow sort of progress. One of the newest fads of the Big City has been to dine outdoors. For years the folk who went regularly back and forth to Paris wondered why we could not have something of the sort here in New York. There were a thousand reasons (apparently) why the thing could *not* be done, and these weighed the balance against it. Two things finally carried the day for it—Repeal and the very pleasant art of outdoor dining as it was displayed at the Chicago World's Fairs of 1933 and 1934. When the new fad finally hit New York, it hit it with a bang, which is a way the Big City has of doing things. Almost overnight Lower 5th Avenue became the Grands Boulevards and demure old Central Park the Bois. True it was that the Casino had been there in the Park a goodly number of years, but in recent years it had been regarded as high-priced and was operated as anything but a democratic sort of resort. A new mayor and a new commissioner of parks, wishing to do something very new indeed, have battled, rather helplessly, against this condition of things and, failing (as yet) to break down the barriers of exclusiveness at the Park Casino, have retaliated by taking an ancient sheepfold (a quaint exhibit of the Gay 'Nineties it was) and making it into a more popular tavern. The result is that there you eat rather indifferent food and drink rather indifferent drinks out in the open, under huge sun-umbrellas while the younger portion of *hoi-polloi* makes faces at you. Still it all is very new and has a certain aura of the grand foreign manner about it, and so New York likes it.

The Opera holds its devotees and so does the Philharmonic, particularly upon those golden occasions when *Il Maestro* Toscanini wields his magic baton. There are big art shows at the Metropolitan

Museum and a thousand lesser ones up and down 5th and Park Avenues and across 59th Street. The annual Flower Show has begun to vie with the long-established Horse Show in social popularity, and again there are a thousand smaller shows, all the way from motor-boats and motor-cars to "hobbies" and small model railroad trains. Madison Square Garden (nowhere near Madison Square) houses a variety of sporting entertainments, including horse shows, ice-hockey, six-day races and the circus. Of course there is the theater; New York clings lovingly to it. And the movies, the glorified ones, with the West Pointish ushers, and the plain garden variety, where you rustle about in the half-dark for your own seats. There are endless parties—high-brow, middle-brow and ones in which you would search in vain for any brows at all. There are four seasons of the year in New York, and they are all popular seasons, even the summer. A good many of the townsfolk, through necessity or habit, leave the city then but are immediately replaced by a noisy, gay crowd from the South and the West. In some ways, summer is the most gracious season of the year in the Big City. The Opera House and most of the regular theaters are closed, but there are really fine concerts in Central Park and the uptown Stadium, a vast variety of side excursions, riding atop the buses or in ancient horse-drawn carriages through the leafy Park. There is sport of every sort, from swank racing at Belmont or polo on Long Island to all-day fishing on excursion steamboats. There really are no dull seasons in the Big City. At all times of year, it is the very greatest of American resorts, not even excepting the national capital.

The variety of fodder that it has to offer the intelligent traveler the whole year round is amazing. Not only has it such vast and internationally known institutions as the Metropolitan Museum of Art, with its fascinating American Wing housed in a rebuilding of the lovely Assay Office that once stood in Wall Street; or the Museum of Natural History, with its brand-new main entrance dedicated to the memory of that lover of clean sport, Theodore Roosevelt; but it also has smaller and more individual collections, such as, to make a most interesting instance, the Museum of the City of

New York, on 5th Avenue, at 105th Street. This last one appeals to me always. Its carefully fashioned dioramas that give clear pictures of the New York that was and that never again can possibly be, get my enthusiasm upon sharp edge. With such guides, one's imagination easily can walk the streets of other days.

Well to the north of pleasant old Central Park, intellect gathers itself into its own grouping, a sort of modern Acropolis, of which the two most sightly features are the great and steadily building Cathedral of St. John the Divine, which may be seen from a long way off, way across the desolation of the flat roofs of hundreds of Harlem tenements, and the four hundred-foot tower of the Riverside Church, a wonderful structure, gift of that same citizen of the town, John D. Rockefeller, Jr., who has just presented it with its newest park, far to the north. I have been in a good many of the great churches of the world, but rarely have I seen one whose interior has greater simplicity and dignity and beauty than this Baptist temple. The new Protestant Episcopal Cathedral, only a few blocks away, has not the same simplicity of design or detail. As a cathedral it hardly could. New York's Cathedral of St. John the Divine has suffered some of the same disadvantages in its fabrication as many older similar great churches overseas, changes not only in architects but in the fundamental plans of its design. Yet it has persevered, and the result is a rather astounding church, whose nave, crossing, choir, apse and north transept, now, after forty years of steady work, approach completion. It is possible that no man now living will ever see the church completed; so very much remains to be done. Yet those of us who refuse to confess to old age clearly recall the day when services were held in the incomplete crypt, and old Bishop Potter was consecrating, one by one, the several lovely chapels that surrounded the chancel. Perhaps after all it will not be so many years before the great tower that is to arise above the crossing is completed, and they are putting its cross in place, final symbol of the completion of the entire tremendous fabric. For St. John's, more than five hundred feet in length overall, is planned to be one of the largest churches in all the world.

The dominating feature in all the briskness and energy of New York's Acropolis is Columbia University. Other colleges, much smaller, have larger campuses. But the campus is no feature of Columbia life. Columbia is truly New Yorkish in that it is compact. Necessity has forced its compactness. Space, the eternal problem of the Big City, has been the uncompromising factor that at all times has belted in the college, which in all its years never has really learned what it is not to grow.

Starting as Kings College in lower Broadway, in 1754, it dropped the name when there no longer was obeisance to the king, and became Columbia College. A few years later it was trekking north to a group of buildings in Madison Avenue, in the 40's, and there it remained until about thirty-five years ago, when it moved to its present site on upper Broadway. It has created for itself a remarkable staff and plant. Columbia University, in all its functions, summer and winter, now has some thirty thousand students. But Columbia College, the core and center of the entire institution, never has had more than a few hundred of these. The rest of the thirty thousand receive teaching in the affiliates—medicine, law, art, architecture, journalism. Around about her, too, are gathered still other great schools, Barnard (her affiliate for the teaching of women), the huge Union Theological Seminary, Teachers College, the Horace Mann School, the Juillard School of Music, the Jewish Theological Seminary.

You see most of this when you go uptown on one of the Big City's showiest thoroughfares, Riverside Drive. Incidentally, the very best way to see the Drive and a good part of the rest of the town is to ride atop one of the Fifth Avenue buses.

The proper way to do the entire thing is to go down to Washington Square (go down by taxi and on the way stop in to see Grace Church at the slight turn of Broadway at 11th Street, designed by James Renwick nearly eighty years ago, and one of the loveliest marble churches in all creation; it once was, and still largely is, among the most fashionable churches in the town).... You will find the long green buses standing there in the aristocratic old Square, which, long years ago, was New York's Potter's Field.

The bus starter in Washington Square will see to it that you get the right bus for your trip up 5th Avenue and Riverside Drive to the Acropolis and beyond. You see to it, if you can, that you get one of the older buses, with no roof whatsoever over its upper deck. Ascend to that upper deck, find yourself a corner seat, and if the day be fine (and the weather reports show that the Big City has a plentitude of that sort of thing) you are in for the best ten-cents' worth in the entire town.

At the beginning is a section of the far-famed Greenwich Village. The dignified Washington Arch follows and then the lower Avenue, with its open-air cafés and its two fine old brownstone churches —the smallish Church of the Ascension, and the somewhat lordly First Presbyterian. Then comes a sort of desolate *marais* of small business, broken only by the pleasant greenery of Madison Square, with its dominating clock tower, speaking the hour, the half, and the quarter to hurrying New Yorkers. A few blocks uptown "the tallest building in the world," the Empire State, with its one-thousand-foot observation tower, is reached and passed.

Now you are right in the heart of the retail shopping district. New York's smartest shops are on either side of you, all the way to 57th Street, where the bus turns sharply to the left. There is much else besides, the Public Library (with the dandified new Bryant Park hidden just behind it), and 42nd Street corner, vying with that of Park Avenue and 57th Street, for recognition as "the busiest street corner in the world," Radio City and plenty of fine big churches—St. Patrick's Cathedral (not excessively large, but very beautiful), the Collegiate Dutch, the stately St. Thomas's, the 5th Avenue Presbyterian. In between them are the last of the important townhouses still remaining in downtown 5th Avenue, including the impressive brownstone mansion of General Cornelius Vanderbilt.

Now you are in West 57th Street—broad and busy but not unusual, save perhaps in its single offering of Carnegie Hall.

After a short drive on West 57th Street and on Broadway, up to

West 72nd Street, you finally reach Riverside Drive. Riverside Drive is Glory Hallelujah. It should be New York's most glorified residential street, not Park Avenue nor Fifth, but somehow it has failed to be. Its single-builded-up edge still has handsome houses looking out upon a strip of park and the flowing waters of the Hudson—of these, the most notable, the great *schloss* of Charles M. Schwab, which occupies (with its lawns and gardens) the entire block from 73rd to 74th streets. . . . Aside from these the street is monopolized pretty largely by apartment houses; and most of these are apartment houses of the better sort. But the street has little of its former swank.

A good many reasons have been advanced for the decline of one of the most beautifully located streets in the world. It has been ascribed to—first, the noise of the switching locomotives on the tracks below the roadway and close to the river; second, the coming, under certain winds, of pungent and none-too-pleasant odors from certain manufacturing establishments over on the New Jersey side of the river; and finally, the bitterness of winter cold and sharp wind along the thoroughfare.

Despite its lower social standing, Riverside Drive remains Glory Hallelujah, as a drive or promenade, all the way to and past the handsome Soldiers' Monument to the homely Grant's Tomb and the Acropolis. Just beyond is one of New York's most delectable restaurants, and beyond all question the most beautifully located, the ancient Claremont, which has defied all efforts to "popularize" it and remains an outstanding eating place, in which you may dine within doors or without, as your fancy may choose. And no book on New York which aims to serve, even in slight degree as a guide to the stranger within her doors may neglect that little grave that stands on the steep slope of the river bank, with its headstone reading

SACRED TO THE MEMORY OF AN AMIABLE CHILD

and no one today knowing what child, or whose. That's the Big City.

Beyond Grant's Tomb, "the Rockefeller church" (as people will persist in calling it) and the delectable Claremont, is a long viaduct, and then still more Riverside Drive. Anything but notable now, but still beautiful. Ahead of you, you begin to see the George Washington Bridge, that Father of all great bridges, gateway to the picturesque terrain of North New Jersey and New York's own west bank of the Hudson. Just why they called it the George Washington Bridge, no one seems to know (beyond of course the general idea of the thing). Most of New York wanted it called the Palisades Bridge, for its great seventeen-hundred-foot suspension span—fine silver cobweb it is—leads directly over to the carved granite lip of the Palisades, and that is the final big scene of Glory Hallelujah.

Only you see none too much of it from the bus. That temperamental vehicle swerves out of the drive just north of the viaduct and once again seeks the vivid charms of upper Broadway. Some of them are quite real charms, such as the Trinity Cemetery, where so many old New Yorkers sleep, the Hispanic Museum, the Medical Center, with a dozen great hospitals rolled into one. A few of the buses continue on to the handsome new park that Mr. Rockefeller has given the town, and which in the summer of 1935 was receiving its final touches, preparatory to opening. It occupies a glorious natural position, a high rocky promontory rising abruptly above the plain of the surrounding terrain and the Hudson and the Harlem. In former years the site was that of many suburban homes, including that of Boss Tweed and of a pleasurable little restaurant, the Abbey, with a wide reputation for its cuisine. It also held George Gray Barnard's remarkable studio, the Cloisters. The Abbey is gone, forever, but Barnard's picturesque studio and its collections are operated for the public, as a branch of the Metropolitan Museum of Art.

If you are still young and energetic you will wish to alight from the bus somewhere in this neighborhood and pursue your journey afoot to the beginnings of the George Washington Bridge. And then you will wish to walk across the bridge, itself. And you will be more than repaid for your trouble and effort. The Hudson is never more beautiful than from midstream. And when you are lifted two hundred feet or so above midstream—with the vista of a mighty city upon the one side, and upon the other, the centuries-old Palisades —you have walked your old feet into something far more heavenly than earthly. You will wish to linger; then perhaps continue on to the Jersey side and a bit of refreshment at one of the near-by taverns. A bus will bring you back, easily and quickly, into the heart of the Big City once again.

This volume does not have any ambition to be a guide-book; yet it seems fast on its way to achieving that very sort of thing. Still, in the Big City it often is the obvious thing that is most quickly forgotten.

For instance, the City Hall. Few New Yorkers themselves ever go to it, unless to make a call upon His Honor, the Mayor, or else to attend the rather labored and exciting sessions of the Aldermen or the Board of Estimates. The fact remains, however, that there is no more charming building in the entire city. Its curving stair is well worth the trip downtown. The place is filled with lovely portraits; Washington, Jefferson, Hamilton, Jay, Lafayette—by the most eminent of early American painters. The Governor's Room—I sometimes wonder how long it has been since a Governor came to visit it—is an exquisite Georgian interior, with the furniture that was used by the first Congress of the United States, when it met in old Federal Hall down in Wall Street. New York's City Hall after a century and a quarter of steady use as its civic heart still is the town's most precious possession. A jewel box of a town hall, it is.

You really can have a pretty fine time downtown. In many ways that part of the Big City has changed far less than uptown, especially of late years. You wander in and out of St. Paul's and Trinity and their churchyards in lower Broadway, visit the Stock Exchange (if you have a friend at court to get you a ticket for the gallery, and the stockbrokers are not having one of their periodical scares and closing it entirely), look at Mr. Morgan's big banking house across the way; then, across the way from both, you visit the

Forty-four stories above the street these riggers are working on the final stories of a new skyscraper. Beyond them is the massive tower of the New York Central Building.

Most of New York's Jewish population live the lower east side Manhattan Island. Chtown, a network of row streets near the Bery, is a favorite spot tourists.

Sub-Treasury, a handsome, classic structure, built upon the site of the famed old Federal Hall. Washington was inaugurated as first President upon the very spot where his statue now stands; and now people go to the building to get passports to visit those very foreign lands of which he once warned all of us. You can lunch in aged Fraunces Tavern (built in 1730) and afterwards go upstairs and visit the room in which Washington bade good-by to the officers of his army. The Battery and the Aquarium are not far away, and both have perpetual popularity. Oh, you can really have a fine time downtown. And friends at court may ask you to lunch at one of the swank lunch clubs that occupy the top floors of many of the skyscrapers, serve one fine meal six days a week and call it all a day's work. In the afternoon the captains, the waiters and the chef go to the uptown restaurants.

And you can have a good time uptown. New York's restaurants may not be the best in the world, but they are far from bad. Rapidly they come and go; and rapidly they change favor. Any well-posted man of the town can give you quickly a listing of the best of them.

If you come to the Big City at almost any time of year you will want to see Westchester and the Long Island suburban country, and if you see them any time from late April to late November you will see them at their very best. Some one once called Westchester "the loveliest county in the world," and she has gracefully accepted the appellation.

Certainly there can be few lovelier vicinages of a great world-city than those which the gods gave New York: sweet old Staten Island, with her softly rounded hills and old houses bathing in the fragrance of the near-by sea; the stern sweep of the Palisades; the lovely banks upon either side of the Hudson stream, and of the Long Island Sound as well, and the glorious lush country that lies between. There are broad parkways making egress and ingress for the Big City easier than that of any other large city in the world; in between them gentle, shaded, narrow, twisting roads that do not seem to have changed in half a century or more, where the buttercups and the daisies still come in June and the American goldenrod in late summer. There are great houses, great estates, along and between these roads, but you do not see many of them. They do not parade themselves; but if you are given an opportunity to partake of their hospitality you cannot but admire their well-ordered existence—servants and service as well-trained and as impeccable as those of Surrey or of Passy, generous food and drink —the American cuisine reaches its highest levels in the well-conducted American home; that is, when it is conducted with at least a passing regard for the amenities of life.

That section of the New York metropolitan district just north of the Harlem River almost always has been known as a land of good living. Long, long ago it first was threaded by two main roads; the Albany, which was a continuation of New York's early Broadway (after it had crossed from Manhattan Island at Kingsbridge) straight up the east shore of the Hudson to the capital of the state; and the Boston, which for years branched from the Albany just above Kingsbridge, and which (many years ago) changed its way into New York, so as to be a continuation of the old Bowery, continuing up the east side of the island of Manhattan to the Harlem and then finding its way to a junction with the earlier road at Eastchester; then along the north shore of Long Island Sound, through Pelham and Rye to the Connecticut line and a good part of New England beyond.

The many indentations of the lovely Sound gave fair sites indeed for the mansions and country seats of the early New Yorkers, and they were not slow to take advantage of this. Some of these families, like the Pells and the Delanceys, had held their acres it seemed almost since the beginnings of things. Jonas Bronck was another very early settler, whose name is perpetuated in that of one of the most populous of all the boroughs, a lazy and idyllic little river, a great park, and a parkway. The Lorillards also came early. Their snuff mill stood (although for many years unused) on the rim of the Bronx River, until March 1888, when its ancient fabric fell, an easy victim to New York's most devastating blizzard. There were other lovely seats in this southeastern portion of the old county of Westchester—the homes of the Hunts, of the Failes, the Dennison-White mansion and, most astonishing of all, the so-called Casanova mansion, known in its day, with its hundred or more rooms, as the largest and finest (but certainly *not* the handsomest) in the United States. B. M. Whitlock built the fantastic house, about 1859, and he was said to have expended over three hundred and fifty thousand dollars upon it. The tales told about it are hardly less than fabulous. It had doorknobs reputed to be of solid gold, a "blue and gold room" dazzling in its decorations, and an ingenious device by which horses approaching the house touched a secret spring which automatically threw open its outer gates. A whole saga of romance wove itself roundabout it. And yet in less than five years its builder, his fortunes ruined by the Civil War, was forced to sell it; to a Cuban planter, one Senor Yglesias Casanova. Casanova was a friend and patron of the insurgent Cubans; and the mysteries that had attached themselves to the place, as a home of a southern sympathizer, became as nothing to those that multiplied with the activities of the Junta in the great and gloomy place.

Most important of all these houses in this portion of Westchester were the homes of the Morrises, Gouverneur and Lewis, close to the mouth of the Harlem River. The Gouverneur Morris mansion in New York (he had another upstate, erected about 1798 and still standing, just outside of Gouverneur, in St. Lawrence County) was in the style of a French château. It was famed for its hospitality and quickly gave the name of Morrisania to the neighborhood. Lafayette was perhaps its most distinguished guest, although John Jay once took Martha Washington to breakfast there.

The house of Lewis Morris (signer of the Declaration of Independence) was hardly less notable, either in structure or in the character of its hospitality. For a while the two men shared a great dream for the future of Morrisania. It was proffered as a suitable site for the capital of the young United States of America; and they were much disappointed when the site on the banks of the Potomac was selected. Yet Morrisania was not doomed to die. The railroad came along and with its widespread yards swept away the fine houses, their lovely gardens roundabout, but their lands commanded high prices, and Lewis Morris made a pretty penny out of his toll-bridge across the Harlem. Presently a great traffic came to use it, and eventually the new Harlem Railroad bought running rights across it for its extension up toward the north. Almost all of these old houses now are gone. One of them still remaining is the stout stone mansion of the Bartow family in Pelham Bay Park. It is a handsome and a sturdy house, surrounded by lovely gardens, and it now serves very nicely as the headquarters of the International Garden Clubs.

Fascinating neighbor to these old houses of southeastern Westchester (much of it now enclosed in the city of New York as a part of the borough of the Bronx) all these years is old St. Paul's Church in the erstwhile village of Eastchester, at the head of a shallow inlet from the Sound. St. Paul's was built in 1763, and with the exception of a rather hectic time during the Revolution and a year when it was a court house, services have been held in the edifice continuously. Its bell in 1758 was presented to a preceding St. Paul's, and when things became pretty alarming in the war with England some one had the foresight to take it down and bury it. After that unpleasantness it was hung again, and it has been calling the godly folk to worship pretty steadily ever since. There is a quiet churchyard, and the names upon the graves within sound like a veritable roster of Colonial aristocracy. St. Paul's has a deal of pride in the fact that the first bishop of the Protestant Episcopal Church in America, the Rt. Rev. Samuel Seabury, was for ten years prior to his ordination as bishop, its esteemed and much-loved rector. In the middle of a none-too-orderly corner of the new New York, it is a pleasant breath of a fragrant past.

There are fine old houses up the westerly edge of Westchester County, as well as the easterly one; and these really begin with the Van Cortlandt House in Van Cortlandt Park. This stone manor house, situated at the edge of one of New York's largest and most popular parks, is but the first of three Van Cortlandt houses along the lower Hudson—the other two are at Peekskill and at Croton. The Van Cortlandts were a powerful and a prolific family in those earlier days. They built well, and so did the Philipse family, whose manorial home still stands near the Albany Post Road in the very heart of the city of Yonkers. For years it served as the Yonkers City Hall. Now the town has a new municipal palace, and the aged Philipse Manor is in a fine *métier,* as a carefully arranged historical museum. As an early American home it shares keen interest with the Jumel house, in upper Manhattan. For it was Mary Philipse, the beautiful daughter of the manor who married Roger Morris, the builder of the Jumel house. That house, overlooking the Harlem, at 162nd Street, did not assume the present name until Morris (the one member of the family who stuck to Toryism) had fled from the country, at the outbreak of the Revolution. After having served as military headquarters both for Washington and (afterwards) for the British commanders of New York City, it was purchased by the picturesque Stephen Jumel for himself and his even more picturesque bride, who later became the wife of Aaron Burr.

There are so many old houses still remaining in Westchester that it would be difficult more than to attempt a mere catalogue of all of them. But for me, no house there is half so fascinating as the old Washington Irving home, Wolferts Roost, at Irvington-on-Hudson. The quaint, rambling old structure remains in the hands of the collateral descendants of its original owners and therefore is not open to the public. There is a very old house at the southwestern corner of Irving Place and 17th Street, in New York, in which Irving is reputed to have lived, although to what extent is much disputed. The late Major George Haven Putnam used to recall visiting the author there. Washington Irving's memory is closely entwined with all this portion of the state; he is said to have placed the iron letters, "1838" upon Bolton Priory over in Pelham Manor. And now he sleeps the long sleep in the ancient graveyard of the old Dutch Church in Sleepy Hollow, just north of Tarrytown. And, in case your memory needs refreshing, please recall that below that old church (reputed to be the very oldest in all the state) is the site of the Post Road bridge over which one Ichabod Crane, profession, schoolmaster, was chased in the witches' hour, by a certain headless horseman, profession unknown.

You can have a pretty fine time also in old Westchester—and its neighboring Putnam, just to the north of it—in just looking at the old churches and their burying-grounds. But most of the times the open road and the little villages of the "loveliest county" are the more appealing. I love the small obscure hamlets—like ancient Bedford, which proudly proclaims its venerability (it was founded in 1681) or the near-by Poundridge, or the Salems, designated South and North, to distinguish them from the other New York Salem, up in Washington County. Salem is about the sweetest name that I know for a town, unless perhaps it is Tranquility, New Jersey.

Some of these small places have hard work retaining their venerability these piping days. The onrush of the Big City forever is upon them. It started almost ninety years ago when the New York & Harlem Railroad finally thrust its rails across Lewis Morris's bridge at 133rd Street, invading Westchester hill and dale, reaching, in due time and solemnity, Williamsbridge and White Plains and finally, distant Brewster and Pawling (chiefly famed for doughnuts and milk in its ancient depot), and even places as far beyond as Chatham, on the railroad from Boston to Albany. At about the same time New York was deciding that it was going to be a metropolitan city, willy-nilly, and that a metropolitan city would have to have, among other large things, a metropolitan water supply. In the northerly part of the "loveliest county" was a stream of clear, pure water, gradually making its way down to the brackish Hudson. This was the Croton, a hundred years ago New York appropriated it as its chief source of water supply, building a dam across it, not ten miles back from the Hudson, and then an aqueduct for thirty miles right down to the island of Manhattan.

That was a mighty enterprise, and when it was completed (in

THE BIG CITY 39

1842) it was the excuse for a mighty celebration, with fireworks and speeches in the little park in front of the New York City Hall, general rejoicing, eating and drinking everywhere. New York had every reason to be proud of her new waterworks. Its thirty-mile aqueduct is a great pipe of masonry close to the surface of the earth (it used to be a pleasant walk to follow its plainly marked course) crossing and recrossing Broadway (at one point on a great stone-arch bridge) until finally it reached the east bank of the Harlem River. Manhattan was just across that stream (really not a river, but a strait of the sea), and to cross it was no easy problem. The engineers of the new waterworks solved it in the most obvious way —they bridged it; with a high stone-arch bridge of many arches, which for sheer beauty and artistry has rarely been equaled anywhere. High Bridge still stands and should continue to stand, for centuries to come—but not long ago, modern engineering did its best to ruin it (and nearly succeeded) by substituting a broad span steel arch for the former central ones of stone. Debit one for modernity.

It was not until the 'eighties that the northward pressure of New York City against Westchester County began to assume large proportions. Even as late as 1890, Yonkers, now the fifth city of the state in population, had only some eighteen thousand people. There were commuters to it from the beginning of the 'fifties; yet these were few in volume, demanding no great batteries of local trains morning and night and vast terminal stations in the city of New York. When Horace Greeley edited the *New York Tribune,* he lived in Chappaqua (his house burned years ago, but his descendants still live within his fine stone barn), rode regularly on the trains of the Harlem road and sometimes wrote pieces about them. There are veteran commuters on the New Haven as well, and in the 'seventies and the 'eighties Morrisania and Fordham and Williamsburgh were brisk suburban stations. No one ever thinks of them that way any more. Now it is Bronxville or Scarsdale or White Plains; Yonkers or Ardsley or even Peekskill; Larchmont or Rye or Port Chester. Mount Vernon is a new town, hardly sixty years old, yet it already has (1930) 61,499 inhabitants. In ordinary seasons some three hundred suburban trains run into the Grand Central Terminal in the morning, out again at night. If it were not for the commuter traffic, that glorified railroad station would hardly have to be half of its present size. The same is true of the Pennsylvania over on 7th Avenue, the bulk of whose one hundred and forty-five thousand patrons a day are users of the Long Island Railroad, co-tenant of the terminal. There are thousands of commuters as well on the Central of New Jersey, the Erie, the Lackawanna, the West Shore, but these go to Jersey night after night, and so they do not quite come within the province of this book.

Within an hour this flood ebbs out of its city and flows—a very great part of it—up into Westchester. It grows steadily all the while. Even Depression fails to halt it. Yonkers becomes a bigger and still bigger town; it is filled with apartments these days, and so are Mount Vernon and New Rochelle and Bronxville and White Plains, apartments nearly as closely built and as minutely divided as those of the Big City itself. There is no end in sight. The Croton system long since ceased to be adequate for the increasing thirst of New York (to say nothing of its other water uses), and twenty years ago the city thrust a hundred-mile arm up into the Catskills (as we are going to see in due time) for more, and now it contemplates invasion of the rural districts to the south of that mountain area.

Eventually Yonkers and Mount Vernon will become boroughs of the greater city, just as the Bronx and Brooklyn and parts of Queens were absorbed into it, forty years ago. The problem of transport will become the more acute. The present fine system of parkways, runing north and south and across Westchester, will not be enough. Just now they are building a super-highway from the north line of New York City down to Spuyten Duyvil, across the entrance of the Harlem into the Hudson by a super-bridge; then more super-highway down the west rim of Manhattan to Riverside Drive and

Whether it is to feed pigeons or to watch the flow of life on Fifth Avenue, the plaza before the New York Public Library is a favorite rendezvous.

Union Square East is the site of "S. Klein on the Square," New York's famous cut-rate dress store.

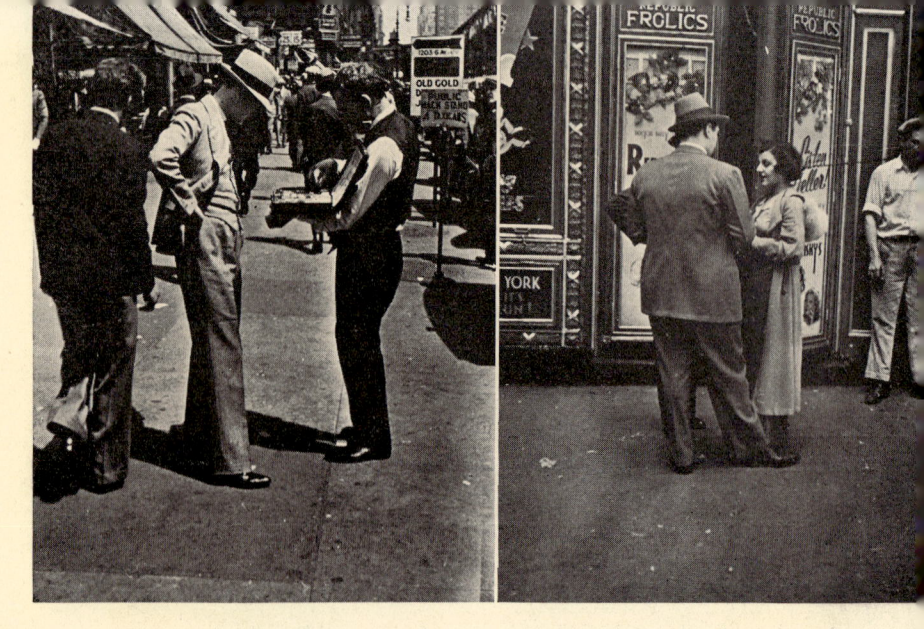

The sidewalks of New York are justly famed for the diversion they offer. Sidewalk vendors along Sixth Avenue will try to sell you anything from perfume to watches. And if you happen to be passing one of New York's many burlesque houses, you may catch a glimpse of a chorine or two.

Streets like Nassau Street, in the heart of the financial district, are packed in the daytime but at night they look like deserted caverns. Mid-town Broadway, on the other hand, is crowded with the traffic of cars, actors, and sightseers night and day.

THE BIG CITY

the elevated highway almost clear through to the Battery. Generous as it is, it will not be more than a drop in the bucket.

The truth of the matter is that no highway system can solve New York's eternal problem of transport. More relief can be granted—a super-elevated highway upon the east rim of Manhattan Island as well as upon the west; long underground roads, connecting 6th and 7th Avenues across the long way of Central Park, similar to the popular depressed transverse roads so many years in use across the breathing place of the great New York. But all of these would be only a few more drops in the bucket.

The answer is mass transportation. And mass transportation is buses—and more than buses—trains. A man riding to his office in the morning in his limousine takes up sixteen to eighteen feet of linear space in the crowded highway. Put another eight or ten feet to that, and you can have a vehicle that will carry, at least fairly easily, twenty to twenty-five persons. Add still another ten or twelve feet, double-deck your bus and you can seat, comfortably, from sixty to seventy persons. That is part of the answer. But not all of it. Buses—many of them—do take room; and they have no right to absorb completely the streets, on which other types of vehicles have inherent rights as well. Then the recourse comes to the steel rail, laid upon a right-of-way that is not part and parcel of the public highway. The day is coming when suburban passenger trains will again run down the west rim of Manhattan to a terminal, probably somewhere in the West 40's. No one knows when that day will be—it is not imminent, but it is inevitable, just as the addition of Yonkers and Mount Vernon to the greater city are inevitable. When this last comes to pass, the present subway lines will find their way into these populous communities now to the north of the line that marks their present barrier. The little branch of the Putnam (never developed as yet to its full possibilities as a carrier) into Getty Square, Yonkers, would make a logical extension of the present city-owned and operated Eight Avenue Subway, jut as the New York, Westchester & Boston (also never developed) would make an extension of one of the east side subways. But not at a five-cent fare. That silly fetish of the politicians will have to be thrown into the discard before a real transport solution ever can be reached for metropolitan New York.

There is a corner of metropolitan New York of which I almost hesitate to speak, lest it become invaded and so become no longer the precious, quiet corner that it now is. I refer to that point on the west bank of the Hudson, immediately above the New Jersey State line, where the Palisades cease to be abrupt escarpment and waterways break through again to the Big River. There are a few little towns in there—Tappan, Palisades, Sparkhill, Piermont (where the Erie originally had its main-line terminus). There are many old houses in this odd corner of great New York, and most of them are very old indeed. None perhaps are more interesting than the old DeWindt house at Tappan, one of George Washington's several headquarters in the Hudson River country. It bears upon its front the year of its construction, 1730. Half a century later it came to its greatest distinction: In its main room General Washington and Governor George Clinton met (May 6, 1783) to discuss the evacuation of New York by the British Army with Sir Guy Carleton and Admiral Digby of the British forces in North America. One William Smith was present, and in his diary he recorded some details of the interview—discussion over the time necessary for the formal evacuation of the city, about preventing the carrying off of American property, especially negroes, and the extension of the government of New York State as far as possible before the entire evacuation took place.

A few years ago the old house was doomed to destruction, but quick action on the part of the Masons has made it a shrine, open to public inspection. A better act the Masons never did.

One of the rarest *little* drives that I know in all New York State is that ten-mile affair at the very edge of the Hudson, from Piermont up to Nyack. You reach it by diverting from the main Route 9–W, just before you reach the Piermont viaduct, pass through Sparkhill, past a curious ancient drinking-well set into the side of the hill which bears this inscription:

O Traveler
Stay the weary feet
Drink of this fountain, cool and sweet
It flows for man and beast, the same.
Then go thy way, remembering still
The well beneath the hill.

then through Piermont itself. Now you are close beside the waters of the Big River. One street is between water and a towering cliff, and upon either side of it are tiny old houses, set very close to the road, with bits of garden—little beauty-spots, each of them. The scene is Old-Worldish, quite unforgettable. There is a tiny brick chapel along the way, with open belfry, which might have been stolen right out of Belgium, itself.

Through and beyond Nyack the road becomes a main route again, impressive, magnificent. It dips under the great hills that line the steep west bank of the Hudson, finally fails to find even the slenderest passage-room between them and the river, swings inland, rounds Rockland Lake (a place of popular resort), then gathers courage, strikes through to the river, reaching it by a veritable mountain pass, just south of Haverstraw, and thereafter keeps more or less in sight of the river, all the way up to the great Bear Mountain Park. Every mile of this is fascinating driving. Sometimes the road is wide and concrete, and sometimes it is narrow and twisting and not concrete. But always it is interesting, not alone in itself, but in the places that it reaches. Stony Point—redolent with its memories of Revolutionary fighting—Jones Point, the Highlands, finally Bear Mountain Park and West Point and Storm King—all within a brief fifty or sixty miles.

Almost every one of these is a stellar attraction. If Bear Mountain Park were situated out in the Far West, almost half America would be finding its way to it, time and time and time again. Here man and Nature have combined forces to create a vast playground of almost incomparable beauty. It reaches from Hudson rim, almost from the Military Academy at historic West Point, back some eighteen miles, almost to the aristocratic and exclusive Tuxedo in the

Ramapo Valley. It is as wild and as remote as anything that you will find in Colorado or California these days—and as beautiful—and yet it is at the very gates of the greatest city in the world. You come to it over roads of great beauty and excellence, by steamer up the nation's busiest river, or by train, and all that is but the beginning of a fascinating trip. For when you have wearied of it—if one might ever weary of Bear Mountain Park—there are the joys of that huge military educational machine at West Point, and beyond these the great highway that winds itself over the very brow of Storm King Mountain and then down again into the old towns of Cornwall and of Newburgh.

The roads that lead up from the Big City to this paradise upon the east bank of the Big River are less dramatic and perhaps less beautiful than that spectacular main highway upon the west, but they are interesting. They are lined with the great estates of Westchester and Putnam counties. They lead to fascinating and abundant lakes—Croton and Mahopac and Oscawanna. Every inch of this ground is ancient and profoundly historic. And when you are come by the very old town of Peekskill, whether you have ascended the new Bronx River Parkway or the ancient Albany Post Road, you will take a turn or two and come to the Hudson in its greater glory, at the very point where it emerges from the beauty of the Highlands. You will follow six or seven miles of steep and winding road, which would be very dangerous road if it were not well constructed, paved and guarded, passing one vista of the river after another, and then you are at the Bear Mountain Bridge, the most dramatic of all the gateways into Bear Mountain Park. The scene forever is dominated by the Big River and its guardian mountains, the mountains with their stillness and the Big River with all its life.

The Big River. It is upon us now—heart and soul upon us. And at once we begin to hie ourselves to its source, just as nearly as we can manage to locate it.

CHAPTER III

The Hudson Flows to the Sea

IT is born of a raindrop on the leaf of a tree somewhere on a mountainside in the hidden depths of the vast and seemingly endless Adirondacks. There are other raindrops, other trees. Pools of water glisten at their feet. From these pools run little rivulets, joining one another and constantly gaining in size. Pretty soon there is a considerable stream. The Hudson is born. The tiny river, like the rivulets that gave it birth, grows in size all the time. It finds its way through the crevices of the mountains, rattles noisily down over stone ledges, brings other and minor streams to it. Now it is a real river, still gaining strength and force. It becomes masculine, lordly, strong; it has powerful sets of muscles, which a little later will be compelled to go to work in the service of man. Adirondack lakes, Wolf Pond and Rich and Harris, pour into it. It makes a definite channel for itself, there in the distant hills of remote Essex County; it comes to North Creek and first attains the dignity of bridges and of dams—the young giant at last is being put to work.

Winging its way swiftly all the while, vigorous and strong in its ebullient youth; rushing through small towns like Warrensburg and Corinth and Luzerne and the much bigger ones of Glens Falls and Hudson Falls; driving their waterwheels, a laughing, impulsive river dancing in the sunlight, growing at each mile of its progress, slowing itself, gaining more dignity; then finally assuming a straight, southerly course toward the open sea—the Hudson begins to take its proper place among the mighty rivers of the land. At Cohoes it quietly receives its distinguished consort, the Mohawk, supplies its final efforts of power; three miles below at Troy it drops to sea level; thereafter it ceases to be power and becomes navigation.

Albany is but six miles below Troy, and there, at the capital of the state and the greatest of all its traffic hubs, navigation begins in earnest. Great ships ascend to Albany, one hundred and fifty miles from the open sea; and its new docks and elevators rank with the best that may be found anywhere. There they exchange traffic with the rail routes that radiate from the town, as well as with barges on the two canals that really terminate there; the one running north to Lake Champlain and to Montreal (using the upper Hudson for some thirty miles north of Troy), and the other almost due west, to Oswego, on Lake Ontario, and Buffalo, at the foot of Lake Erie. It all has come to be a considerable traffic, even though ice closes the canal for four or five months of the year. They have succeeded in keeping the river open for the big ocean ships below Albany for much of the entire twelvemonth. How difficult this is, the river folk know best. I have both walked and ridden (in a taxi) on the ice across the Hudson at Kingston. But I must confess to something of a quaking feeling when the floor of the river began to creak and sigh and boom in ominous fashion.

From Albany to the sea, the river becomes most majestic. Yet there is rare beauty in its banks as it thrusts its difficult young way past Corinth and Luzerne and the impasse just west of Glens Falls. Below Albany it is a different sort of river—an estuary of the sea, if you please, so very wide, that until recent years it defined the efforts of the bridge-builders to span it. True it is that there has been a railroad bridge at Poughkeepsie for nearly fifty years; but the river there is comparatively narrow, and very, very deep. The only deeper spot is in the Highlands of the Hudson, where the solid bot-

THE HUDSON FLOWS TO THE SEA 47

tom is over a thousand feet below the surface of the water. A tunnel (carrying much of the city water supply of metropolitan New York) passes under it here, at eleven hundred feet below the water surface. Cut from solid rock, a fine dry tunnel it was, too, before the Catskill waters were turned into it. I know, because once I walked through it, from Storm King Mountain to Breakneck Hill. I have crossed the Hudson in many ways; but never in more interesting ones than walking upon its surface and more than a thousand feet beneath that surface.

There are other tunnels under the Big River,—at New York City, which carry the rails of the Pennsylvania lines and the rapid transit lines into New Jersey, and which are also used by hundreds of automobiles and trucks every hour, but none of these reach anything like the depth of the aqueduct at Storm King. There are several bridges below Albany nowadays, in addition to that already ancient structure of the New England railroad at Poughkeepsie. The George Washington is one of the largest and finest suspension bridges in the world. There are two other suspension bridges; the picturesque one in the Highlands at Bear Mountain Park and the comparatively new highway bridge at Poughkeepsie. The railroad structure at Castleton (ten miles below Albany and carrying the through freight lines of the New York Central) and the newly completed Rip van Winkle at the village of Catskill, just a few miles further down, are of truss and cantilever type. The crossing of the wide lower Hudson is also furthered by the operation of many ferries, most of which have hung on persistently, even after the development of the bridges.

For any sort of proper appreciation of the Big River one should plan to make its ascent, preferably by steamboat. The motor-car is possible, although the main highroads that parallel it from New York to Albany do not always run close to its shores. The traveler upon the railroads (on either side of the river) has much better opportunity to see it, particularly if he rides upon the trains up the east bank.

But the steamboat is the real way to do it. The practical steamboat was born upon the Big River, away back in 1807, when Robert Fulton first began to operate his doughty little *Clermont* between the chief town of York State and its main seat of government. Upon the Hudson the steamboat has always thrived, until very recently at any rate. The *Clermont* was quickly succeeded by larger craft; the progress in this form of transport for almost an even hundred years was rapid indeed. The steamboat chugged and paddled itself into immediate popularity. Hudson River boats grew bigger and bigger. Almost always it could be said that they were the biggest in all the world. Three decks, four decks, two stacks, four stacks—they became vast white bulks, seemingly unmanageable, but the skill of the river pilots in making their way through the long and sometimes rather difficult course of the river as well as heeling them into dock became a marvelous thing indeed.

For many years no railroad dared directly to parallel the Hudson, and many of its more important towns were almost completely dependent for their transport upon the river and its craft. Steamboats formed the first swift and easy method of transit between New York and Albany and thrived accordingly. At one time there were not less than seven competing lines of boats between the two cities. And how they did compete! Their captains stood upon the ancient steamboat dock at the capital; they lied and fought and swore and cajoled for business down the river to New York, until bedlam was exceeded and the Albany police nearly driven crazy. Out of all this commotion two or three powerful "trades" finally emerged—the historic Peoples Line (night-boats) and the almost equally historic Day Line between New York and Albany; as well as the Citizens Line to Troy. There were other sizable lines upon the Hudson that survived until recently; night-boats from the metropolis up to Saugerties and Catskill, and local boats as well to West Point and Newburgh and Poughkeepsie and Kingston.

As the steamboats upon the river multiplied, they not only grew larger, but grander. Dr. Eliphalet Nott, the famous early president of Union College at Schenectady, developed the use of anthracite as marine fuel to replace the steadily dwindling supply of wood; gadgets and refinements of every sort were added to the boats. They became swifter, as well as finer, but not safer. The fierce competition between them at the outset led to their owners and their masters taking all manner of risk in their operation. Steamboat racing became a mighty sport upon the Hudson. A mighty dangerous one as well. Sometimes boilers would explode and fires start, which, with the wooden tinderbox construction of these craft, became holocausts and great tragedies. Sometimes boilers would explode and the steamboats mysteriously catch fire, without racing, and sometimes they would go ashore upon the river banks in heavy fog and manage to wreck themselves. The casualty lists upon the old-time river boats became long and most appalling.

Yet gradually travel on the Hudson was made reasonably safe. The many accidents upon the river in the early development of its steam navigation made for restrictions and improvements that hedged about the well-being of the travelers. And for years past, there have been few consequential accidents. The average age of the steamboats has been greatly lengthened. The *Drew,* of the Albany night line, was one of the finest river boats ever built. When she was completed (in a Jersey City shipyard in 1863) she was longer from stem to stern than any ship crossing the Atlantic Ocean. She ran her course for more than forty years, with never an accident of any sort, wore herself out in steady duty and finally was taken to the graveyard of many ships, at Perth Amboy, off Staten Island. There she was dismantled and sunk in the mud—a sort of inglorious fate that comes to many boats that merely have done their duty, and done it well.

As the *Drew* came forth in '63, so, in that selfsame summer, came the *Mary Powell,* in many respects the most famous of all the Hudson River craft. The *Powell* was designed for day service only, as a sort of glorified ferry between the Big City and ancient Kingston, some ninety miles north. In the sixty long years that she plied the river there was no variation to her run. She left Rondout (the ancient port of Kingston) in the very early morning and reached her berth at New York just before noon. At three in the afternoon she began her dignified return up the river; and came into Kingston at about nine in the evening. Six days in the week, from early in May until late in October, she fulfilled this program. On the Sabbath day her giant paddle-wheels never ruffled Hudson water. Her skippers were God-fearing men, who stuck stoutly to their principles. I knew the last of them very well indeed: Captain A. E. Anderson, who succeeded his father as master of the *Mary Powell*. He was one of the few remaining river men who owned and operated their own ships, as they pleased and when they pleased. It pleased Anderson to take the Saturday before the *Powell* went into commission for the summer to entertain the children of a certain Sunday School in Poughkeepsie as his guests for a trip up the river to Albany and back; on the Saturday after she had ended her season he took the boys and girls of the Sunday School in Rondout for a similar expedition to the capital.

"Would you believe it," he used to say to me, solemnly, "when we make the Albany trip it's just next to impossible to make the *Powell* go outside Kingston breakwater and continue on up the river? She's just that used to making the turn up Rondout Creek and into the harbor."

The master of the *Mary Powell* took his task very seriously indeed. He was a slim, dapper man, who wore double-breasted suits of blue serge and took a sort of gentle, personal care of his passengers, as if they were members of his own family. Early in the morning when the *Powell* pulled out of her berth in Kingston harbor, he stood at the gangplank of his craft, inspecting closely each person that came aboard; greeting his many friends cordially and at rare intervals rejecting some one whom he deemed unfit to make the journey upon his boat. He detested drunkenness. He repeated the process at all the landings, Poughkeepsie, Milton, New Hamburgh, Newburgh, West Point, Highland Falls, and when in the shadows of the evening, the huge white bulk of the steamboat made her way up the Creek again, so silently that you would not have known of her coming, save for the whistles and the catcalls of the boys along the stringpieces of the wharves, it was Captain Anderson, himself, who saw the last of his patrons safely off the gangplank. They do not make that kind of captains any more, on the Hudson or anywhere else.

The whole world was his patron. Boys rode on her when first they came to "the Point," brought their brides upon her for the honeymoon and rode again upon her when they had become distinguished generals in the Army. The cream of the valley was proud to be enrolled upon her passenger lists. Those lists read like a bluebook of Hudson River aristocracy. They all were the captain's guests. And they all knew him. And once, on one of his almost innumerable winter trips to far corners of the world, while he was riding on a steamboat up the Nile he presented his card to the captain of that craft and was immediately welcomed in royal fashion by a Britisher whose pleasantest memory of a long-ago trip to America was a ride up the Hudson on the *Mary Powell*.

It *was* pleasant to pull out of New York harbor in the middle of a broiling-hot summer afternoon and to run into the soft coolness of the evening up the most beautiful of all American rivers; an experience that you never forgot, and of which you never tired no matter how often you ventured upon it. The *Powell* was swift, but silent. She rarely used her whistle. But above her wheelhouse she had mounted a silver bell, of ineffable sweetness, and this gave the warning to the little towns along the Hudson bank of the long-acclaimed "queen of the river"—that and the voice of Seymour Darling, for thirty-four years head deckhand of the *Mary Powell*, calling the landing, with a sweetness of musical inflection that seems to be the exclusive possession of the negro.

One could write a good deal about the *Mary Powell*. There probably never was a swifter side-wheel steamboat ever built. Her designer, once the craft had been finished, burned her models and her drawings. When, years afterwards, the Day Line, inheritors of much of her prestige, sought to build the great *Hendrick Hudson*, and to make it the fastest, as well as the largest, steamboat that ever ran on inland waters, they put the old *Powell* in the drydock and measured her hull with rules and giant calipers; and fashioned their new craft just as nearly to the lines of the old as they could make her. For no steamboat going in the same direction ever passed the *Mary Powell*. Perhaps in her latter years some of them could, but no one ever did. There is a good deal of etiquette after all among these river captains.

The Day Line has always had the same veneration and respect for Hudson water tradition that the owners of the *Mary Powell* had. For many years the Van Santfoord family owned the line; and in those years their boats never ran on Sunday either (the most profitable day of the entire week for the steamboat business); and, like the *Powell,* never dispensed liquor in their restaurants or cabins. In my early days, the service of the Day Line was performed by two fine steel steamers, the *New York* and the *Albany*. The *New York* burned years ago in winter storage in Newburgh, but the handsome *Albany* still is in good running order and occasionally used. The *Mary Powell* went out of commission at about the time of the World War. Her fine old master died, and they ran the boat up Rondout Creek well beyond the shipyard and there, just out of sight of Hudson water, they dismantled her—after all her years of wonderful service without the loss of a single passenger or a serious accident of any kind. Once she was caught in a hard blow in the wide waters of Tappan Zee and her tall smokestacks blown off, all with a good deal of attendant excitement; but Anderson and his men worked coolly, and the boat made her way to the landing under her own power.

Many of the fine old boats remain in service. The *Hendrick Hudson,* the *Robert Fulton* and the *Alexander Hamilton* still have few rivals upon inland waters anywhere. Even those giants of historic nightboats, the *Morse* and the *Berkshire,* still operate under pressure of extra heavy traffic. Unfortunately that pressure comes rarely these days; the smaller *Trojan* and the *Rensselaer* seem abundantly able to take care of most of the night business up to Albany and Troy, even in the hot months of midsummer. And the boat service to the mid-Hudson has become a rather sketchy and uncertain thing. It begins to look as if steamboating on the Hudson after a splendid hundred-year career and a brave fight for existence at the end of it, was about to go the way of steamboating on the Ohio and the Mississippi. Credit that to the motor-car. The railroad may have worked devastation to the steamboating of western rivers, but it was never able seriously to affect the mighty water traffic of the Hudson, for it was not all passenger business on the Big River. Long tows of barges, hauled by stout and efficient tugs, ran up and down the entire navigable length of the river. The center of this traffic was at Kingston, chief gateway to the Catskill country and once the main terminal of the historic Delaware & Hudson canal. That canal company, formed much more than a century ago, was chiefly responsible for the introduction of anthracite coal to profitable commercial use through the entire East. Its canal ran more than a hundred miles into the inland country back of Kingston, as far in fact as northeastern Pennsylvania, and brought the shining new fuel—"stone coal" they called it in those days—from the collieries on the far side of a barrier mountain near Honesdale.

Two Philadelphia dry-goods dealers, named Wurts, were really responsible for the conception of the Delaware & Hudson enterprise. They had mined over a thousand tons of hard coal from that far side of Moosic Mountain, when the unpleasant fact began to be forced upon them that they could not sell their product unless they could transport it to good markets. William Wurts went afoot all the way from Honesdale to Kingston and made a rough location of the projected canal. He took his maps and his ideas and a trunkful of the stone coal to New York and there demonstrated it to ex-Mayor Philip Hone and a group of other influential citizens in a grate in the old Tontine Coffee House. That was early in January 1825. A few days later the Delaware & Hudson Company was incorporated, with Hone as its president. And that summer, work began on its new canal, at a small settlement then called Mamakating, but which quickly was renamed Wurtsboro. That name has remained from that day to this. Three years saw the 108 miles of canal completed, with its 110 locks and 137 bridges, at least two of which—the suspension aqueduct over the Rondout at High Falls and the long three-arch one over the Delaware near Lackawaxen, both of them designed by John B. Jervis—were real triumphs of engineering. The High Falls aqueduct disappeared some years ago, but the structure across the Delaware makes a fine highway bridge and probably will be used for years to come. Motor-cars slide easily through the bed of the aqueduct; it is more than forty years since the quiet waters of the once-busy canal rested placidly there. For the Delaware & Hudson Canal is but a memory now; its honorable name is perpetuated by an extensive railroad, which runs across New York from Binghamton to Albany and the Canada line.

One still can easily trace the old canal's course for a dozen miles or more back from the Hudson at Kingston. And a more picturesque and enjoyable walk can hardly be imagined. The canal really began at Eddyville, a very small village about three miles back from Hudson water. High hills here encompass the Rondout and its tributary, the Wallkill. Here once was the center of a great industry. Rosendale cement seemed to have a virtue and a vogue all its own. Now it is gone. Only hills with their hearts burned out remain; industry is forever stilled; there is nothing but silence and summer boarders and the bed of the canal, still half filled with water, becoming clogged with small brush and sizable young trees. At Eddyville stands the old structure that housed the weighlock, where the fat-bellied little canal barges were carefully weighed and checked as to their loads (in the last days of the ancient water town, from 125 to 150 tons each) after two strenuous days down from the Honesdale terminal.

On the high bank of the Rondout Creek in Kingston Harbor you still can see the old-fashioned brick structure that once housed the offices of the canal; below were the docks and the slips. Three staunch steamboats of a still earlier day would gather up large groups of the canal barges and carefully convey them down the

Big River to the Big City. These steamers had done with their duties as passenger-carrying craft; their cabins and their decks long since had been removed; their upper works stood out in gaunt nakedness to the gaze of a younger world. But they had not lost their efficiency—the old *Alida* and the *Norwich* and the *Syracuse*. It was no small trick to bring a long tow of thirty or forty canal-boats down around the sharp turn and swift channel at West Point, particularly with a stiff wind coming up the river. No one must have known that better than these old boats themselves. They had been at it too many years to take it as any light responsibility.

There still are many tows upon the river; but nothing like the old days when it was said (with exaggeration) that there were times when one could walk or jump from shore to shore in the Narrows of the Highlands by crossing the decks of the barges in the tows when they became wedged in thick traffic. Now, in place of the tows there are ocean steamships, big five-thousand-ton craft with lumber bound from Portland or Seattle through the Panama Canal to Poughkeepsie; or from Scandinavia, bringing pulp or pulpwood from Stockholm or Oslo or Bergen up to the new docks at Albany. Trim modern barges of the Standard Oil, cleverly devised to fit the prisms of the locks of the Barge Canal, further upstate, also use the Hudson. The Big River is far from dead.

The towns that line its banks are apt to reflect a past of some omniscience. Some of them sleep in the sweet serenity of a day when they played a valiant part in the making of a new nation.

Can there come to this valley once more the stout and sturdy spirit of a colonizing nation like the Dutch; and, after them, the English? Does history repeat itself? Will there ever come again the day when an invading army from far-off shores seeks to take advantage of such a God-given natural water path as this? The ancient hills that hem in West Point cannot have entirely forgotten the strong chain of iron that was wrought in distant Ramapo Valley to be stretched across that narrow part of the river against the ascent of a British navy. The hills around Saratoga are softer, but they too have heard the echoes of hard cannonading, of the deadly rattle of musketry; have known of the presence of a hard-fought battle of worldwide significance.

It may take a holocaust of such importance along Hudson stream ever fully to awake the old Hudson River towns again. Better let them sleep. They are not dead—far from it. Their streets still pulse with life and activity, are lined with smart and handsome new buildings. Try to poke your way through Market Street, Poughkeepsie, with your motor-car on a busy Saturday afternoon, or down the narrow hillside streets of Newburgh, and you will think that the circus certainly has come to town, or some other attraction of not less magnitude. These are all important hubs, of merchandising attraction, of legal authority, of education and, to no small extent, of manufacturing. We will eliminate Yonkers and everything else up the banks of the Hudson to Peekskill and to Haverstraw, as being in large sense a part of metropolitan New York; and still find before we reach Albany a group of rather important cities and towns—Newburgh, Beacon—a sort of conglomerate of several old towns—Poughkeepsie, Kingston, Saugerties, Catskill and Hudson.

Of all of these, to me, Kingston has the largest measure of personal appeal. Perhaps because I have known it rather better than the others. In it are blended all that the Hudson Valley has of charm, tradition, beauty, history. As the ancient Dutch village of Wiltwyck, it was one of the earliest points in the entire valley to be settled. Many of the descendants of those sturdy Dutch emigrants still are resident in and about the place. It changes but slowly and sticks most loyally to all its fine traditions. As a renamed loyal British town it grew apace. Equipped with a fine harbor, it became a natural gateway to a really vast back country. Already we have seen how a thriving canal enterprise made it its chief terminal; how a stone-paved turnpike ran all the way over the Catskills to the distant village of Oneonta and the swift and somewhat navigable Susquehanna. But the more important hinterland to old Kingston was up the Valley of the Huguenots along the course of the

THE HUDSON FLOWS TO THE SEA 57

Rondout Creek. If you continued far enough you passed the head waters of the Rondout, crossed a slight divide and descended those of the Neversink until you came to Port Jervis at the turn of the Delaware at the point where New York and New Jersey and Pennsylvania come together. Eventually this valley became the route of the Delaware & Hudson Canal. An obvious route it was. But long before the calls of the boatmen began to echo against the hills it was a busy valley; busy in agriculture and curiously interested in the development of lead mines which began to push their way into the hearts of those high hills. The railroad did not come into the lower valley until comparatively recent years, along in the 'nineties. By that time the old lead mines were deserted and the canal abandoned. The sole memories of yesteryear were the low gray stone vine-clad houses of Old Hurley and Stone Ridge and Kerhonkson and Warwarsing and Napanoch.

These still line the highroad and serve as a gracious link between past and present. As you drive today along that road you find that it frequently takes and follows an elevated ridge down the middle of the valley and then presents a succession of exquisite views; on the one hand, of the Catskills and their foothills, and on the other, of a parallel range, the Shawangunks. These last mountains are nearer. They rise abruptly from the Valley of the Huguenots; sometimes in sheer ascent; and at one place, where there is a great gash in the skyline, there is a tower, and if you journey up to the handsome summer hotel there you will find that it watches its reflection in a gem of a lake, set like a teardrop, high upon the mountain.

For such a hinterland, Kingston makes appropriate gateway indeed. It is, as it should be, a county-seat. The law business of Ulster County is done in the handsome old gray stone court house, built back in 1818. Law faces Religion. Across narrow Wall Street—Kingston once upon a time was a walled town—is the churchyard of the Dutch Reformed folk, with its great trees and its crumbling stones and, set sternly amid it, a sizable high-spired church. This is not the original Dutch Reformed of old Wiltwyck. That disappeared two centuries or so ago. The present church is modern, but not too modern. That Upjohn, who designed Trinity Church in lower Broadway, New York, built it, and it is hardly less handsome than its slightly older brother at the head of the Wall Street of the Big City. It is a spacious and a splendid edifice and, if you are interested, you may wish to notice the well-preserved letter of George Washington to the deacons of the church at Kingston, which is displayed in the vestry. To be a deacon of Kingston church was no slight honor. One feature of the old Dutch high church there should not be overlooked. Annually, in November, the "First Dutch" gave its "turkey supper"—one dollar and eat all you can. The women of the church spent much time making preparation for this sweetly solemn festivity. Such mountain-ranges of good foods. Such cake! Such preserves! And such turkey! Supper was served at a quarter of six, and an hour before that the line formed outside the door. At a quarter after six there was no more food. They have appetites (also digestions) in Ulster County.

We used to have a good deal of a time each fall in Kingston, carefully reading the *Freeman* each evening and checking the turkey suppers being given all around the county. By working it out rather carefully you could eat about four a week. None of the others cost a dollar; but none of the others ever reached the super-pinnacle of excellence of the "First Dutch." There never was as much dollar's worth of food anywhere else in the world.

Kingston is another conglomerate. Originally there were two towns: Kingston, set on the upland above Esopus Creek, three miles back from the bank of the Hudson, and Rondout, at the point where the creek of that name empties itself into the Big River. A broad highway connected the two villages, and gradually they grew together, ribbonlike, upon it, until there was a continuous line of buildings all the way and a horse-car line to complete the marriage. They paved the street and it became Broadway, and they united the two villages and became the city of Kingston. They were united politically, but not so well united in some other ways. For a long time bitter rivalry prevailed between the two ends of the town; each was rather jealous of the other. When it came to the placing of its public buildings—the City Hall, the Post Office and the High School—it was tactful, to put it moderately, to locate them on Broadway just halfway between the two former business centers. When the West Shore Railroad first was built to and through Kingston, it had the wisdom—and the tact—to place its station midway between the two centers. Even visiting circuses learned long ago equally to divide their morning parades between Rondout and Wiltwyck. Circus men nearly always are diplomats. They have learned to be.

The chief showplace of Kingston is the aged Senate House, which is carefully preserved in a small park of its own (with a historical museum closely adjacent). To this long, low, gray stone building, running close to the sidewalk and so very typical of all the early houses of the old colonial town, the first governor of the state, that "country lawyer," the Honorable George Clinton (he lies buried in the quiet churchyard of the High Dutch Church not far distant), called the first Legislature of the state of New York, the Senate of which met under its roof September 10, 1777. The Assembly organized that day in the near-by tavern of Evert Bogardus with Walter Livingston, son of the distinguished Philip Livingston, New Yorker and signer of the Declaration of Independence, as its first speaker; then joined with the Senate (already organized) at the Ulster County Court House to hear the Governor speak most enthusiastically of the American victories in the north and of the Highlands of the Hudson, strongly fortified against any possible British invasion. Clinton boasted all too quickly. Within the month the forts in the Highlands fell to the invaders, and, to add insult to injury, the British incontinently burned Kingston on the evening of the 16th of the following October. Thereafter the meetings of the New York State Legislature became sketchy indeed. Poughkeepsie was used. It was not until several years later that the capital was moved to its permanent location, at Albany, up the river.

The older Kingstonians are immensely proud of their fine town and its traditions. In recent years there have been many changes; you can sense some of them as you read the names on the street signs in the two business hearts of the town. One of the two ferries has disappeared—the ancient *Skilliput,* which hung on a chain across the mouth of the Rondout Creek; it boasted a charter dating back to the days of George II. A fine new suspension bridge has replaced it. But the other and more important ferry, down the creek and straight across Hudson water to ancient Rhinebeck, still remains. It is nearly as old. And the venerable *Transport* still operates and prints its charges for cattle and sheep and hogs and human beings. For the last the toll is thirteen cents, which is about as close to the original sixpence permitted, as can be figured out in our coinage.

The Catskill country has nearly always been tourist area. The Catskill Mountain House, which still stands on the sharp eastern slope of the mountain, has looked down into the villages of Saugerties and Catskill for over a hundred years now. You can see it clearly against the mountainside, like a lady wearing a white pearl against a dark green evening gown. The first travelers who risked the ascent to its hospitable great public rooms and wide verandahs made the trip by coach-and-four and probably spent much time writing to their relatives about the difficulties of the trip. Then came the boon of the railroad; first a little line up from Kingston by a most roundabout route (Phoenicia and Tannersville). And then the far more direct one of the "Narrow Gauge."

This curious little railroad, which was one of the triumphs and the joys of Greene County in the 'eighties and the 'nineties, has now disappeared. It was in three sections. You went up to Catskill on the steamboat, or the West Shore Railroad, and there you found the "Narrow Gauge" awaiting you. It went around sharp curves and some rather stiff grades until it came to the base of the mountain in the middle of an open field. There you transferred, bag and baggage, to the Otis Elevator, one of the most remarkable constructions in the entire East, a funicular to delight the heart of any Neapolitan.

It made the lower part of its very steep ascent up a spidery-looking steel trestle and the upper part within a cutting; but every inch of it revealed to passengers a panorama of dazzling beauty, with the Hudson in the middle foreground and off far to the east, the sharp-cut rim of the Berkshires. When you had come to the platform at the very top, you were within short walking distance of the Mountain House (to all the natives known as the "Old Beach," because of the family who ran it so successfully for many years). If you wanted to go a little farther back into the Catskills you transferred again at the upper landing-stage; this time to another little "narrow gauge," whose small locomotives hauled their heavily laden trains, as far back as Tannersville.

Hunter and the Grand Gorge were about the far limits of the tourist invasion prior to the coming of the motor-car. Yet beyond these there are some of the most charming villages of the Catskill area; Roxbury—home of the great naturalist, John Burroughs, and birthplace of Jay Gould, whose old family homestead still is carefully preserved—and Stamford and Prattsville amongst them. Of these, the last and least picturesque has greatest appeal to me. Perhaps it is because of Zadock Pratt.

Zadock Pratt was a man of personality in these parts, a hundred odd years ago. He was the greatest tanner New York State ever knew; the bark fires of his giant tanneries night and day threw their yellow smoke up against the blue sky that hung above the mountains, in order that there might be plenty of leather for man and beast, shoes and saddles and harnesses and what you will. But Zadock Pratt was much more than tanner or founder of the small tidy village that still bears his name; his name was identified with all the major projects of that part of the state at that time, post roads and railroads and canals and every sort of manufacturing enterprise. But I like him best because he was fond of horses. He buried his pets in a small burying-ground at the end of the village cemetery; on the hard rock of the mountainside above, he caused a sculptor to make an enduring bas-relief of his favorite. A man cannot be far wrong who likes horses that way.

Zadock Pratt in course of time became a member of Congress and introduced many radical changes into that body. He had an equally distinguished son, George W. Pratt, who headed a distinguished New York fighting regiment and was killed in action in the battle of Manassas. Colonel Pratt shares the curious memorial at Pratts Rocks with his father. But the monument to the older Pratt's animals is the most interesting feature of the place. It stands in a small clump of pines just above the road and reads:

Of over a thousand horses owned and worn out in the service of Z. Pratt, the following were favourites:

BOBB, A Sorrel
AE 24 Years

BOGUE, A Bay
AE 18 Years

PRINCE, A Gray
AE 30 Years

DOGS

CARLO, AE 12 Years

RUFF, AE 11 Years

MINGO, AE 10 Years

At the top of the headstone, in a circle, are small bas-reliefs, oddly carved, of a horse and a dog, the one above the other. This was a man's tribute to his animal friends, erected many years ago and venerated by the mountain country to this day.

The beginnings of mighty rivers other than the Hudson are in the Catskill mountain area, the Delaware chief among these; and also the Schoharie, which did not come to Hudson water until it had traveled far to the north and emptied itself into the Mohawk. But nowadays the waters of the stream come *under* the waters of the Hudson, in a far more direct fashion. The newest dam and reservoir to supply the insatiable water appetite of metropolitan New York is at Gilboa, on the upper waters of the Schoharie. By this great dam these waters are turned directly back in their course and diverted through an eighteen-mile tunnel to the head waters of Esopus Creek, which in turn leads into the Ashokan reservoir, twenty-four miles in length and from two to four in width.

This artificial lake, held high above Kingston in a dimple of the mountains and into whose waters they cast their noble reflections, long since became a magnet for motorists. They admire the tremendous dam, which is the key of the entire extended structure of dykes and smaller dams, and cast "ohs" and "ahs" at the system of aerating fountains in the parklike area before the gatehouse and the beginning of the hundred-mile aqueduct right down into the heart of Manhattan. But they do not realize that where the deep waters of this lake now mirror the Catskills there once was a deep valley with little houses and farms and seven little villages and a dozen graveyards and the ancient highroad and the railroad from Kingston to Oneonta, all within it. What a mighty trek began when the edict went forth that this valley was to be no more, that the shiny surface of the reservoir would be more than a hundred feet above the cock on the spire of the church at West Hurley, and that water from above would mock at Olive Bridge, which had spanned water below all the many years. Now, after nearly a quarter of a century, they are nearly all forgotten. The city's drink of water rests securely in the mountains; in the hundred-mile tube from it to the Big City, you could run two railroad trains side by side; water, to the height of a man's shoulder, passes through it, as rapidly as if a man were afoot and strolling down Broadway.

Newburgh and Poughkeepsie present their own charms. They are today brisk and attractive cities, without having sacrificed much, if any, of the glory of yesteryear. Newburgh is built upon the west shore of the river upon a steep slope close to the Hudson bank; Poughkeepsie, rather back from the eastern shore of the stream.

Newburgh has, as its chief attraction, the carefully preserved structure where Washington made his headquarters in the winter of 1777; and Poughkeepsie has Vassar College. Newburgh is the shiretown of Orange County; and Poughkeepsie, of Dutchess. It would be hard to pick between them for loveliness. It certainly is safe to say that there are no two lovelier *twin counties* in all America. Both were formed away back in 1683. If Dutchess has Vassar College, Orange has West Point—and there you are! Both are horsey; probably Orange, on the west bank, with Goshen and its trotting races and Hambletonian tradition, the horsier of the two. But Dutchess has but little to yield. The very names of its towns—Pleasant Valley and Silvernails and Red House and Amenia, connote a kindly sort of old-fashioned living. At Washington Huddle, just beyond Pleasant Valley on the hard road from Poughkeepsie to Millbrook, there once was a fine race-track and fair. Traces of it remain. I never saw the races there. But the memories of the Dutchess County Fair and the Grand Circuit races under the great trees on the outskirts of Poughkeepsie are not eradicable.

In an editorial, entitled *Restocking Dutchess,* in the New York *Herald Tribune* a year or two ago, the anonymous writer paid full attention to this phase of the rural situation along the easterly shore of the Hudson, saying:

Dutchess County less than fifty years ago, was still famous for its animal husbandry. The smart pacers that drew its top wagons, the oxen that helped out the team with heavy drawing, the hams hanging in the smokehouse, the cows that gave leathery, yellow cream, the sheep obligingly cropping forage no other stock would touch, the frozen beef, the justly boastful Dominiques and Buff Cochins, all were raised within their own confines. Now and then in summer a tumultuous string of horses from "the West" would be driven along the dusty roads, and farmers would take a few as a sort of adventure, but the county's celebrated stockfarms supplied finer and better-mannered horseflesh. For there was always a stockfarm in the neighborhood and a proper number of "well-known local horsemen" who had their own racetracks and that bred-in-the-bone horsiness of men who have grown up with horses and tended them in sickness and in health, in days when running races were regarded as coarse, when real horsemen gave their attention to trotters and pacers, and a portrait of Rex Hambletonian hung in the dining room.

Every autumn, then, saw the Dutchess roads busy with blue-ribbon contenders being driven to the Poughkeepsie or the neighboring Danbury or Carmel fair. The bright boys of Dutchess County broke bull calves and trained teams of chubby steers and curried their own sorrel coats until they shone like copper. Box wagons paused on thank-you-ma'ams, full of crated Poland-China boars. Yearlings and glowering rams, with their feet carefully tied, lay on their sides in soft hay, jogging to the fair. All is now a part of the county's gracious past, it might be thought. The new blood doesn't raise fine stock; doesn't know how; has no crumbling blue ribbons in the top bureau drawer. . . .

All of which is preface to comment on the part of the *Herald Tribune* to the effect that animal husbandry *is* again returning to the fat farms of old Dutchess. The far-sighted and progressive owners of some of its finest estates are giving thought again to the breeding of cattle, large and small, of sheep and of horses.

Dutchess County also has the summer home of the present President of the United States and the interesting little group of workshops conducted by his ambitious and energetic wife. There are homes on Hudson bank even more pretentious than that of the Roosevelts. Many of the old houses remain; and some of them are in the hands of the original proprietary families. Not many of them can be seen; not from the road at least. You do rather better from the water, which the old houses seem to delight in facing; turning their backs upon *hoi polloi* and the rush and racket of the highroad.

One of these houses I shall never forget. I came to it through a narrow riverfront street of one of the sleepiest and most decadent of the Hudson River towns. Quite sharply, as we made a sudden turn of the car we faced a neat brick lodge, or gatehouse, painted a fine red, with a woman in black sitting on its porch, knitting.

"You're expected up at the big house," said she. "Up this road, about a quarter of a mile and then a sharp turn to the right." And went on with her knitting.

The "big house" faced a gently sloping, well-cropped lawn and a vision of the Hudson and its mountains that would give the most case-hardened old city sinner pause. On the river below, a white steamboat made leisurely progress downstream, a tow and an ocean-liner, Albany bound, breasted the current upstream. The gentleman and his sister who lived in the house, both elderly folk, gave gracious welcome to one who had not before met them, but who came only by note of introduction. They showed me the house, dark and rather forbidding within its high Victorian rooms, lined and sealed with walnut, almost grown black in shade; and the garden, bright and beautiful. In that garden there were, literally, miles of boxwood hedge. There were pools, too, filled with yellow and red goldfish and silver globes whose rounded faces reflected the glories of the trees above and of the cloud-flaked sky. There these two folk lived; and triumphed in the serenity of a life that seemingly could know no defeat.

To bring into this single picture all the charm and wonder of the Big River and its valley is well-nigh impossible. One would have to take you to the parade ground of West Point (as well as to the daisy chain at Vassar), to see one of the almost matchless bodies of well-trained and well-drilled young men march in steady rhythm before you. You would have to go into the far reaches of the great Bear Mountain Park, with its deep forests and its endless chains of lake. You would take a stout motor-car and ride around the stony breast of old Storm King. You would park the car and take the thrilling trip up the steep funicular to the top of Beacon Mountain; resume it again, ride north, tarry for tea at what claims to be the oldest hotel in America (and probably is) at Rhinebeck, dine gorgeously (if invited) at the exclusive and ever glorious Yama Farms in the Valley of the Huguenots, ascend to the near-by Sands Points, where George Inness and other important painters long years ago established headquarters, and drink in the view to the south from there.

If you are interested in the painter folk, their work and their recreation, you certainly will wish to go back from Kingston, a dozen miles, to the small village of Woodstock; which in recent years has become a sort of Mecca for the craft, comparable with Lyme or East Gloucester or Taos or Carmel. Good craftsmen have worked and still are working up at Woodstock, in the shade of Overlook Mountain. There is much play there, a harvest festival under the August full moon (called the Maverick) that is the astounding talk of the countryside and to which it comes in great numbers each year and waits till the coming of the dawn. There are plenty of "quaint shoppes" and "olde nookies," for people who like that sort of thing, and Saturday mornings all summer long a market on the village green where one can pick up curious works of art and the like. But this of course is *not* the real Woodstock.

The real Woodstock originally was a small, sleepy, unspoiled York state village on the banks of the Sawkill, with a white-spired church and an ancient hotel with a two-storied porch, and the town hall looking down upon the village green; a quiet group of God-fearing folk with their own traditions, and not many ambitions. The late Ralph Radcliffe Whiteside and his associates, Bolton Brown and Hervey White, were scouring almost the entire Atlantic seaboard in a search for a location for an art colony where not only painting, but all manner of hand craftsmanship could be encouraged and developed. They hit upon Woodstock. And Woodstock promptly ceased to think of its traditions, and began to develop its ambitions, until it found itself, for three or four months of the year at least, seething with a sort of pseudo metropolitanism. The sweet old hotel with its porches burned, and they substituted an atrocity of pressed brick and stained glass in its place; the invasion of "olde shoppes" and Hungarian restaurants came in, like an inundation. People swam in a deep hollow of the Sawkill (which incidentally is the city water supply of Kingston). Woodstock became a second Coney Island!

Yet judge not Woodstock too harshly for all this fuss and flutter. Go behind this veneer of gayety; get admittance (if you can) to one of the studios where the real work of the colony is being done. The fuss and flutter may yet conquer; if it does Woodstock as a real art center is doomed—just as other attempts of the same sort have doomed themselves. The real artists will disappear. And the little village will have to bury its new ambitions and try to live again in the old traditions.

The main street of Woodstock, which leads due east from the market green in the center of the village, forks just beyond the swimming hole. The road to the right leads to the Ashokan Reservoir and down to Kingston; the one to the left to Saugerties. If you choose to follow it and then up the west bank of the river to Albany, you will shortly come by Malden-on-Hudson. Here stands the old Bigelow home and a warm welcome by John Bigelow's equally distinguished son, Poultney. In other years Poultney Bigelow was wont to have a Maverick of his own. Annually he chose the first Saturday of October for this *fête champêtre;* for the genial Poultney always has hung to a pet theory that it never, never rains on this particular Saturday. At any rate, the entire countryside was pretty generally invited—and the entire countryside made a point of coming. The hospitable old Bigelow home furnished the soup and the bread and the coffee. The three or four hundred picnickers did the rest. Some of the folk from swagger Rhinebeck or Hyde Park over across the Big River even brought their butlers, to help in the service. Everybody brought sandwiches and cold meats and salads and cake and whatever else came into their imaginations.

At just noon Poultney, in his open-throated shirt and French peg-top pants, pushed the old greyhound out of the front door and appeared, frantically ringing a huge dinner-bell. That was the signal for the line to form and file solemnly by him through the long library into the great kitchen and there get the soup and coffee. Bowery style, but great fun. Then everybody would go out into the yard again, and plunge into the basket lunches. It was share and share alike. After an hour or so, the music of the village band would be heard coming up the street, lending more gayety to the scene. There was more music afterwards, perhaps a singer up from the Metropolitan or a famous harpist down from Syracuse. After that, oratory. It seemed as if almost always he had the Japanese Ambassador for a guest. He always liked Japan. And weeks before he would have had the children of the Malden school properly rehearsed in singing the Japanese national anthem. In exchange for their performance they received ice-cream and cake.

The parties are but pleasant memories now. *Who's Who* says that Poultney Bigelow has now reached the comfortable age of eighty; and *Who's Who* ought to know. And at eighty men do lose a little of their zest for parties—big parties at any rate. Some one else ought to take up that Malden custom. But probably no one else ever will. You do not get Poultney Bigelows and their generous hospitalities every day in the week.

If Saugerties and Malden-on-Hudson and Poultney Bigelow are out of your ken, you might turn your car out of the village green at Woodstock and head it due west instead for a twist through the loveliness of the High Catskills. This will give you the chance to come down through Palenville Cove, and there are in the entire East few more dazzling drives than this. The still-smart community of Twilight Park is left behind, and your car begins to dip . . . dip . . . dip . . . until you begin to feel that you surely have dropped from a lofty upper world to a very much sunken nether one.

If this is motor meandering up the valley of the Big River, it might be well to cross the new bridge at Catskill to the east bank of the stream again; or, better still, to use the ferry from Athens to Hudson. Then you will see, right in the sleepy little village of Athens, one of the loveliest doorways in all the state, and come straight up the main street of Hudson, 125 miles from the sea and once— believe it or not—one of the chief centers of the American whaling industry. Third city of the state in point of age, it once was its second port, with its Folgers and Macys and Husseys and Coffins sending their fine ships for the sperm all the way down the river and far, far out into the open sea. Yet Hudson, with all its onetime importance, would never have been, had it not been for little Claverack just behind. In fact Hudson for some long years was quite content to be known as Claverack Landing; such was the prestige of the interior village of which all that now remains is an ancient church, Dutch Reformed of course, and a group of fine old houses spread along the village street. In a near-by village, Kinderhook, the shrewd Martin Van Buren was born, and in Hudson he lived the earlier years of his life; so Columbia County can hold its head high with Dutchess as having housed a primeval Democratic President of the United States. In fact, *practically* two presidents. For Samuel J. Tilden was one of its most distinguished sons.

As the names of its first settlers would indicate, Hudson was, of a truth, an offshoot of Nantucket Island and Marthas Vineyard. The Nantucket Navigators first sailed up the Big River in 1783 seeking a site for a new colony; their numbers and industry had quite outgrown their two native islands off the Massachusetts coast. Just why they decided upon Claverack Landing is not clearly known. They renamed the town Hudson, after Henry Hudson, to the infinite disgust of Governor George Clinton who had wished it called after himself. They began at once to build their shipyards and after them their staunch ships, sometimes five of them on the stocks at one time, which reached out as far as the South Pacific; and these at once began to make a great deal of money for their owners and for the new city of Hudson, which grew apace. It was said in 1800 that, with the single exception of Baltimore, Hudson was the fastest growing city in the United States. On a March day in that year more than two thousand eight hundred sleighs arrived in town, from the back country. The produce they brought was said completely to fill five large warehouses.

For forty-five years Hudson continued very largely as a whaling town. There was a slight intermission in the days of the most unfortunate War of 1812, when several Hudson whalers were the victims of British ships enforcing embargo regulations. Some also fell into the hands of the pirates of Tripoli. But the trade persisted for three generations after the Peace of Ghent, and it is a matter of record that the ship *American,* Captain Solomon Bunker commanding, once brought to Hudson's wharves the largest cargo of sperm that ever had been obtained. When whaling declined, Hudson began to decline; to turn its interest to other and more profitable forms of industry. But it never lost its pride in its fine ships, which sailed more than halfway round the world in search of the treasures of the seas.

Hudson did not lose its pride in itself, or its ambition. Once it aspired to succeed its neighbors down the Big River, Kingston and Poughkeepsie, as capital of the Empire State. Albany, not only proud and ambitious but intensely jealous, was determined to be the capital. A bitter fight arose in the Legislature, and Hudson lost by one vote. It decided that it was a nobler thing, after all, to be shiretown of Columbia County, and set up a court house in which such brilliant local attorneys as Martin Van Buren and Samuel J. Tilden might come, to plead and to battle.

Albany and her sister cities of Troy and Schenectady deserve chapters of their own in this book; and cannot have them. Schenectady and Troy will be treated elsewhere. Schenectady is not on the Big River anyway; merely upon its lovely tributary, the Mohawk. But Albany, next to New York, has always been the chief city of the river trade. Close to the head of navigation (it really is Troy that stands at the actual head), it became centuries ago the seat of interchange of brisk traffic between river craft and inland routes. So it was when the Dutch began it, called it Rensselaerswyck, and then built their stout little city, with the gabled ends of its brick houses all facing the narrow streets; so it was—in increasing measure—when it became an English colonial town and took its name from that vain old soul, the Duke of Albany. By that time there was navigation (of sorts) upon the Mohawk and steady improvement of the highroads into the back country. And Albany the *entrepôt* of all of this.

In the stirring conflict of the Revolution the town did not play an outstanding part. Its mind always was chiefly upon its commerce. Commerce was its life-blood, and life-blood always must be carefully conserved. And so as early as 1701 one finds a party of Albany traders pushing its way through the wilderness north to Montreal, a sort of Chamber-of-Commerce visitation as it were. The pathway to Montreal was a natural and fairly easy one. It consisted of the Hudson as far as Fort Edward, then an easy carry or portage across to the present Whitehall, at the head of Lake Champlain. After that it literally was rather plain sailing; down Champlain and the Richelieu to the mighty Saint Lawrence itself.

The pathway west from Albany—through the valley of the Mohawk—was only a whit more difficult than that to the north; and here was a far vaster area to be served. But the territory was far less settled and developed. There really was little development in York State west of the Big River until after the Revolution. Sir William Johnson had come into the valley of the Mohawk as early as 1738, and during the next thirty-six years this shrewd Irishman had built up vast estates for himself and had captured a title as well. But his acres were still mainly wilderness, and his chief job in those years was to keep the peace—and his blessed acres. The Indians still were powerful. Johnson's post as colonel of the Albany County militia showed very clearly what was destined to become his chief occupation in life. One could not carry forward a large industrial development with a redskin and a tomahawk lurking just outside the doorstep.

But with the Revolution over and the Indians relegated to a form of subjugation, York State breathed in peace again. And the traders of Albany town turned their eyes and their thoughts toward the west. They promoted post roads through the valley of the Mohawk and to those of the Susquehanna and the Genesee. The roads from south and east focused quite naturally at Albany, and the Albany ferry became one of the very busiest in the entire length of the Hudson. With the enterprise of the Erie Canal, leading right to the West and the waters of the Great Lakes, it was no wonder that the inns of Albany town multiplied, and that when (in 1814) Congress Hall was first completed it was hailed as one of the chief hostels of the entire country.

Of this traffic the *National Advertiser* was to write, in 1827:

Probably there is no point in the United States where so many public stages meet and find employment as at Albany. They issue thence upon every point of the compass and it has become a business in which a large amount of capital is invested and much enterprise and competition enlisted.

No wonder, too, that here was a fair field for the beginnings of the railroad as well as the canal in York State. In the late 'twenties, when the Erie Canal was completed and the railroad to the West fairly begun, Albany was a place of seething importance. Its brick warehouses lined its waterfront and piers for more than a mile and, back of them, up a fairish steep hill, rose the rest of the town, with the Capitol itself at the crest of the hill, surrounded by a group of other public buildings—the City Hall, the first State Hall and the Academy.

Through rare good fortune two of these fine old buildings have been suffered to remain until this day, the State Hall and the Academy. Two finer Colonial structures it would be hard to discover the Atlantic seaboard over. The Academy is the older of the two. It was built about a century ago, of Nyack red sandstone, and within its walls one Joseph Henry studied and taught and there gave to the world the tremendous principle of electro-magnetism.

The State Hall, now the headquarters of the state's Court of Appeals, was completed in the 'forties. It is a simple and appealing granite structure of classical design, with its most unusual feature a long flight of stairs which spring apparently unsupported, save by a single side wall from the first floor to the second. Tradition has it that this surprising piece of masonry was designed by a lifetime prisoner in Sing Sing Prison, and that for this accomplishment he was given his freedom. It would seem as if he had fairly earned it.

The Albany of a century ago was an exceedingly substantial and handsome city. Then, as now, State Street, leading directly back from the river and up the long hill to and past the Capitol, was the chief thoroughfare of the town, and a noble one it was. Upon it faced many of the showiest edifices of the place; the Museum, gradually becoming a sacred temple of the drama; the earlier State Hall (later Geological Hall); the New York State National Bank (built in 1803 and to this day used as a bank, the oldest bank building in the land); the ancient Dutch residences of Lydius and of Staats— the curious "palace" of Vanderhuyden, so well described by Washington Irving in his *Bracebridge Hall* had just been torn down— and the town house of Philip Livingston, the patroon, with an elm tree in front of it which still bore the iron ring whereat slaves were fastened and publicly humiliated and lashed.

The Capitol, which stood at the top of the hill facing down State Street, was then new and did credit to the place. Just back of it stood Congress Hall; no more famous hotel ever existed in Albany. It was a curious edifice, formed by a solid row of city houses thrown into one another. Plenty of distinguished guests came to it—Jenny Lind, Louis Kossuth, and finally the Prince of Wales, who had one of the houses allotted to his sole use and a dinner given in his honor. Much of the political history of the Empire State was made late at night within its upper rooms. That is apt to be the way with principal taverns in capital towns. When old Congress Hall disappeared (in 1878) to make room for the new Capitol, old Albany swallowed a big lump in its throat. It seemed to matter very little that there remained Stanwix Hall and the Delavan, also hotels of fine tradition and repute. The passing of the old hotel was bitter medicine indeed.

But what was the passing of Congress Hall compared with the rape and wanton destruction of the old Capitol? That was a crime, nothing less. No wonder that the rusted ancient scales fell from the statue of Justice upon the dome as they tore down the fine old building, the chief architectural pride of the town. No traces of it whatsoever remain. The few Albanians still living who remember it, recall it as a rather charming structure, a good foil and companion piece to the Academy across the street. It is a pity that it could not have been retained. In its place there began to be built in the 'seventies and the 'eighties the present ungainly Capitol, which combines all the architectural vices of that generation and none of the virtues. At one side of the Capitol is the state's Education Building, with its imposing pillared front, and directly back of it the towering thirty-two-story state office building, a piece of modernism almost at its worst. The contrast between this ill-assorted group of public buildings in the capital city of the greatest state in the Union and the beauty of a similar group at Harrisburg in the neighboring commonwealth of Pennsylvania is rather startling.

Yet Albany has good architecture and plenty of it.

Once I was riding on a train north from New York, and when the cars began the long turn into the lower railroad bridge across the Hudson, two women in the seat in front of me exclaimed over the dignity and beauty of a building at the water-edge at the foot of the town.

"That's the New York Capitol," said one of them.

I felt constrained to interrupt.

"Sorry, but you are wrong," said I. "That's the freight house. The Capitol is not nearly so good-looking a building."

When Leonor F. Loree began the thorough reconstruction of the Delaware & Hudson Railroad, one of the large problems that confronted him was the Albany terminal. The passenger facilities already were taken care of in the large and handsome Union Station. He decided to build a combined freight house and office building at the foot of State Street and, railroadlike, to make it as plain and as simple as concrete construction would permit.

A local architect and inspired creator of much of the new Albany, Marcus A. Reynolds, went to Loree and pleaded with him. The dominant location of the new building, right on the river front and facing the town's chief street as it climbed toward Capitol Park, made it bound to be a landmark, good or bad. Reynolds and his fellows had worked for a long time to rid the town's waterfront of a congested block of dingy old brick warehouses, long since rat-infested and deserted; and had succeeded in making that waterfront rather beautiful and dignified and parklike, a place at which any steamboat might be proud to make a landing. Loree saw the point and capitulated. And the Delaware & Hudson freight house, as designed by Reynolds, became a thing of great beauty, with a medieval tower rising from it that would have done credit to any handsome German city. Loree did more. He induced the late William Barnes, who was planning a new home for his famous Albany *Journal,* to join forces with him and to build in the same manner and beauty as the adjoining railroad building. The thing that these men did for the state's capital city cannot easily be forgotten.

There are many other handsome buildings in the town, two of the most famous of them being the Episcopal Cathedral, just back of, and unfortunately obscured by, the Education Building; and the City Hall, designed by H. H. Richardson, that master architect of half a century ago. Around this group of public buildings there sprang up years ago handsome residences, narrow-fronted in the metropolitan manner but with wondrously fine and dignified façades. The onrush of the motor-car has greatly changed the scheme of living in Albany, as in most of the other larger cities of the state. The Albanians have begun to build their fine new houses out to the west of the town; in fact as far out as Loudonville and New Scotland. The place has astonishingly handsome suburbs; and Thacher Park, atop of the Helderberg Mountains, has a view hardly inferior to that from the "Old Beach" in the Catskills. In all directions you see mountains eternal, and the towering state office building down in the city is reduced to the proportions of a white pinhead, and trees to a green tapestry.

Yet, despite the beauty and the popularity of these suburbs, many of the older families of Albany hang on to their downtown homes of other years. That is the Albany way.

Not very much else of the older city still remains.

There was the distant day when Albany was patroon indeed. That ancient feudal system, always flowering in the entire lower length of the Big River, reached its apotheosis at Albany in the vast Van Rensselaer estate. The manor house of the Van Rensselaers stood at the northern bounds of the town, set in a deep grove of trees, and was an awesome structure. It represented an old and rather unpleasant order of things to Albany. For long years the patroon system, with all its manifest evils, had hung like a millstone around the neck of the town. The old Van Rensselaer house was the symbol of these evils. Therefore Albany breathed something like a sigh of real relief when some years ago the old house was carefully dismantled, torn down and moved, brick by brick and timber by timber, to Williams College, just across the Massachusetts line, to be restored there as a chapter house for one of the fraternities.

So died the old order of things. The days when the Van Rensselaers, the Schuylers, and the Livingstons dominated the politics of Albany County and Albany City are long since gone, as the domination of the Philipse, Cortland, Morris and Heathcote families, still further down the river. In Albany they were followed by the overlordship of the Regency of the middle of the past century, exemplified, perhaps, in the person of Erastus Corning, a local merchant of much ability, who became the first president of the first New York Central Railroad and a politician and social leader of highest rank. Martin Van Buren preceded him. The Lansings, the Pruyns and the Parkers also were powers of those days. But the Regency, like the patroons, is a matter of history. The old families still rule Albany, but now their rule expresses itself socially rather than financially. The town, moving much more slowly than many of its fellows, in some ways has changed radically. What American town has not?

So flows the Big River past its guardian cities to its sea. Americans will always speak of it with pride, foreigners with admiration. The sheer dignity and majesty of the Hudson are hardly to be overestimated. Its beauty is compelling. Sometimes men attempt to do bitter things to that beauty. It is an unending struggle between beauty-lovers and men who see no beauty in the giant pathway of a great river, forcing its way through the mountains to the sea; men whose commercial instincts are so crass that they would seek to tear down those mountains for their own purposes. The state has spent no end of money to maintain and perfect the beauty of the Highlands of the Hudson, yet within the past two or three years an ugly excrescence of a stone quarry with its ungainly apparatus has begun work against the helpless Mount Taurus. Legal forces and public opinion already are moving against this latest offense. But the law moves all too slowly in these things, and much damage may be done before the thing is officially stopped and removed. Pennsylvania went through the same thing but a few years ago, when a similar operation was begun in the Delaware Water Gap but finally was stopped and removed before serious damage had been done. At Niagara there is perpetual reminder of the evil that can be done in just this way. . . . Yet nature seeks quickly to heal these wounds. Time, which levels all things, smooths out the hurts inflicted by the puniness of man upon a noble mountainside; the underbrush and the trees come again; nature is triumphant and man righteously defeated. And the Big River flows on to the open sea.

CHAPTER IV

The Mohawk Flows to the Hudson

IT actually starts at Cohoes, where the Mohawk takes a final tumble off a high shelf and disappears into the Hudson. But for our own purposes, let us assume that the valley of the Mohawk really begins at the ancient Dutch city of Schenectady. Practically, it does begin there. The old Erie Canal bent through and past the town, crossing the river twice below it, but it was at Schenectady that, once the little Mohawk & Hudson Railroad finally had been completed, it received and discharged most of its passenger traffic. The canal from Schenectady down to the Hudson water was a long and tedious trip, with many locks and all the delays inevitable to them. The new railroad across the level plain from the state capital, but seventeen miles distant, took hardly more than an hour for the trip and offered agreeable contrast to the more leisurely canal travel. And so from the beginning it was much patronized.

It began its service in 1831. In August of that year the well-famed *De Witt Clinton* made its historic first trip from Albany town to Schenectady town, amid much acclaim and much ado. Horses took fright and ran away. And burning embers from the locomotive's tall stack set afire the parasols of the ladies who sat atop the stagecoach bodies, which had been remodeled for the first train upon the railroad.

Despite many minor mishaps, the *Clinton* finally succeeded in bringing its train through to Schenectady in a little over an hour, which was unheard-of speed for those days. It was a glittering day indeed that first opened railroad history in New York State. Thereafter the Mohawk & Hudson settled down to the workaday business of a railroad. Another small road was at once built from Schenectady north to Ballston and Saratoga Springs, both of which already were attaining large popularity as watering-places. The road to Saratoga had no money with which to bridge the Mohawk, and so it found it necessary to place its rails through the many spans of the tremendously long covered bridge that connected Schenectady with Scotia. For several years it used this makeshift passage (for its cars only, engines being attached at the far end); but its cars soon grew too large and too heavy for the old bridge, and so the Saratoga Railroad built its own structure.

From the very beginning, both of these small railroads out of Schenectady were most successful. They made a pleasant span between the Hudson River boats and the state's chief spas. The trip from the capital to Saratoga was done in four hours and a half. You alighted from the night boat at Albany dock, caught the six-thirty morning train on the Mohawk road, breakfasted royally at Schenectady and reached the springs at Saratoga just at eleven. What comfort! What ease!

Toward the setting sun from Schenectady the railroad made much slower progress. To begin with, there was the canal. The canal was all-powerful. It always was politically entrenched over at Albany, and its friends were both zealous and jealous. It mattered not that there were five months of the year when it was completely out of business, icebound, impotent. The railroad, none the less, was not even to be tolerated. And when, finally, under the powerful leverage of public opinion, the iron horse was permitted to parallel the sacred ditch he was hobbled in every manner possible. For instance, he was distinctly forbidden to haul freight of any kind during the months when the canal was open for business. It took several years to remove this obnoxious provision from the charter of the Utica & Schenectady Railroad.

Yet the Utica & Schenectady was built (opened in 1836) and, like its neighbors to the east, proved to be an immediate success, so much so that it was at once double-tracked and entered upon the pleasant experience of paying dividends—something that a good many little roads of that day seemed utterly to forget. People liked to ride upon its small trains, despite the much-heralded comfort of the packet-boats upon the Erie. You cannot easily divest the American of his passion for speed. He had it a hundred years ago; and in all these years it has grown upon him steadily.

The packet-boats of the Erie Canal represent a pleasant phase of the romantic era of American travel about which much can be said. Almost immediately upon the completion of the Mohawk & Hudson Railroad they ceased to attempt the tedious trip up and down the locks east of Schenectady, and began making that town their eastern terminal. There they connected with the Albany trains and began the placid trip up the valley of the Mohawk, not on the waters of the river but within the rather narrow prism of the canal. It was not until close to a century afterwards that there was any serious attempt again to use the river itself for navigation. For the Mohawk is, in the very nature of things, a temperamental stream. When winter comes, and in the spring that follows, it is anything but placid. Its waters rise alarmingly. Ice-jams form and must be broken, sometimes by dynamite. Trees and bushes and shanties and even houses come sailing down its mad rush in a way that bodes no good to anyone. One of the classics in the saga of the valley is the story of how Fonda bridge once floated down the river and embraced Amsterdam bridge and then they did a sort of fatal lovers' leap together.

When, two or three decades ago, the pretentious Barge Canal was planned, to replace the historic but antiquated Erie, all the way across the state from east to west, the engineers finally decided to "canalize" the river; and they have done magnificently with the idea by making great movable spillway dams and guard-gates of steel from Rome down to Schenectady. These have proved effective. Even though there still come times when the river goes on a rampage, and it becomes necessary for a time to close this section to traffic. In the long run, the Mohawk seems to have a good deal of contempt for man's contraptions. And it would make away with every one of them, if it could.

So it was that the planners and builders of the original Erie, De Witt Clinton and Benjamin Wright and James Geddes and John B. Jervis, decided to let the river have its own way. They felt that, if it were not cheaper, it were far better (and possibly, in the long run, cheaper) to parallel the river with the canal. And so they did. And even then, upon occasion, the river would rise up in its wrath and make the lowlands of the valley into inland seas and with these wash away the canal banks, with impunity. When things became normal once again, you sometimes would find a canal barge or two a quarter of a mile or more away from its accustomed pathway. And sometimes it was cheaper to leave it there in the middle of a dry field or an orchard, than to attempt to haul it back to the canal again. Upstate New York became quite accustomed to that sort of thing.

These occasions were the rare exceptions. As a rule, the old Erie was on good behavior all summer long. As soon as the snow showed signs of disappearing on the tops of the hills that line the Mohawk Valley and the sap began to force its way up through the sweet maples, the boatmen began to think of the pleasantness and excitement of life on the canal wave and to dig themselves out of their winter quarters in the comfortable farmhouses of the uplands. The *Mary of Lockport* or the *Eliza Jane of Pultneyville* began to appeal once more. Farm life might do in winter, when there was nothing better to do. But in the summer, the Grand Canal! What cracking, rough times were had in Buffalo and in old Coenties Slip, on the lower edge of New York City; and there was also plenty of excitement in all the ports and locks and docks in the five hundred miles of river and canal that intervened. For the Hudson, itself, is canal for 142 miles. *It* never is temperamental. It is too majestic, far too dignified, to let little things like melting mountain snows ever upset its equilibrium. There is something, after all, in being known as an arm of the sea. The Mohawk never could call itself anything like that.

The packet-boats, the *Lions of the West* and the *Seneca Chiefs* and all the rest of them that plied between Schenectady and Buffalo (a little later Rochester was substituted as a western terminal for most of them), were of a far different stamp than the *Marys of Lockport* and *Eliza Janes of Pultneyville*. They were the aristocrats of the old Erie, carrying passenger traffic, top-hat traffic, nose-in-the-air traffic, if you please; traffic to look contemptuously down upon mere freighting-craft. Packet-boat men on the old Erie were of a far different (and far superior) caste than those of the freighters. Yet, it was the freighters that survived. The packet-boat era of the Erie was comparatively short-lived. It was never profitable. The trouble was that Americans, then, as now, demand speed. The best packet-boats could not compete with the swift Albany-built and Troy-built and Concord-built coaches upon the parallel highways. The natural limitations of the canal were about four miles an hour. Four horses and a good coach and a good driver on the box could easily make twice that. It did not matter that the early New York State highways left much to the imagination, that those handsome Albany-built and Troy-built coaches rocked and pitched fearfully over them. They made the time. And time counted. Moreover, remember always, too, that the canal season in New York State is limited by weather. This also cut down the earning capacity of the packets. The stage-coaches not infrequently made better speed in winter over ice-hard roads than in summer through mud and dust. And speed always counted. As the iron horse grew bolder and bolder and finally did not hesitate to parallel the state's pet child, the canal, there no longer was question as to the fate of the packet. It was doomed, irrevocably doomed. You could ride upon the cars of the new railroads at fifteen or more miles an hour, with far better speed promised.

A good deal has been written about the romance of riding on the packet-boats of the old Erie. I doubt if it was all so romantic. Unquestionably it was nice, on a pleasant summer day or an even pleasanter summer night, with a round moon hanging over the valley, to throw sweet and shadowy light upon the trees, the big barns and the little houses, to sit upon the packet deck and drink it all in. (Probably drink in other things as well.) But there were drawbacks. Not the least of them were low bridges. The economy in planning the old Erie led to a reluctance on the part of its engineers to elevate properly the many highway bridges that crossed it. It must have been the least bit disconcerting when you were absorbed in a game of whist or of bezique with fellow passengers, or in Fenimore Cooper's latest exciting romance or, possibly, just the scenery, to have the captain or helmsman shout abruptly "low bridge"; and to realize that if you did not give promptest heed to the warning, that there was excellent possibility of your being swept into the muddy waters of the canal.

The packets, being necessarily very small craft, had most limited sleeping accommodations and (with a very few exceptions) no restaurant ones whatsoever. This last deficiency was made up, rather generously in a few places, by the hotels that sprang up at intervals upon the banks of the Erie. To this day, a few of them still exist, but not as hotels. Sturdy old fellows they are, generally of red brick, abundant in verandas and with the hurts that time has made upon their earthly frames, covered in part by nature's blanketings of vine. Great tradition exists as to the superior quality of their cuisine—mountains of steaming hot biscuits, chicken with gravy (for hen and biscuit alike) coffee . . . all the rest. Cheap whiskey. Albany beer. This, like the food itself, I should take with a grain of salt. Most of the food probably was pretty bad. It is no doubt like the fanciful tradition of the railroad eating-houses in New England, particularly those at New Haven and at Springfield. The Massasoit House in its prime was before my day, but I have vivid recollections of the smoky, greasy, four-sided lunch-counter in the middle of the waiting-room of the old depot at New Haven, and it was not so much. We did far better in our New York State, even at Syracuse and at Poughkeepsie. Utica was always good. We never bragged about the cuisine of *our* railroad stations. We knew better.

Sometimes the hotels along the tow-path bedded the packet-boat travelers at night, as well as fed them, but this was not usual. Most of the packets had two small cabins; one for the men folks and one for the women. The facilities in each were about the same. Two or three tiers of hard, narrow bunks, with flapping curtains of red or green cotton, as a slight concession to ordinary modesty. It is said that George M. Pullman got his original concept of the sleeping-cars from the packets on the Erie. That probably is true. He was a carpenter at Albion on the western end of the canal in that era. And in a slightly later one he took a prehistoric New York Central night train to New York and "rode day coach." After which he probably decided that the worst sleeping-car that might possibly be devised would be a vast travel improvement. At any rate the idea seemed to have sound business sense. Pullman died, far from a poor man.

In de Veaux's amusing and interesting guide to Saratoga Springs, Niagara Falls and Canada (published in Buffalo in 1841) he gives some interesting suggestions to prospective travelers which throw light upon the difficulties of travel in an earlier day. After having devoted himself to the highly practical problems of money and of baggage, he writes:

Packet Boats

Enter your names as soon as you get on board, that you may have a berth, if you should remain over night. Do not put your head out of the cabin windows; keep below as much as practicable, and when on deck look ahead for the bridges, and before passing them come down on the lower afterdeck. For the feeble, and those who are worn with fatigue, the canal-boat offers the best accommodations. It glides along so quietly that you can repose and slumber as undisturbedly as in your own chamber.

Stage Coaches

Of these old-fashioned conveyances little need be said. Ladies are always accommodated with the back seat. The middle seat is the easiest, the front seat the best to sleep on; but if you are subject to sickness when riding, always avoid it. Post coaches, if not crowded with too many passengers, over good roads, in fair weather, afford the most safe and agreeable mode of transit of any other; but the flyaway character of travelers is fast driving them out of use. From these vehicles the scenery of the country can always be advantageously viewed; and as the wheels roll on, the hours pass in social chat, free remark, amusing anecdotes and gay sallies, often truly pleasant and interesting.

De Veaux devotes himself to further comment and suggestion for the prospective traveler of 1841. He does not neglect the steamboats. It is suggested that it would be well to engage one's berth as far from the boilers as possible, as being both safer and pleasanter. Nor does he forget the railroad. After warning that the traveler should never ride in its cars at night—"very uncomfortable . . . and attended with more danger than during the day," he adds:

. . . The cars from the engine to the centre have the least motion and are considered the easiest, and those in the rear, the safest. . . . Do not suffer yourself to sleep in the cars; take your seats before the cars start, and do not get out until they have stopped. . . . Ever have your eyes around you and keep out of harm's way. . . .

The last bit of advice is not to be ignored, even at this present late day.

The era of the packet-boat upon the Erie was a passing short one. There remained, until that ancient ditch was replaced by the modern canal and its power-driven craft a quarter of a century ago, the old freight barges, drawn by teams of horses or by mules. These craft persisted, even though they became less and less a factor in the state's transportation system—the Erie Canal had its period of highest use in the decade between 1862 and 1872—and more and

THE MOHAWK FLOWS TO THE HUDSON

more devoted to short-haul or local cargo. When the day came that the last of them disappeared there was a good deal of sentimental anguish across York State.

The stage-coaches supplanted the packet-boats and made no bones about it. When the railroad in turn came through the valley and replaced the stage-coach there, that vehicle remained entrenched up in the hills. It plomped its way to and from the railroad stations along the Mohawk's edge, and still found its way, unchallenged, the entire length of the famed Cherry Valley Turnpike.

That turnpike did not officially go out of business until about ten years ago. On March 16, 1927, the board of directors of "the President, Directors and First Company of the Great Western Turnpike" met in New York City and prepared to wind up its affairs, after a century and a quarter of its existence. Long before—in connection with its contemporaries, the Albany and Schenectady (incorporated April 1, 1797) and the Albany and Columbia (leading off to the east from the capital and incorporated April 5, 1798) —it had divested itself of its physical property and turned its right-of-way over to the public weal.

The Great Western Turnpike Road then, as now, more popularly known as the Cherry Valley Turnpike, was incorporated March 15, 1799. It had been preceded by a very bad road which always had much trouble in maintaining itself, and which finally had suffered a fatal blow in the loss of its bridge over the Schoharie at Esperance (fifty-five miles west of Albany). The new turnpike company was authorized to establish toll-gates for each ten miles of its length (seventy-five miles, from Albany to Cherry Valley) and at each of these to charge tolls, according to the following schedule:

Each score of sheep or hogs	$.05
Each score of cattle	.12
Each horse and rider or led horse	.04
Each sulky, chair or chaise, with one horse	.12
Each chariot, coach, coaches or phaeton	.25
Each stage-waggon or other four-wheeled carriage, drawn by two horses or oxen	.12

Each additional horse or ox .03
Each cart, sleigh or sled, drawn by two oxen or horses .06
Each additional horse or ox .02

The legislature later ruled that persons going to or from their usual places of public worship and to or from the gristmill used for grinding flour for family use need pay no tolls whatsoever.

Construction was begun upon this important road soon after its incorporation, and, despite grave difficulties encountered, it was finished through to Cherry Valley by 1807. From the outset, heavy traffic awaited it. The route which it traverses is an extremely beautiful one. Running generally parallel to the Mohawk and south of it from ten to twenty miles, it makes its way over the tops of the high hills. There are fair vistas from those hilltops and many villages situated in between them. To the south at the outset are visions of the Helderberg Mountains and the more distant Catskills, and to the north, for many, many miles, the peaks of the Adirondacks—a fine road to traverse, then and now.

Great traffic came to it. W. J. Coughtry, historian of the Delaware and Hudson Company, and a student of these ancient pathways in Eastern New York, has written of it:

The turnpike was a necessity to the pioneers of Central and Western New York and it also had its part in the settlement and development of the middle western states. Lines of heavy freight wagons drawn by four and sometimes six horses operated regularly over it, transporting supplies from Albany and the seaboard to the settlements in the central and western portions of the state and returning with farm and forest products to the markets at Albany . . . from which they were forwarded to New York by water. Regular stagecoach lines were also operated. These constituted the life of the turnpike. Dashing along at a gallop, the four and often six horses attached to the ponderous coaches formed a marked contrast to the slowly-moving teams drawing heavily laden freight wagons. It is stated that in 1803 there were twenty-eight taverns of various kinds located along the road, to the open doors of which the stages of the various local and through lines drew up for refreshment.

By 1815 the number of taverns had increased to seventy-seven, fifteen of which were located at Cherry Valley. During the War of 1812 the turnpike was traveled by hundreds of teams transporting munitions and supplies for the government to the patriot army on the Niagara Frontier. . . .

By the middle of the past century, this once sizable traffic had slackened greatly. The competition of through railroad and canal just to the north was too much. The turnpike company began to sell off its road to the state, which promptly abandoned the tollgates and opened the road to the full use of the public. First (in 1853) was sold the section west of Esperance and, ten years later, the road west of Duanesburg. The old corporation hung on for many years, however, to the prosperous short-haul traffic in and out of Albany and reluctantly, and under large public pressure, gave up its final toll-gate at the edge of that city, as recently as 1906. So ended a once-powerful monopoly. The highway gradually was improved and, in due season, paved from end to end.

Until five or six years ago its chief monument remained—the covered bridge over the Schoharie at Esperance. This structure, of three arched spans, was built by Theodore Burr, a distant cousin of Aaron Burr, who achieved no small fame in constructing bridges of this sort throughout the entire East. Even after the Cherry Valley Pike had become fully "motorized" this bridge stood faithfully to its task and there seemed to be no wearing it out. Finally (in 1930) the New York State Highway Department pulled it down. And there was much sorrow at its passing.

State highway departments seem to have a sort of vicious delight in tearing down these fine old bridges anywhere and everywhere. As a patient collector of covered bridges (with my Kodak) I should like here to record my humble protest against such vandalism. It was bad enough to have Esperance Bridge go; even worse to have the two fine structures at Hoosick (within two or three miles of the eastern boundary of the state) torn down ruthlessly. In this last case, as at Esperance, there was no need for the demolition of the old bridges. The fine steel structures of the concrete highway (efficient, but not beautiful) were placed in slightly different locations. A public protest against the destruction of the old bridge at North Blenheim in the western Catskills (said to have the longest span of any covered bridge in the world) led to its retention, as a sort of museum piece. And Rifton Bridge (near Kingston) also has been suffered to remain. Yet for charm or beauty or antiquity, neither North Blenheim nor Rifton bridges were to be compared with Esperance or the longer structure at Hoosick.

There are but few of these covered bridges left upstate. Most of those remaining are in the Catskills, particularly along the east and west branches of the Delaware River. The last one in Erie County, within ten miles of Buffalo, was torn down only this past spring; the year before saw the final three in St. Lawrence County go. The fine double-roadway structure at Northampton, at the south edge of the Adirondacks, disappeared in the creation of the Sacandaga Reservoir. The tremendously long one at Jacks Riff, in the marshes just west of Syracuse, went all of a dozen years ago. Yet both Scotia Bridge and Waterford, the one across the Mohawk and the other across the upper Hudson, exceeded it in length. I recall Waterford Bridge very well. Theodore Burr had built it, and it grew to be a hundred years old.

Its stout timber arches carried the heavy trolley cars of the Hudson Valley Railway (now abandoned) on their way from Troy up to Glens Falls. I spent the summer of 1903 in Glens Falls, and it was at about that time Waterford Bridge burned, a tremendous conflagration. Old Man River had tried many times to conquer it by bringing down his armies of high water and floating ice and had met with the contumacy of utter and wringing defeat. Old Man Fire made a thorough job of it. Covered bridges always were just white meat for him.

Pennsylvania and Vermont and New Hampshire, even Massachusetts, seem to be much more sentimental about their old bridges than we New Yorkers. One of the finest specimens remaining in the East is that whose five spans cross the Delaware from Portland

(Pennsylvania) to Columbia (New Jersey). In recent years this bridge, the only one of many which formerly spanned the lower Delaware, has been rebuilt and restored. It is an interesting bit of Americana. Motor vehicles are permitted to cross Portland Bridge at ten miles an hour maximum; only last summer I was reprimanded for absent-mindedly letting mine get to twelve. I apologized to the traffic officer for my oversight. It was like trying to waltz too rapidly with a very old lady.

The motor vehicle really was the chief cause of the disappearance of the old covered bridges, even though our New York State Highway Department might have saved them in the few instances just given. Two-ton, four-ton, six-ton vehicles at twenty to thirty miles an hour were quite too much for ancient structures—no matter how honestly and how soundly built—that long before had been compelled to forbid passage to horses "faster than a walk."

Yet, on the other hand, you may credit that highway department with having created, within the confines of the Empire State, one of the finest roadway systems in all the world. And almost every mile of it well graded, well paved, and clearly marked.

This system ranks with the state's waterway system, as one of its major extravagances, and one which not only has brought the once wealthy commonwealth (as recently as twenty-five years ago it boasted that it had not one dime of bonded indebtedness) close to bankruptcy, but which has compelled its citizens to pay almost extortionate taxes. You cannot have extravagances of this sort without paying for them.

The chief difference between the state's highway and waterway extravagances is that the one is highly popular and much beloved of the great mass of the taxpayers, while the interest in the other is largely confined to those who benefit financially and directly from it. Comparatively speaking, there are not many private or pleasure craft upon the waterways, but a great many of them upon the highways. Which accounts quite largely for the distinction between the affection that is lavished upon the one and quite largely withheld from the other.

Schenectady, at the base of the Mohawk Valley, is a curiously interesting town. For more than three centuries it has stood, sentinel at the gate; watching life flow through and past it; taking its toll of the varied commerce that the valley has ever brought to it. Yet until quite recent years, it has not been a particularly important town or a town of large fortunes. Its neighbor, Albany, ever keen, sensitive, jealous of its own commercial prestige, grew rich years and years ago, while the towns roundabout maintained a studied indifference to that progress. Schenectady was one of these.

For nearly two centuries out of the three she was content to be gatekeeper and guardian of the valley that she has loved so dearly. The first bridge across the lower Mohawk was to Scotia, just across the river from her waterfront. Before that there had been a ferry there, established long before the days of the Revolution. The bridge was a real boon, for the swollen and tempestuous river often made ferriage a difficult and dangerous problem. Scotia Bridge was an ungainly thing, of many spans and tremendous length. It was a covered bridge, to be sure, for many of its years, but never one to be catalogued among the fine covered bridges of the state, although one of the most important early ones. Over it there passed always a vast traffic. We have seen how even the early railroad to Saratoga took it to itself for a time. After a while the upper structure of the bridge was removed; it was such a tunnel-like and gloomy thing. And then (in 1873) the wooden bridge, itself, was replaced by wrought-iron spans of rather light construction. But it stood to its task. And again a railroad ran over Scotia Bridge, only this time it was electricity that was the motive power. Schenectady had entered her electric era; big interurban trolleys, bound for Amsterdam and other points up the valley, now crossed Scotia Bridge. These are almost all gone, and the old bridge, which still stands, is stoutly barricaded against highway traffic. It has been replaced by the new Western Gateway Bridge, a short distance up the river, a really fine concrete and steel structure and one of Schenectady's chief prides. Scotia Bridge today is neglected and forgotten; the job it did so

THE MOHAWK FLOWS TO THE HUDSON

faithfully for so many years, out of memory. The real wonder is that it stood so long, against the impetuous Mohawk.

Before the second of her centuries was over, Schenectady became a college town. It was Dutch, as Dutch could be. But the new Union College was not Dutch. It was not even denominational, as were most of its fellows of the year of its foundation, 1795. Its very name indicated a desire of a group of churches to bury their differences in the cause of education. That eminent Albany architect, Philip Hooker, who designed the state's first Capitol and the Albany Academy, was responsible for the design of the first building erected by Union College, not far from the bank of the canal in the closely built Dutch settlement. The Rev. John Blair Smith was its first president (for a short time only), and then Jonathan Edwards (son of the great Jonathan Edwards of Northampton, Massachusetts) was called to the post and great promise he gave. He died soon afterwards, however, and Dr. Eliphalet Nott was made president, and for more than half a century thereafter, Eliphalet Nott and Union College, Schenectady, were synonymous. Union College was Eliphalet Nott; nothing less.

Nott was a sort of Nicholas Murray Butler of his day, always getting his teeth into things and getting away with them. He was the man who introduced the use of hard coal as steamboat fuel; his steamboat, the *Novelty* (over on the Hudson in 1836) was classed as one that just simply could not be equaled. He liked boys and the boys liked him. He was a broad-minded educator. When other college presidents frowned on fraternities, Nott encouraged them; and six national fraternities were founded at Union College, three of them of great importance. He was the first college president in America to recognize French, with Latin and Greek, as an essential college requirement; the first to permit engineering to enter college walls.

The boys liked Eliphalet Nott, and they kept coming to his college until it came to be the largest in the land. Occasionally one of those energetic schools over in New England, Yale or Harvard, would slide ahead of Nott for a year or so, but never for long. He turned out men of quality in quantity. In after years it was to be Union's pride that not less than ninety college presidents were enrolled among her alumni. In the days of the Civil War two rival Secretaries of State, the New York Seward of the Union and the Alabama Toombs of the Confederacy, were both Union College graduates. Up to the time of the war the Southern boys came in great numbers to Union. They liked it and the quiet, narrow-streeted Dutch town by the river in which it was situated.

Dr. Eliphalet Nott remained with Union, as president, for sixty-two long years, a record never equaled at Union, or any other college in this land and not apt to be repeated. The impress that he made upon Schenectady, as well as the rest of the country, could hardly be overestimated. In the two decades between 1830 and 1850, Union generally led the college world in thought as well as in enrolment. Then came hard days. Other and younger colleges forged ahead. Plant and faculty at old Union declined until, in the 'nineties of the past century, the abandonment of the ancient college was seriously considered.

Fortunately there came at that same time a meteoric change in Schenectady's commercial fortunes. Never well known as a manufacturing center, even though for years past it had a creditable reputation for its locomotives and its agricultural machinery, a man named Edison had hit upon it as a suitable point for the manufacture of electrical apparatus. America was just entering upon its Electric Age (curiously enough the son of the early Schenectady manufacturer of agricultural machinery, one George Westinghouse, was himself showing remarkable ability in this very sort of thing), and Edison, a pioneer in it, was beginning to capitalize his dreams into manufactured output. A group of uncompleted and unoccupied buildings at Schenectady enabled him to go to work, without delay. Out of that came one of the greatest single industrial manufacturing enterprises in the state, with twenty thousand men at work in its widespread workshops in normal times.

Aladdin rubbed the lamp and old Schenectady woke up. It was no longer a sleepy Dutch town. In the single decade of the 'nineties it more than doubled its population and became a real city at last. Three hundred of the four hundred acres that Eliphalet Nott had purchased so long before for the future extension of his college went into homesites for General Electric officers and Union College was saved—with a vengeance. It wiped the dust out of its eyes and bade the past farewell. It began to live in the present and in the future. The presence of so huge a manufacturing enterprise in the town was a stimulus not to be ignored. It built new buildings and took a fresh lease on its collegiate life.

General Electric in itself is a great college of technology. You feel its influence in every far corner of old Schenectady. No city in the land can offer more cultured and more brilliant companions at its dinner tables. Three thousand scientists are enrolled within the research laboratories of the manufacturing plant, and at least three hundred of these are men of widespread international reputation. Is this small stimulus to Union College?

And so the old college has thrived. And when depression came upon the land, and few engines came out of the shops of the American Locomotive Works, and even General Electric was forced to lay off workers by the hundreds, Schenectady awoke to one very interesting thing; there was no depression at the college. It never had flown high, therefore it had no great depths to which to drop. And Schenectady turned to it once again, with fresh affection and renewed support.

You can spend a long day in the town, very pleasantly indeed. If you are scientifically-minded, General Electric gladly will give you a peek at its House of Magic, which has more mysterious and interesting things in it than you might ever have dreamed existed. It represents all manner of curious experimentation on the part of scientists, strange optical illusions, superfreezing, illusions of sound, a perfect orgy for a man with a taste for that sort of thing. Playthings perhaps. But in the catalogue of G.E. the plaything of today is the tool of tomorrow, and tomorrow it will be turned out in its workshops, by the hundreds of thousands.

If you are not scientifically-minded, you will find plenty else in Schenectady to keep you occupied. The narrow streets of the old town have been but little changed in nearly two hundred and fifty years. They follow the plan of its founders. The houses are newer; it has been repeatedly burned, once, in 1690, by the French and Indians, a cruel and bitter experience of midwinter, for which both afterwards paid most dearly. One relic of the past still stoutly stands—the stone St. George's Church, built in 1762, and, in its interior at least, changed but little. The antiquarian will also wish to cross to Scotia and see the old Glen-Sanders house there, a public monument restored to its oldtime appearance.

And then the college. Perhaps they will show you the old chapel, so dear to the hearts of the older Union men, in South College, with its curious woodwork, its low ceiling, and the balcony running around three sides of the room. Since 1920 it has been supplanted (as a chapel) by the fine new structure just across the way. And new as this chapel is, it fits perfectly into the picture of the lovely old campus.

The next town as you ascend the valley of the Mohawk is Amsterdam, a manufacturing center of some importance but not devoid of historic interest or association. Amsterdam may boast loudly of its ability to make fine carpets and rugs—it is the second city in the world in its output of this sort of thing—but no local citizen, if he could help it, would ever let you pass through the long narrow town, stretched along both banks of the Mohawk, without taking you to the two fine stone houses at its far western end. Both were built by the Johnsons, one by Sir William himself, in which he lived for fifteen years before building Johnson Hall at Johnstown, and then turned over to his son, John. The other, on a narrow strip between the highroad, the railroad and the river, he built for his son-in-law, Guy Johnson. Of the two houses, Guy Park (as it always has been known) is the more formal and elegant mansion. Both are preserved as public monuments and are generously open to the public. In the course of an average year, literally thousands of tourists visit them. Special preparations have to be made for parking their cars, and there is not a state in the Union which is not represented by the signatures in the guest-books.

It is curious how the memory and personality of a man may dominate a countryside nearly two centuries after he has lived and died. I have referred to Sir William Johnson before in the pages of this book. We have seen him as a colonel, in command of the Albany County militia, seeking always to maintain order and peace in a primeval country. Remember, if you will, that this entire New York countryside was the kingdom of the redskins, and that they came by it honestly, through inheritance, and were to undergo the unpleasant experience of having their own taken away from them; in many instances, forcibly and unfairly. Of this kingdom, nothing was more sacred to them than its luxurious river valleys. The chiefs of the Six Nations built their "castles" and their "long houses" upon the hills of the valleys of the Mohawk, the Onondaga and the Genesee. To take away these prized lands of the once-proud Iroquois nations required all that a white man might possibly possess of force and determination, of tact and an innate sense of fairness.

Sir William Johnson combined all these qualities in remarkable degree. The Indians loved him, even after he had battled against them and taken their beloved acres away. They fought him, but they respected him. He fought squarely when he fought, and that was often. And in the end it was to be said that he probably was the largest single force in establishing order for the white man west of the Big River and so prepared a vast area for settlement upon the conclusion of the War of the Revolution. That area was the greater part of the present state of New York.

Johnson first came into the valley of the Mohawk, without many resources, without title, without position of any sort, in 1738. It was then a reeking and miasmic wilderness. His title came from his victory over the French and Indians at Lake George. He bought a house on the north edge of the Mohawk for his residence, tore it down and built a bigger and a stronger home—it really was more like a fortress; and to this day it is generally known as Fort Johnson.

From a family near by he purchased, for sixteen pounds sterling, a young German girl (by name Catherine Weissenberg) for a housekeeper and general servant and liked her so well that, tradition says, after a little time he took her up the river to old Fort Hunter, and, in the Queen Anne Chapel there, the Rev. Dr. Henry Barclay married them. All of Johnson's legitimate children were born of this woman. Yet in the end she was to have shared his affections with a most curiously interesting woman, whose life and history has become more closely interwoven with the memory of Sir William Johnson. This was Molly Brant, Indian-born and sister of Joseph Brant, the last great chief of the Iroquois.

After all these years, Molly Brant has become a rather romantic memory of the Mohawk country. All the saga of the valley tells us that she was dashing, beautiful, brilliant. According to these traditions, Johnson is said to have first seen her at a militia muster at Fort Johnson. She was but sixteen. She had asked one of Sir William's officers for permission to jump and ride on his saddle. Jestingly, he assented. With a pantherlike leap the next instant she was behind. The horse, badly scared, started to run away. Molly hung on. The officer paled, but not the young girl.

"By Gad," shouted Sir William Johnson, "there is the woman I want and that I am going to have."

And, as usual, he had his way. Molly was taken to Fort Johnson and installed as the mistress of the house. Her own dusky brood were educated, by herself, under its roof, while a governess, imported from London into the Mohawk wilderness, taught the graces of European standards to Catherine Weissenberg's daughters. Of them, Benjamin Lossing (in his *Field Book of the American Revolution*), afterwards was to say:

These two daughters were left by their dying mother to the care of a friend, were educated almost in solitude. They were carefully instructed in religious duties and in various kinds of needlework, but were themselves kept entirely from society. At the age of sixteen they had never seen a lady except their mother and her friend (who was the widow of an English officer) or a gentleman, except Sir William, who visited their room daily. Their dress was not conformed to the fashions but always consisted of wrappers of finest chintz over green silk petticoats. Their hair, which was long and beautiful, was tied with a simple band of ribbon. After their marriage they soon acquired the habits of society, and made excellent wives.

The record of the progeny born to Sir William by the "brown Lady Johnson," as she came to be pretty generally known by the countryside, is not so definite. There were other "brown ladies." He was said to be the father of over a hundred children. Yet it is recorded that visitors who came to Fort Johnson (and afterward to Johnson Hall at Johnstown) treated Molly Brant "with much respect." In which there possibly was as much wisdom as courtesy.

Johnson was a hot-headed young Irishman when he arrived in America at the behest of his uncle, Sir Peter Warren, with a vast enthusiasm at the very thought of entering a new land known to few white men and peopled with tribes of powerful and not overfriendly Indians. In such a situation he had need for tact, as well as impulse, and this he developed. And when he had built Fort Johnson and brought Catherine Weissenberg to it, his whimsy led to a desire that this structure, half residence, half fort, should be possessed of a leaden roof, such as the English country houses of that day were wont to have, and without hesitation he sent to London and imported such a roof, bringing it by ship across the Atlantic and up the Hudson, and by small *bateaux* up the Mohawk. He was a man who almost always got what he wanted. By dint of great energy, as well as his natural charm and affability, he succeeded in accumulating wealth, an outstanding position upon the frontier, two wives, and a title from the British crown. Yet he was not content. He wanted more land. And more land seemed to be the thing that he could not have. Not on the banks of the Mohawk. It all had been preëmpted. So, after twenty years' residence upon those banks, he suddenly quit Fort Johnson and went a dozen miles to the northwest and there founded a town, a shiretown; to this day a shiretown and known after its distinguished founder, Johnstown.

On the edge of the new town he built his new house for Molly Brant and himself (the unhappy Catherine Weissenberg had died) and named it Johnson Hall, in true baronial fashion. Like its compeers upon Mohawk bank, Fort Johnson and Guy Park, it still stands, as a historic monument, for public inspection. In recent years it has been carefully restored—it had become covered with many architectural excrescences through the passing of the decades. There also stands, like a big watchdog, one of the two stout whitewashed stone blockhouses, originally built to defend it.

Your antiquarian may tell you that the fact that Sir William built this final residence of wood rather than of stone and finished it much less elaborately than its predecessor, indicates that it was only a temporary structure. I am not so sure. It also may have indicated that Sir William was not as flush as when he built Fort Johnson, or that he might not have cared as much for Molly Brant as he cared for Catherine Weissenberg. There are a dozen different guesses, one as good as another. But Johnson Hall is a fine old house, none the less. And it is with much unction that they show the gashes upon its mahogany balustrade wrought by the tomahawk of Chief Joseph Brant in a fine frenzy. How much of that frenzy came from firewater is not related. But it is easy to picture that wide hall and that broad and easy stair that rises from it filled with redskins, and towering above them the big chief of all the Iroquois, the still bigger chief of the white men and his squaw wife, her progeny and her relatives. Let your imagination run away with that sort of a picture.

Sir William Johnson died the year before Bunker Hill. He left behind him his brown-skinned wife, a large number of children, recorded and unrecorded, including his son Sir John Johnson and Guy Johnson, who had married one of his daughters by the faithful sixteen-pound (sterling) Catherine Weissenberg; also the three fine houses, the court house and the jail at Johnstown, every one of them now standing. The courthouse at Johnstown, New York, to my mind ranks in interest with the similar edifice at Williamsburg, Virginia. The Johnstown courthouse has a cupola, a curious, ungainly and ill-proportioned thing set astride the roof of a long squat building, whose red bricks are believed to have been imported from England when it was constructed (1772).

Sir William Johnson died in 1774 and was buried in the churchyard. His grave still is there, having been rather rudely disturbed in several ecclesiastical building operations; his body was finally set to rest in peace with prayers by the distinguished (first) Bishop Henry Potter, of New York. He died at the outset of the Revolution and thereby was saved a very embarrassing situation. Subject of the British crown and bearer of one of its titles, a valiant fighter for it, what would have been his attitude in the American Revolution? There was no question as to the attitude of his son and his son-in-law. They were thorough and consistent Tories and as such were compelled to leave the young United States of America in haste and in disgrace, while the new state of New York proceeded to confiscate their estates—for the glory of God and country and the benefit of the exchequer. That scant cupboard was nearly bare. In the meantime Joseph Brant "acted up" in a way that brought for himself only the fear, the hatred and the contempt of the countryside. Massacre after massacre, the burning of houses, the trampling down of fields, the putting of women and children to the torch, as well as the tomahawk—many of these things were charged to the last chief of the Iroquois. Whether this be true or not, the saga of Joseph Brant is not a pleasant one to read.

Yet men there are, and wise men too, who argue, convincingly, that Sir William Johnson, like George Washington, would have thrown his lot in with that of his fellow countrymen in their emergency. The contumely that was attached to those around him, and who succeeded him, has now left him, at last, in this day and age, quite unscathed. He has emerged in history a rather fine as well as a distinctly colorful figure.

This is not a book of history. If you would know more of the days when this now peaceful valley was a swift center of highly dramatic events, when Indian and Frenchman and Briton and the citizens of the new American republic marched to drumbeat up and down its length, and fought and swore and battled with one another, let me commend to you a reading (or rereading) of Harold Frederic's classic novel, *In the Valley*. There never will be, never can be, another such a story of the Mohawk country. It gives exquisitely a picture that I would not even attempt to render.

Yet one cannot sit in a railroad train or a motor-car and today go up or down the valley of the Mohawk without reflecting as to the tremendous part it has enacted in the upbuilding of present-day America. Every mile of it has played its part in the making of the nation. . . . The little Dutch houses in the lower valley, which still stand, as if defying Time, itself . . . the old Abram Yates house in Union Street, Schenectady . . . the Arent Bradt and the Mabie houses, only a few miles further up the river . . . the Drumm house at Johnstown and the Van Alstyne at Canajoharie . . . the scene of the ghastly tortures of Father Jogues and Brother Goupil and his fellows, now commemorated by the great Auriesville shrine to which thousands of faithful souls make pilgrimage each year . . . the ruins in the narrow gap of the river at Little Falls of the stone locks of the Inland Navigation Company . . . the brick house on the bank of the stream just below, which belonged to that doughty old patriot Herkimer, and upon the front lawn of which his leg was so cruelly and blunderingly amputated . . . the sentinel shaft of the great monument on the hill at Oriskany which marks the battle in which General Herkimer received the wound that was to cost him his life . . . these are but a few of the high spots of American history as it has trod this lovely valley.

Some of the more interesting places that are closely interwoven with that history lie some miles back from the stream and quite out of sight of it. The old, old neighboring villages of Schoharie and Middleburgh in the valley of the Schoharie, whose waters eventually find their way into those of the Mohawk—at least such of them as have not been diverted by the new Gilboa Dam of the New York City waterworks enterprise—stand out conspicuously amongst these.

Both Schoharie and Middleburgh have their ancient churches,

well worth a visit by any man who finds that an occasional delve into the past is good for his well-being. Schoharie also boasts a massacre; it happened back in 1780 and like more of these affairs was both brutal and tragic. It seems to be a pretty poor sort of Mohawk country village that cannot boast at least one massacre.

Beyond the north rim of hills that mark the precise limits of the valley of the Mohawk lie other towns of historic interest. We have already spoken of Johnstown, chief of these. Just beyond it lie Ephratah and Stone Arabia and Palatine Bridge, each of which saw bitter fighting in the War of the American Revolution. Each has its old graves and its old stone church. Palatine Church stands within but a few feet of the steady throb of traffic through Route 5 and looks serenely and without interest upon it. I like the old stone church at Stone Arabia best of all. Not many months ago I visited it. The young minister came from his parsonage adjoining and opened it, showing me the square pews with the doors, the low balcony around three sides of the room, one wing of which was dedicated to a dining room and the huge kitchen which ran all the way across and above the vestry.

"The Dutch folk always liked their eating," he said with a smile, then added: "I hope that you will tell people to come and see our old church. They are always welcome here."

Which invitation is hereby repeated.

In Mohawk country also, please remember, is the route of the Cherry Valley Turnpike. The old towns that line that old road also had their part in history, and it also was no small part. Springfield had its massacre and so, of course, did Cherry Valley. But among the more interesting places along this old route to me are those ancient watering-places, Sharon Springs and Richfield Springs. Richfield has a lovely lake of its own and Sharon has none. But Sharon has a view—and such a view! From the high colonnaded piazza of its ancient Pavilion Hotel the entire Mohawk country seems to spread itself before you; light green and yellow and brown fields, patchwork-quilt style, and dark green copses and bits of forest. In the distance the deep indentation of the pathway of the river, with the smoke of its trains and factories arising from it; far off to the north the blue silhouettes of the great Adirondacks, the prescience of silence of eternal forests.

Richfield also has its old hotel; and a very old hotel it is, which for more than a hundred years has complacently faced the main highroad and served those who traveled upon it. The ancient stagecoach bills upon the walls of its office tell the story. Across that same highroad today, now hard paved and known to the world as the Cherry Valley Turnpike, is the village park, with the grandstand set under the trees and the springs, neatly housed, just beyond. In that park also stood, until about a quarter of a century ago, the famous old Spring House, a rambling two-storied hotel which at one time was the Mecca of the smart folk of New York and other large cities of the Atlantic seaboard. Then one summer night it burned, with a great flurry and confusion. It never was rebuilt. After which Richfield Springs had to look backward to find its future.

There are many other old houses and old inns along this turnpike. A little way after you have driven out of Albany, you will discover a rare, historic group of houses at Duanesburg, which is the point where you really should head south for a visit to near-by Schoharie and to Middleburgh. And if you weary of the purely ancient, turn north from the Pike at Springfield, wend your way through the hills for four or five miles over a well-paved side road and you will come to Van Hornesville. Once, not so long ago, I might have said "sleepy little Van Hornesville." Like so many of its fellows upstate, it seemed to have had its day and to have gone to sleep for all time. It had begun as a town a century ago, when old Abraham Van Horne made his way from his native New Jersey up into the Mohawk country, found an excellent power, dammed it and built his stout stone mill. Other typical industries followed the first mill into young Van Hornesville, a foundry, a plow-and-axle factory, a distillery, a cotton mill. Van Hornesville men financed and built the good plank road (not corduroy) from Fort

Plain, on the bank of the Mohawk, to Cooperstown, at the foot of Otsego Lake.

Then came hard days. The railroad refused to attempt the high hills to reach the little York State village. It thrust its rails into Cooperstown and into Cherry Valley (it long since had placed them through the valley of the Mohawk) but showed no interest in Van Hornesville. Without rail transport, industries ceased to thrive. The local ones closed up and were dismantled. The largest of the town's two hotels was burned. Prohibition ended the distillery. The plank road had long since fallen into ruin; within sixty years of its founding Van Hornesville was a wreck, thoroughly decadent.

So it seemed to a smart local boy at least. That boy's name was Owen D. Young, and soon he cast aside sentimental ties and found his way down the big valley to the Big City, where he went into law and then into the electrical business and made quite a success of it. He achieved much success elsewhere in the world. But he never forgot his native village. He returned to it often. And a few years ago he thought out the plan for its renaissance, in the twentieth-century manner. He gave Van Hornesville a new birth by making it stand once again firmly upon its own legs. The plank road was gone and there never would be a railroad, but a concrete road did pretty well by it. Owen Young rebuilt the old stone mill and put it to work again. He fostered the creation of a modern dairy and made it pay. The concrete road made its collection and distribution necessities easy. He also built a fine modern school in the town, which was planned by a city architect and constructed by the townfolk themselves. It was a central school for a wide area roundabout and thus displaced many shabby and outworn single-room district schoolhouses.

You no longer can call Van Hornesville decadent. It has had a rebirth indeed. It is an object lesson and an inspiration. Henry Ford must get a good deal of kick out of all of it.

The Mohawk is born in the southwestern wilds of stony Lewis County—no one seems to know or care exactly where. Up there the

Black River or the Canada Creek is more important. Like its big brother, the Hudson, the Mohawk gains size and strength and minor streams as it works its way toward the south. It first comes to public attention at Rome, the former Fort Stanwix, an isolated and bitterly defended outpost on the ancient trading route from Albany on the Hudson to Oswego on Lake Ontario. It is an indolent river always, albeit a temperamental one, and gives but comparatively little of its power until it almost reaches its end and drops precipitately over its great falls, seventy-five feet high and nine hundred feet broad, at Cohoes, where it drives the wheels and looms of the huge textile mills of that industrial city. But between Herkimer, where the river leaves the broad flats through which it has wended its way for more than sixty miles and enters the seeming impasse between the high hills at Little Falls, the drop to Schenectady is one hundred and seventy feet. A good part of this, however, is at Little Falls, and here there is a considerable development of power and a thriving industrial town. After this, the river becomes leisurely again; and, as we already have seen, in these days, part and parcel of the Barge Canal itself. Its course is marked by navigation buoys and locks, all splendid engineering works, although the star exhibit is in the gorge at Little Falls, where Lock 17 has a forty-nine-foot lift and is boasted of as the "highest lock in the world," a statement which is hotly contested by the little town of Peterborough in Canada, some fifty miles north of Lake Ontario. Peterborough also has a star exhibit in the way of locks.

But for the first ten or twelve years after the Barge Canal was finished, the men who were responsible for it were alarmed at the refusal of traffic to take to it. Even if it had been conceived in error rather than in sin, there must be boats to operate upon it. A couple of hundreds of millions of dollars had been thrust into the enterprise by a rich commonwealth which seemed to know neither the meaning nor the value of money. Vast mistakes had been made in its designing and in its building. It was of bastard size—too large for a barge canal and far too small for a ship one. Its promoters did not dare risk the outbursts that would come upon them if they installed lift or draw bridges, similar to those in use upon the old Erie and thoroughly damned by the citizens of Utica and Syracuse, and Rochester in particular. They built bridges of a fixed low height instead, which absolutely precluded the use of lake vessels upon New York's new waterway.

And so, was tickled the heart of Buffalo, which for years had watched uneasily the declining traffic of the old Erie Canal and realized more than vaguely what was happening to its own docks and elevators. Any canal scheme that obviated the necessity of a transshipment of through cargo in Buffalo harbor was bad for Buffalo. At least so that city reckoned it. Therefore, it cast its lot with New York City, which had something of the same premonitions, and the vast political power wielded by the two largest cities of the state sufficed to make the new canal across it (in practical effect, from the one to the other) of the bastard size.

Oswego the earliest freshwater port in the United States, and with a fine God-given harbor at the foot of Lake Ontario was, and still is, the logical western terminal for any real canal across the state of New York. Why parallel a perfectly navigable lake for one hundred and fifty miles? So has the War Department, and every other Federal agency that ever went into the matter, always reported. But Oswego unfortunately is a small city—something of a weakling, both politically and financially. A fine old town, always with more than her fair share of ill-fortune, she certainly was not able to stand up against cities such as New York and Buffalo. She was told to keep quiet. The reward for her silence was a generous expenditure for the improvement of her own harbor and canal; this last branching off from the main stem near Brewerton, at the foot of Oneida Lake, which, quite logically, became a link of the waterway across the state. She took the mess of pottage and kept her silence while the barge canal went on apace. A sop was thrown to a portion of northern New York by the building of a canal (canal and canalized river) north from Waterford to Whitehall, at the head of Lake Champlain, and so on through the Richelieu River to the St. Lawrence, at Sorel, below Montreal. A similar sop to the southern part of the state was in the form of canal extensions south from the main stem to Lakes Cayuga and Seneca.

All of these canals were built to the same size, a twelve-foot depth, a fifty-foot width, with lock-chambers three hundred feet in length. When they were done they were too large for the old horse-drawn barges, whose owners retreated to their homes in the hills for the rest of their natural existence. And, with a twelve-foot depth and the fixed bridges at fourteen feet above the surface of the water, they were entirely too small for any craft suitable to operate against the hard weather conditions of the upper Great Lakes. Buffalo rejoiced. And so, in a lesser degree, did New York. The canal enterprise never was quite as important to her as to her upstate sister. . . . And Oswego? Well, Oswego just continued being Oswego. Which is what she has done for many years past.

Gradually, of late, traffic has increased upon the canal—even though in no measure comparable to the size of the enterprise. The state still loses some ten millions of dollars annually upon its operation. It is of large service to a few of the oil companies which operate fine, efficient tankers upon it. It hauls some local freight and a little heavy tonnage; but mighty little through traffic. Despite elaborate efforts on the part of the state to compel the railroads to coöperate with it, they have pretty much refused to do so. Originally barred from participation in it, like the devil from a Sunday School picnic, they now have lost their interest in the enterprise, despite the important fact that, as the chief taxpayers of the state, they pay rather dearly for its waste and impotency.

The canal, the inland waterway, is a splendid theory. And the day may come when a proper canal (and canalized rivers) across New York State from the Hudson to Lake Ontario will be a pride and a joy to the state. But that day will not come until we have honesty and efficiency in public office that will bar personal ends and ambitions and work to the good of the public as a whole. Unfortunately that day does not seem to be near at hand.

It is far pleasanter at this moment to turn from the contemplation of public transport in upstate New York to that of private industry. The indolent Mohawk, save at its Great Falls (Cohoes) and its Little Falls, does not often raise its muscles to drive the waterwheels of men's factories, but that has not prevented its valley from becoming extremely industrial—from the textile mills at Cohoes, past the great locomotive and electrical works at Schenectady; the carpet mills of Amsterdam (the Sanfords came to weave carpets and raise fine race horses there nigh unto a century ago); the fancy foodstuffs of Canajoharie; the dairy products and textiles of Little Falls; typewriters and guns (a curious combination) at Ilion, more textiles at Utica; and at Rome, pipes and beds and many other things wrought of brass or copper. Oh, the valley of the Mohawk is highly industrial, indeed.

Yet the charm of life—of good living—has remained with it.
Take Trenton Falls, for instance.
Trenton Falls, some twenty miles north of Utica on the West Canada Creek, is all but forgotten by this day and generation. Yet the day was, and that not so long ago, when it was a resort mecca not to be ignored. N. P. Willis was an early New York author who took great joy in describing the beauties of his native state. The Trenton Falls that he knew was a place visited by many, both Americans and foreigners. Of it he once wrote:

. . . The company of strangers is made somewhat select by the expense and difficulty of access. Most who come stay two or three days, but there are usually boarders here who stay a longer time. . . . Nothing could be more agreeable than the footing upon which these chance-met residents and their daily accessions of newcomers pass their evenings and take strolls up the ravine together; and for those who love country air and romantic rambles without "dressing for dinner" or waltzing by a band, this is "a place to stay." These are not the most numerous frequenters of Trenton, however. It is a very popular place of resort from every village within thirty miles; and from ten in the morning until four in the afternoon there is gay work with the country girls and their beaux—swinging under trees, strolling about in the woods near the house, bowling, singing and dancing—all of which (owing, perhaps to a certain gypsyish promiscuousity of my nature that I never could aristocrify by the keeping of better company) I am delighted to be at least a looker-on. The average number of these visitors from the neighborhood is forty or fifty a day, so that breakfast and tea are the nearest approach to "dress meals"—the dinner, although profuse and dainty in its fare, being eaten in what is commonly thought to be rather "mixed society." I am inclined to think that, from French intermixture, or some other cause, the inhabitants of this region are a little peculiar in their manners. There is an unconsciousness or carelessness of others' observation and presence than I have hitherto seen only abroad. We have songs, duets and choruses sung here by village girls, within the last few days, in a style that drew all in the house to listen very admiringly; and even the ladies all agree that there have been pretty girls day after day among them. I find they are Fourierites to the extent of common hairbrush and other personal furniture—walking into anybody's room for the repairs which belles require on their travels, and availing themselves of whatever there was within, with a simplicity, perhaps a little transcendental. I had obtained the extra privilege for myself of a small dressing room apart, for which I presumed the various trousers and other merely masculine belongings would be protective scarecrows sufficient to keep out these daily female invaders, but walking in yesterday, I found my combs and brushes in active employ, and two very tidy looking girls making themselves at home without shutting the door and no more disturbed by my *entrée* than if I had been a large male fly. One of the girls (a tall figure connected by a hyphen at the waist) continued to look at the back of her dress in the glass, and the other went on threading her most prodigal chevelure with my doubtless very embarrassed, though unresisting, hair-brush, and so I abandoned the field, as of course I was expected to do. . . . I do not know that they would go to the length of "fraternizing" one's tooth-brush, but with the exception of locking up that rather confidential article, I give in to the customs of the country, and have ever since left open door for the ladies. . . ."

Which tells the story rather thoroughly. Except that a little later Mr. Willis made some excerpts from the hotel's register, which must be put down here. On the pages of that ancient book was written, below the entry of a gentleman "and servant," the following:

> *G. Squires. Wife and two babies. No servants, owing to the hardness of the times.*

Another entry follows:

> *G. W. Douglas, and servant. No wife and babies, owing to the hardness of the times.*

It has been a good many years since folks went to Trenton Falls to spend any length of time. Long ago a power company took over the ravine and dammed the West Canada and put it to work lighting the houses and the streets of Utica. And one more resort of upstate New York passed out of tourist existence, without fuss or feathers, yet not without regret.

CHAPTER V

Central New York — Empire of Beauty

CENTRAL New York and the Lakes District have their beginnings at Otsego Lake, sixty miles west of Albany. Cooperstown is at the foot of Otsego, at the precise source of the far-reaching Susquehanna River, and it is as good a place as any to begin a tour of the region.

Otsego, beautiful as it is, is hardly to be considered one of the Finger Lakes. This far-famed chain begins at the village and lake of Skaneateles, a few miles southwest of Syracuse, and there are but six of them—Skaneateles, Owasco, Cayuga, Seneca, Keuka and Canandaigua. Otisco (near Auburn) is a little too small to count as a finger, hardly a thumb even. In a strictly technical sense these six are the Finger Lakes and so will be considered. Only what are we then to do with Otsego and Oneida and Hemlock and Conesus, all of them also sizable lakes and situated within the general area of Central New York? Or with smaller ones, too numerous to be set down here in detail? The Lakes District of upstate New York is far more comprehensive than just the Finger Lakes. And so we begin our tour of it at Otsego, which I grant you is perhaps *not* one of the Finger Lakes but in beauty and historic interest is not exceeded by any one of them.

America, on the whole, has produced, in the past three hundred years or so, many lovely villages, some of which have kept their loveliness; but in all America there is no town more beautiful or more filled with romantic charm than small Cooperstown. And it has only been a century and a half in the making; that is, man's part of it. God's part began many, many centuries ago. He fashioned the high hills that rim the deep lake, and the valley in which it rests so securely. Man—in the person of one William Cooper, gentleman and judge, originally of Burlington, New Jersey—chose the precise point where the twelve-mile lake becomes a far-reaching river as the site for a village which should have both dignity and quality; and which, within the first two decades of its life, should house one of the early American authors—James Fenimore Cooper. Three outstanding American novelists and essayists have lived most of the years of their lives and have died and been buried in upstate New York: Washington Irving, at Sleepy Hollow; Mark Twain, at Elmira; and James Fenimore Cooper, in the yard of ancient Christ Church in Cooperstown, built only a few years after Judge Cooper first founded the village (1790). The manorial home of the Coopers, close by, in which the novelist died (in 1854) was burned many years ago. Its site is now marked by a small park, in which stands a bronze statue of an Indian hunter.

More interesting by far is the near-by churchyard. The Coopers reserved for themselves a small private plot, and here the novelist and his wife are buried. Not far away is buried Fenimore Cooper's slave. Three other negro slaves are buried in this northern churchyard. The church is one that Judge Cooper originally built for his town and people. It is a simple edifice, English, not Colonial, with an exquisite marble altar and reredos. The ancient timber pillars, that mark the nave from the aisles, have recently been replaced. A fearful wind storm not long since sent two giant trees, lifetime companions of the old church, crashing against its fabric. That fabric withstood the shock, also the slender spire; but it was found advisable to replace the inner pillared construction, which had been removed years before.

I know of no sweeter thing than to come upon this old Christ Church at dusk of a summer Sabbath, at evensong, to pass through the lych-gate (memorial to a recent and much loved rector, the Reverend Ralph Birdsall) and to stand under the giant trees of the churchyard and listen to the tones of the organ within the old church. Just beyond lies the small town and beyond it, in turn, the soft surface of Otsego Lake, the Glimmerglass of some of Cooper's romances.

Very well do I know my New England. I know its Litchfield, its Lyme, its Stockbridge, its Williamstown, its Old Bennington, its Walpole, its other towns of almost holy beauty. I revere them and love them and again and again return to them. Yet not one of these exceeds in beauty, in charm, and in tradition, Cooperstown, New York. With its rare setting at the source of the mighty Susquehanna, hemmed in by the lofty wooded hills, God indeed did do His part. The village has been favored all these years by being the residence of persons of good taste, as well as of means, and these have labored together to the end that it might have all that was good in architectural creation and restraint; that the work of man might be built to dovetail well with that of nature. The new houses and the old both reflect this feeling. The public and semi-public buildings are almost invariably of neat grey stone, admirably laid by master masons. The streets are broad, tidy, and lined with fine York state trees. Cooperstown is serene and dignified in her beauty, never rowdyish or wanton in her architecture.

The village has the distinction of possessing what undoubtedly is the handsomest railroad station in the United States. Yes, that *is* a statement; in the utter superlative. I am acquainted with those handsome stations that the Santa Fé and other railroads built for themselves and for their communities in the flush years, now past. Hardly one of these can hold the proverbial candle to the Delaware & Hudson passenger station in Cooperstown, of gray stone (after the town's prevailing mode) and set in a trim small park; exquisitely furnished with Chippendale chairs and settees. On nipping days there used to be a roaring wood fire on the broad hearthstone of the waiting-room. Instead of timetables and tariffs on the wall or a battered and fly-bitten poster or two, there are really fine oil paintings of the great men of the town.

But no more trains come to Cooperstown; soon its historic railroad will be but a memory. Already the handsome depot is locked, its windows tightly boarded up. . . . For Sale. . . . What town wants a handsome railroad station? No response. I am afraid that there is little demand for railroad stations these days.

Further distinction comes to this village at the foot of the Lake of Otsego, as being the town where one Abner Doubleday first developed the very American institution of baseball. The small field on which the first game was played, in 1839, is still carefully maintained. Cooperstown also has the oldest agricultural fair in the state, still showing each autumn.

To go by motor-car from Cooperstown and Otsego Lake to the west you will find yourself using the Cherry Valley Turnpike. You will be shouldering yourself past Canaderaga Lake and Richfield, at its head, and then heading straight up and down over the hills toward the setting sun. And what hills! In the entire East there are not stiffer grades than these by which Route 20 makes its dignified progress across the Empire State. They rank with those of Colorado and California; hills to test the pride and the fortitude of any motorist and his car, hills to make him curse and to make him rejoice. Carefully they have been paved and more than carefully graded. The state's highway department has done its best with them. But they could not remove them.

The biggest of them begins just west of the point (the four corners at Bouckville) where the equally historic Genesee Turnpike comes out from Utica and joins the Cherry Valley road as the main stem of Route 20. You climb up a tremendous grade above Morrisville Depot, mount a tall hilltop, pass through little Morrisville, once rejoicing as the shiretown of Madison County and now reduced to the ranks, up three more hills, and then you come to another of the really pretty and distinguished villages of upstate—old Cazenovia, with a sizable lake of its own and the stirring Chittenango Falls nearby. Cazenovia is but twenty-two miles from Syracuse and a favorite country-seat of its folk. But Route 20, that ancient Genesee Turnpike, does not deign to pass through Syracuse, or Rochester. It runs some miles to the south of both those cities, as if making an almost-bee-line for Buffalo, at the west gate of the state. And, so doing, it intersects the heads of practically all of the Finger Lakes, the larger ones, at any rate. It swings through a succession of rather lovely villages, Richfield, Cazenovia, Skaneateles. . . .

And Pompey.

Pompey high on a hill. For nearly a century it has stood firm on the ridge of the highest of all the high hills of Onondaga County, stoutly defying the wind and bitter cold of the northern winter. Its white church, with its graceful Christopher Wren spire, might have been stolen from the oldest of New England villages. How often this York State betrays at almost every turn, outside of the Hudson and the Mohawk valleys, the New England influence that played so large a part in its making!

Pompey, originally known as Pompey Hill, is about the oldest town in Onondaga County, as well as the highest. You will find the graves of Revolutionary heroes in its churchyard. Horatio Seymour was born in Pompey. And, in case you may have forgotten, Horatio Seymour twice was governor of New York, a rather important one at that, and once nearly President of the United States.

For years Pompey Hill was isolated, far from the railroad, all but forgotten. You saw it from the rest of the county, on its high hill in the far distance, but somehow you never came to it. Now this new Route 20, cutting straight cross-country from lovely Cazenovia to lovely Skaneateles (and sort of thumbing its nose at Syracuse as it goes) passes right through Pompey. And you may possibly wish to rest your engine and take a look at the old town and the superb views that it commands in every direction.

The cities of upstate New York, west of the Hudson, divide into two rather distinct classifications: There are the larger industrial towns, a bit noisy, a bit self-assertive, confident that they still are far from their maximum populations, that their greatest future is still ahead of them. Among such towns one would surely find the three largest of the upstate cities, Syracuse, Rochester, Buffalo, possibly two or three others, among which Binghamton and Jamestown would certainly wish to be included.

Of a somewhat different caste is the other type, the older cities and towns, whose pasts give them sufficient assurance. Some of them are industrial, some of them are passing wealthy; all of them have had old families, old ties, old friendships. In this class, not to be scorned, are Utica and Rome and Oswego and Auburn and Lockport and Elmira; some others, too. But these stand out definitely.

How could one ever scorn such a fine old town as Utica? What would not some of our ambitious western states give if old Utica could be picked up, bag and baggage, streets and houses and fine old trees and sheltering hills, history and tradition, and moved out to one of their prairie or mountain sites and there set up by a river reminiscent at least of the lovely Mohawk? A good deal, I fancy.

Most of us North Country people in years gone by used to think of Utica as a sort of super railroad junction, created chiefly to let us get off the yellow trains of the Black River road and take the red ones of the Central on to the Big City. We recall to this day the funny old brick station, with all its activity and the very tall windows of its waiting-room and the clanging of the trains outside and Baggs Hotel adjacent. Baggs had been a hotel ever since the Year One; actually it was first opened and operated as a hotel in 1797, and it was torn down less than ten years ago. A long dark and winding passageway once connected it with the railroad station, and in this passageway a man was murdered. After which they tore the passageway down, and travelers had to brave the weather to go from one to the other. But there were no more murders in Baggs Hotel.

Now the old hotel is gone, and there is a stone memorial building on the plot it once occupied, filled with its registers, its faded bills-of-fare, and other memorabilia of a distinguished life. And there is a handsome new station for the New York Central Railroad, instead of the funny old one. But that still is the spot where Genesee Street, all Utica in fact, begins. You go up Genesee Street through the rather solid and prosperous-looking heart of the town, and then the street widens and the fine trees begin. The lawns are deep and the houses of the fine old families—the Whites and the Shermans, the Proctors and the Maynards and the Baggs—still stand amidst them.

Utica is the hub or center of a considerable surrounding country. Her most important suburb is New Hartford, and as you go out Genesee Street it is hard to tell where Utica ends and New Hartford begins; the one town is really a continuation of the other. The Sauquoit River comes through a narrow valley past New Hartford and New York Mills on its way to the Mohawk; and for seventeen or eighteen miles it is almost a continuous industrial community, with many textile mills. Off to the north, however, the terrain is distinctly agricultural, with good farms and farming communities all the way to Boonville at the top of the ridge. That is a sort of borderland of the North Country, considered elsewhere in this book.

The broad flat valleys to the south of Utica also are agricultural. But one of their once-important crops, hops, has all but disappeared. You used to see the hop houses all over Oneida County, with their queer ungainly ventilators mounted upon their roofs, and in the winter the long poles neatly stacked together, awaiting another summer. In the spring they would place these poles in even rows and string stout cords between them, making, in effect, tremendous trellises, on which the ambitious young hops were bound to grow. By mid-August they had grown; and a tremendous hegira of hop-pickers into Oneida County began. But it has now all ended. The same prohibition that ended the distillery over in Owen D. Young's town in Herkimer County, raised hob with the hop industry in Oneida. With repeal it may come back to its former importance.

More pleasant it is to contemplate Hamilton College on the ridge of a hill at Clinton, just eight miles outside of Utica. It is the veritable nestor of upstate education, antedating even Union College, by four or five years. Its buildings, set New England fashion, in a row, reflect its antiquity. It has a wonderful list of alumni, among whom the names of Elihu Root, Chester S. Lord, Alexander Woollcott, Gerrit Smith and Samuel Hopkins Adams come to my mind.

Hamilton began as the Hamilton-Oneida Academy and later attained collegiate status. A paragraph from a recent issue of its *Bulletin* tells the whole story, succinctly:

Hamilton College is the outgrowth of the labors of Samuel Kirkland, missionary to the Oneida Indians through the last half of the eighteenth century. At the beginning of the Revolutionary War, Kirkland's influence drew many Iroquois to the Colonial cause, and materially contributed to the successful issue of the Battle of Oriskany and the relief of Fort Stanwix. This service and others during the Revolution, followed by frequent interposition in behalf of friendly relations between the Indians and the white settlers, won for Kirkland the confidence and regard of Washington and Hamilton. When Kirkland determined to establish a school for the Indians and the sons of pioneers, Hamilton gave his support to the project, and became the first trustee of the Hamilton Oneida Academy. The Academy was chartered by the Regents of the University of the State of New York, January 29, 1793. The state and the Indians had granted to Kirkland in 1788 a tract of wild land in what is now the town of Kirkland, a portion of which was set aside for the new institution. Here, in a small clearing, at a point just south of the present chapel, the cornerstone of the first building was laid by Baron Steuben, July 1, 1794. The school expanded until in 1810 its students numbered 170. Two years later, May 26, 1812, the college charter was granted.

So much for beginnings. It is sufficient to say that Hamilton's growth all these years has been both steady and dignified. . . . And as for Baron Steuben, that poor old gentleman, who had given all that he had to give to the winning of the War of the Revolution, had been most glad to accept the gift of a farm in the northern part of Oneida. To that he repaired and there he lived and there he died. You still can find his grave in a sandy, high-set plateau, not far from the village of Remsen. A movement is now on foot to make the simple log hut, in which this valiant soldier and gentleman lived and died, a national memorial.

Never, not in a million years, would you find Peterboro, New York, unless you deliberately set out to find it. And perhaps not even then. For Peterboro straddles no high hill tops. She squats herself down in a deep valley and keeps aloof from the main highways and the numbered routes. No guiding signboard arrows point her way. She is aloof and modest. And yet it was in Peterboro that one of New York's colorful personalities lived, was the central figure in a constant drama for most of the days of his life, and made such an impress upon the town that it is hard to believe that Gerrit Smith has been dead for all of sixty years now.

He was born, in 1797, son of that Peter Smith, who had been partner with John Jacob Astor in some of his earlier fur enterprises and had, a little later, become a settler and the first merchant of Utica. Gradually he became the richest man in the entire state and one of its heaviest landowners. He had several children, but Gerrit seems to have been the apple of his eye. He was graduated at the then-new Hamilton College in June 1818, and soon after married wealthy Ann Backus, the daughter of the first president of that college. Wealthy Ann died within seven months of the wedding, and Gerrit Smith did not marry again for nearly twenty years. He devoted himself (with signal success) to increasing his father's vast estates.

In the earlier days of Peter Smith there had been but one county in great New York, west of the Hudson River ones. That was Montgomery (originally Tryon); and west of Utica, but one township, Whitesboro, which extended all the way through to the Niagara River, and which had a population of less than two hundred white persons. As the state gradually was carved into smaller geographical divisions, and counties and townships began to acquire genealogies, the first comers had more than a little to do with it. That is why there is in the present pleasantly rural county of Madison, today, a village of Peterboro in the township of Smithfield. Peter Smith owned both. He built his first house in the place in 1804, and thirty or forty years later his son tore it down and used some of its timbers in his own great house, which still stands in the broad village street of Peterboro, maintained in the elegant manner of its pristine grandeur.

It is a generous, square three-storied mansion, with high pillars in front, after the neo-classical fashion everywhere so popular in Central New York, and it still is surrounded by its broad acres and a large and interesting group of out-buildings: Gerrit Smith's little brick office, the greenhouses, the workshops, the stables, and all the rest of it. Even a great English baronial estate, such as Blenheim or Cliveden, could not be more manorial. The many servants who still staff the house and the grounds are all negroes, and this and the fact that it is of classical architecture might make you think that you were in a great house upon the banks of the Mississippi.

Gerrit Smith was, with William Lloyd Garrison and John Brown, the greatest of the abolitionists. The score of years that he spent in loneliness as a really saddened man served to increase his sensitiveness to the wrongs of oppressed peoples. His father had given help to the Indians, as, slowly but surely, they were being driven out of their rich holdings in Central New York; in Gerrit Smith's day their descendants at times still filled the halls of the new house. But Smith gave his greatest force to the negro and became, with his vast means, the strongest of his supporters. He was one of the founders and chief directors of the Underground Railroad, that unseen but very active pathway that led diagonally up across Central New York from Pennsylvania, and the slave states to the south of it, to the distant freedom of Canada. Gerrit Smith's great house was a chief station upon the Underground Railroad. His grandson, who still lives within it, recalls him, secreted in an attic room with old John Brown, planning weird plans indeed. After the runaway left Peterboro he found his way across the upper Mohawk valley and to Houghs Cave or Whetstone Gulf or some other refuge in the Black River country, and finally he was whisked right across the Canada line. It all was very bleak and cold for a black man, but it was freedom.

Sometimes fifty black men slept (or tossed in fugitive terror sleeplessness) of a night in Gerrit Smith's attic in Peterboro.

Gerrit Smith was an eccentric. A man of unusually handsome build and countenance, with black eyes and hair and flowing beard, he was unusually benign and affectionate, and filled with many whimseys. When he was thirty he gave up tea and coffee (he was an almost violent foe of alcohol in any form); and even before that he had abjured the use of what he was pleased to call "castors" (condiments). He cut himself off from meat, then fish and butter. Foodstuffs that came from slave labor he simply would not touch. His diet, as a consequence, became an extremely simple one. Yet, despite his fine physique, the man suffered much painful illness. Toward the end of his life he spent some time in the Utica asylum for the insane. But when it came to business sagacity or to benevolence his sanity could not be questioned. As Central New York grew and prospered, Gerrit Smith almost always was to be found in the forefront of it. He went to the House of Representatives and there distinguished himself. At such times he was wise and shrewd. But he could not help being generous as well. Once he gave a thousand colored men from forty to seventy-five acres of North Country land apiece, signed each deed himself, and enclosed a ten-dollar bill as a measure of good faith. When finally he died (at the age of seventy-seven) he was mourned, as few other men in Central New York ever have been mourned. His house, his library, his books, his pictures, his open desk, still stand, unchanged, as a living memorial of his simple grandeur.

Somehow I always think of Syracuse as a town which does not exactly know where it came from or where it is going. It is quite a handsome town, with a business district that is decidedly better-looking than most of its compeers upstate, despite the presence, for nearly a hundred years now, of the main-line passenger tracks of the New York Central right down the middle of one of its important streets. To the country at large, most of which at one time or another has ridden upon the main-line trains of the Central, Syracuse is better known by this unique feature than by any other. Foreigners comment upon it, unfavorably, despite the fact that once I found the same sort of thing in the old French city of Nantes. Formerly this intimate dalliance between street and railroad was a feature of a good many of our important eastern towns. And soon it is to pass out of existence in Syracuse. People there will hardly realize what it is not to have their every-day existence punctuated by the slow and dignified (six-mile-an-hour) passage of the *North Shore Limited* or the *Empire* up and down Main Street, with all the Syracuse folk staring at the passengers in the cars and the passengers in the cars staring, with equal unintelligence, at the Syracuse folk. As these lines are being written plans for the new union passenger station in Syracuse are being approved by the many powers-that-be. With it goes a grade-removal project, in a slightly different part of the town, and then the tearing up of the tracks through Washington Street. I think that Syracusans are going to miss the long, fine trains, much more than the trains are going to miss Syracuse. They brought a curiously alien touch at all hours into the workaday life of the brisk town; a sort of daily, almost hourly, rubbing of its shoulders by New York and Chicago and St. Louis and Detroit.

The beginnings of Syracuse are comparatively recent. The earliest growth of Onondaga County was up in the hills, towns like Marcellus and Manlius and Pompey Hill. The site of its present chief city was a marsh, very swampy and unhealthy, which bordered upon a pleasant small lake, Onondaga, which the Indians knew, and liked, as being different from other lakes since it was impregnated with a curious saltiness. For this it acquired a widespread fame amongst them.

The editor of the New York *Commercial Advertiser,* who came to Syracuse in 1820 and again in 1840, was particularly impressed with the place. Of it, he finally wrote in his paper:

It was only in the autumn of 1820, the year in which the middle and first-constructed section of the Erie Canal was opened for navigation, that your humble servant made the passage from Utica to this place, alone with Mr. Forman, a distance of sixty miles. The country at that time from Rome to Salina (predecessor of Syracuse) was wild. The canal pierced the wilderness at Rome only to emerge therefrom at this place. The land almost the entire distance was low, marshy, and cold. The forests, most of the distance evergreen, were deep and dank; and the advancing settlers had eschewed the region as unfit for cultivation. But the clearing for the canal let in a stretch of daylight, which enabled people to see more distinctly. The marshes were to a considerable extent drained by the canal; and its banks, instead of the shades of the gloomy forest, now for the most part refresh the sight by the prospect of a well-settled country, smiling under the hand of well-rewarded industry.

The New York editor gives credit to Judge Joshua Forman, not only for having been one of the large forces in the promotion of the Erie Canal, but for having been, to no small extent, founder of the city of Syracuse.

Forman and his associates saw large commercial advantages in the manufacture of salt from the marshes that surrounded the edges of the lake of the Onondagas. It was the water from these marshes that had impregnated that of the lake. It was a comparatively simple matter to collect and "boil it down" into good salt. And this presently was begun and carried forward, in increasing scale. The editor from New York comments upon this too, saying:

I lodged for a night at a miserable tavern, thronged by a company of salt-boilers from Salina, forming a group of about as rough-looking specimens of humanity as I had ever seen. Their wild visages, beards thick and long, and matted hair, even now rise up in dark, distant and picturesque perspective about me. I passed a restless night disturbed by strange fancies. . . . The few houses . . . standing upon low and almost marshy ground, and surrounded by trees and entangled thickets, presented a very uninviting scene.

"Mr. Forman," said I, "do you call this a village? It would make an owl weep to fly over it." "Never mind," said he in reply, "you will live to see it a city yet."

The editor concedes that Forman's words were "prophetical." In twenty brief years he returned to Syracuse and noted the contrast between its appearance then, and that of 1820. He adds:

A city it now is, in extent, and the magnitude and durability of its buildings, albeit it may not boast of a mayor and common council to oppress the people by insupportable assessments, and partake of turtle and champagne for the benefit of the poor. But as I glanced upwards and around, upon splendid hotels, and rows of massive buildings in all directions, and the lofty spires of churches and well-built streets, thronged with people full of life and activity—the canal basins crowded with boats lading and unlading at the large and lofty stone warehouses upon the wharves—the change seemed like of enchantment.

In other words the editor of the *Commercial Advertiser* liked the Syracuse that he found in 1840. It must have been an interesting and a busy town. The canal passed through its very heart, with the chief buildings of the place—the courthouse, the theater, the famed Syracuse Hotel, the banks—ranged round a long open plaza, down the middle of which the busy Erie squarely ran—and continued to run for many years thereafter, until long after it was of any real transportation value to the town. By 1840, the railroad had found its way into the town, from the east and west, had placed its rails down the center of a street closely parallel to the canal and had taken Vanderbilt Square for its first station. The spreading trainshed of Syracuse's depot spanned the square, until one day, soon after it had been abandoned, the mayor of the town rose up in his wrath, commandeered a switch engine and a cable and went and pulled it down, at one fell pull.

That was before my day. I first recall the long depot at the west of the business center of the town, with the eastbound trains of the Central halting on its south side and the westbound ones on the north, and the busy little local trains to Auburn and Geneva arriving and departing at the far end of the building. Our Watertown trains had their own depot, closely adjacent. Along in the 'nineties, the famous old Leland Hotel, on the other side of the main station, burned (with considerable loss of life), and then they tore down the ruins of the hotel and built the present station, now, in turn, to be abandoned.

In 1840 there was no New York Central Railroad, merely a chain of lesser and independent lines, all the way across the state from Albany to Buffalo—320 miles. We have already seen the Mohawk & Hudson and the Utica & Schenectady, the first two links of this chain. The Utica & Syracuse was the next to open (July 3, 1839) and soon after it the road on to Auburn, which gradually was extended to Rochester. At Rochester a railroad already had been completed to Batavia and to Buffalo, so that when the Auburn road finally was put through, there was continuous track across the state. There also was a very early railroad from Syracuse up to Oswego, thirty-six miles distant, on Lake Ontario. A canal paralleled it, and for a time there was a certain amount of competition between the two; but not for long. The railroad won.

It was not until 1853 that the first New York Central was created by Erastus Corning of Albany, Dean Richmond of Batavia and Buffalo and a group of their commercial and political associates. It was a chain of seven links, each of these a small and independent railroad, and up to the creation of the first New York Central, you changed cars at each intersection, a slow and tedious business, which made the journey from Albany to Buffalo, in 1843, take twenty-five hours. There were many halts, nor were all the halts at the interchange points. Intermediate stations, such as Oneida and Auburn and Canandaigua, had their eating-houses and bars, and these demanded from fifteen to twenty minutes stopping time of each and every passenger train, and got it.

The creation of the Central obviated many of these delays. The chain sagged a good deal between Syracuse and Rochester, again to avoid directly paralleling the Erie Canal, as well as to take in the important towns of Auburn and Geneva and Canandaigua. The places along the canal between these two cities were less important. Corning and Richmond and their fellows, with the immense political power and prestige of the Albany Regency behind them, were able finally to parallel directly the Erie between Syracuse and Rochester and so save twenty miles in distance and no end of time and worry to through travelers. They eliminated the changes of cars between Albany and Buffalo, at the former of these places making connection with the steamboats and the newly completed Hudson River Railroad up from New York City, as well as the older one across Massachusetts from Boston; and at the latter, with the railroads along the south shore of Lake Erie to Cleveland and to Chicago. A branch of the new system, which thrust itself off at Rochester, led straight to Niagara Falls, where, by means of the new Suspension Bridge there, it made connection with the Great Western and Grand Trunk Railway systems of Canada, to Toronto, to Detroit and (by the recently finished Michigan Central) from Detroit on to Chicago.

So was really born the present-day New York Central, long before Commodore Vanderbilt ever entered the picture. When he finally forced himself into it and the remnants of the once powerful Albany Regency crowd out, he also had the Hudson River and the near-by Harlem roads under his control, and it was a comparatively short business for him to create the New York Central & Hudson River; which continued under that name until 1914, when the Lake Shore (leading west from Buffalo to Cleveland, Toledo and Chicago) and some other roads were merged into the parent company and the shorter and more euphonious title of New York Central again adopted for the road. The Vanderbilts, father and son, were both hard-headed and immensely progressive, and from 1869 the railroad system that they created across Central New York forged ahead, with great force and speed. They bridged the Hudson at Albany and at Troy, built new shops and terminals and locomotives and cars and prepared for the great rush of traffic that a new trunk line railroad of such magnitude was bound to attract.

And they received more traffic than either of them had ever hoped to get.

When Cornelius Vanderbilt (the father) went into railroading he already was an old man. It was in steamboating that he had won his laurels as a "transportation king." His son, William H., never "steamboated." All his life, New York Central was his god. He carried on the work that his father had started—with new vigor and enthusiasm. He four-tracked the line between Albany and Buffalo, a thing almost unheard of in railroading anywhere sixty years ago, and speeded the trains and service. It was William H. Vanderbilt who inaugurated the most spectacular train that America had then seen—the *Fast Mail*, from New York to Chicago—and painted its cars a dazzling white and gold, so that one could see them from afar, as they literally tore their way across upstate. When these two Vanderbilts passed away, the New York Central ceased to be the personal railroad that it had been up to that time and became a quite impersonal sort of a corporation, even though the Vanderbilt name was to stick closely to it for years afterwards.

Syracuse, standing four-square as it does to the central and to-day the most productive portion of the state, came fairly into her commercially prominent position. Her salt industry, once reckoned as her leading industry, sickened and died, even though it was kindly supported for years by a patriarchal state. Others, far more profitable to the town, arrived to replace it. She was a pioneer in the manufacture of typewriters, of automobile gears, and of automobiles as well; although for some reason or other, the manufacture of motor-cars in the United States east of the Great Lakes never has been particularly successful or permanent. Rochester, where George B. Selden made one of the earliest "horseless carriages" and, after bitter legal battle, compelled the other manufacturers, for some years at least, to pay him large sums for infringements on his patent rights, tried at one time to manufacture motor-trucks, and failed. Similar attempts by John Brisben Walker, at Tarrytown on the Hudson, were not markedly successful.

Yet Syracuse has one industry that has rather outshown all her others. Attracted by her natural saline advantages, the great Solvay Process Company set up its works just west of the town about a quarter of a century ago and made it a dominant industrial power. Like the General Electric over at Schenectady it quite perceptibly changed the character of the town. It soon rated a new metropolitan hotel and a skyscraper. One noted the springing up of many new houses, in fact of whole new residential quarters. Syracuse began, at last, to foresake the flats where it had huddled all these years and to take to the hills roundabout them. The motor-car had its part in this transformation. It could climb the steepish hills more readily even than the trolleys and certainly much more so than a man afoot. Originally James Street, the Genesee streets (East and West) and Onondaga Street, tree-lined and beautiful, had been the showy residential thoroughfares. The only large house upon the hills was the pretentious Yates Castle (designed in the Gothic by Renwick, architect of Grace Church, New York) off to the southeast of the town. It still stands, lodge-house and all, as a part of the large University near-by.

The Yates family and the Crouses and the Whites are irrevocably linked with the history of Syracuse. Andrew D. White, born in Homer (the David Harum town to the south), was a prominent man of Syracuse, even though he spent much of his life elsewhere. His nephew, Hamilton White, was one of the most unusual men in the town and one of the most loved. His passion was fires and putting them out. He gave the town a fire station, completely equipped, and then he built a private firehouse of his own with signals and drop-harness and all the rest of it. All the doors in his house opened outwards, and when the big gong in it struck the box number, White was off and away, before you could say "Jack Robinson." He became famous. Yet he did it once too often. One night—he was no longer a young man—he hurried away from the dinner table at the strike of the gong. He raced to the fire in his little surrey and when he got there he died. And that was far greater news than the fire itself.

Syracuse in those days used to have some rip-roaring fires. There was the Leland Hotel holocaust, with men losing hands and arms by sliding down the icy ropes, and the night when the old Weiting Opera House burned, a glorious conflagration for Hamilton White. There was that other night when two great fires burst out simultaneously in quite widely separated sections of the business center, and the solid men of the place felt that all was lost. And the next morning one of the largest churches in the city became a blazing torch, and an exhausted fire department, half dead from lack of sleep, fought it!

Onondaga Lake means but comparatively little to Syracuse, possibly because of its slightly saltish tinge, more likely because the modern motor-car tempts Syracusans a little farther away from the home plate. Brewerton (with an old restored fort), at the foot of Oneida Lake, seems far more attractive to them. And also the uplands to the south, with Cazenovia and Skaneateles. We have already seen Cazenovia, and as for Skaneateles—

It is a trim and precise village, seated, like so many of its fellows, in a wealth of abundant and grateful foliage. And Skaneateles has one advantage that a great many must envy. It faces a charming and considerable lake, which at the present time furnishes the water supply for Syracuse, twelve miles away. Skaneateles being set far higher than Syracuse, the water flows easily down to the larger place. If you follow it, by highway, you will come, just before you reach the city, to one of the fairest prospects in the entire state. Syracuse, lying far below you, seems with its towering buildings almost Italian in the soft light of late afternoon, almost like a Florence on its Arno.

Skaneateles is famous for Krebs and teasels. Teasels are those funny little things that carpet and other heavy textile weavers use to raise the nap upon their goods, and Krebs is one of the unusual places to eat in upstate New York, of such quality and quantity that its fame has long since spread beyond the distant boundaries of the state. There used to be another such place over at Canandaigua (oddly enough an oyster-house, four hundred miles from its private oyster-beds down in Chesapeake Bay), equally famous, but of recent years its luster has dimmed a bit. But Krebs with the passing of the years only seems to gain glory. It never has advertised, only recently has it put a modest sign up. But you do not have to hunt to find it. A hundred or more motor-cars stand in front of it any pleasant summer day. Unless your reservations are pretty precise, you may have to wait an hour or two for a table, but that ought only to whet your appetite. By and by your moment will come; when you are done, you probably will not wish to eat again for at least twelve hours. Krebs serves no liquors, no beer (if you like that sort of thing, you can get a very good cocktail at the excellent inn down the street facing the lake) but it serves about everything else in the world. It opens at seven in the morning, and it continues cooking and serving until the kitchen help are nearly dead with fatigue at night. Sometimes in a single day Krebs, a simple country-town white cottage in a broad lawn, serves over a thousand dinners, and thinks nothing of it. They are reputed to have refused half a million dollars for the name and good-will. I know of no place quite comparable with it, unless perhaps it is the gatehouse of the reservoir at Rush (just south of Rochester) where they cook codfish in yellow cream. They have been cooking codfish that way for the privileged at Rush for over sixty years now, which makes Krebs seem like a mere infant-in-arms. Things upstate do not change quickly.

CHAPTER VI

The Finger Lakes Country

THEY call him Copper John, and for the past 116 years he has perched himself atop of a lofty tower over a dull gray stone building in the old city of Auburn. Dressed in the Continental uniform is he, and with a soldier's gaze and a soldier's heart he has watched men go and men come through the clanking iron door of the gray building he surmounts. But a soldier may have the heart of a gentleman as well, and if old Copper John has a gentleman's heart, he must long ago have nearly sobbed it out in his longish century atop of Auburn Prison. The railroad station is across the way, and Copper John can also see the trains come and go and the files of men, handcuffed to their keepers, arrive upon them; sometime later, single men, shabbily dressed, come through the gate underneath to freedom once more and a society to whom they are an eternal problem.

For many decades past, Auburn has had two outstanding institutions, the Presbyterian Theological Seminary and the institution of the Copper Soldier—perhaps a little better known as one of the earlier penal colonies of the state. Now it is about to lose one of them; and some of the goodly folk of the town wish that that one was to be the state prison. No such luck. It is the Theological Seminary that is about to pick up, bag and baggage, after a century of residence in the old town, and move to the newer and more progressive Rochester. It is a bitter blow to Auburn's pride, and pride it has aplenty, despite the depressing influence of that great prison within its heart.

Yet the same Auburn that for years has had to bear the curse of the prison, brought forth in recent years a man who set his strong heart and soul to correct the patent abuses in things of that sort. This was Thomas Mott Osborne, and he needs no introduction to any man who has followed prison reform in America through the past quarter-century.

For many years the Osbornes have been "quality folk" in Auburn. The family fortune has been made in the manufacture of agricultural machinery, good machines, honestly made and widely distributed. When the Harvester Trust was organized, at about the turn of the century, and took over the Osborne Works in the process, Tom Osborne found himself out of a job, and long in pocket money. The sequel is pretty well known now; a man of culture and of breeding, who has the stamina to pose as a convict and go through the rigors of prison life in order that he may see for himself, uncolored, the fate of the poor wights behind the cell doors, only comes along about once in several generations. He gave, literally, his life to this cause; and he perhaps was one of the largest single factors in bringing about real reforms, not only at Auburn but in the other great prisons of the land. Copper John, atop of the tower, must have relaxed his grimness the least little bit, when Tom Osborne walked out of that barred door. . . .

A lovely town, a decently cultured one as well, Auburn has suffered her own trials and tribulations. Like her neighbor a few miles to the north, Oswego, she has had her own fine dreams of greatness. At any time, up to the middle of the past century, it looked as if she would be, without doubt, the chief city of Central New York. Once she dreamed of becoming capital of the state and named one of her thoroughfares, Capitol Street. Center of a rich and prosperous farming country, she welcomed the coming of the railroad with avidity and set forth to be a manufacturing center of prominence. So did Syracuse. But Auburn was the larger town and bade fair so to remain. Then came the blow: the newly-formed New York Central found that by building a more direct line (well to the north of Auburn) across level country from Syracuse to Rochester, it could largely supersede the bad curves and grades of its existing main line and shorten its through route between Albany and Buffalo. It was the logical thing and the road did it. And Auburn was left high and dry on the branch. Within five years its population had declined, perceptibly, and that of Syracuse had shot ahead.

The building of the so-called Direct Road, also dealt a body blow to Oswego. That town, rather overserene in her confidence, because of her seeming strategic location, had thrived mightily in the first five decades of the past century, at least in the final three of them. She had built for herself extensive piers and breakwaters, grain elevators and other harbor improvements, dreamed of metropolitan importance. She was the terminal of a busy branch of the busy old Erie Canal; she also had important railroad connections to the south and east; and the solid men of Boston were planning to build a trunk-line railroad right through to her harbor.

For Oswego, in those days, prosperity was not around the corner; it was right at hand. She even dreamed of dealing a death blow to her eternal rival, Buffalo.

Buffalo had been a bit prone to be extortionate in her harbor charges. Oswego helped to check her. The Welland Canal across the narrow tongue of Canada between Lakes Erie and Ontario had been completed and opened in 1829, and its promoters were shrewd enough to place upon it, at the outset, a very low tariff of charges. All of which benefited Oswego mightily, and she responded to it quickly. She drew much traffic to her harbor, made much money for herself, planned big things.

Eventually all of them came to nothing. The welding of the relatively unimportant little railroads across New York into the powerful New York Central was to Oswego, as well as Auburn, almost a death blow. She tried to rally from it by planning her own railroad into New York—the ill-fated Oswego Midland. Gerrit Smith, who had thrown much of his money into the fortunes of the place, was a heavy promoter of the Oswego Midland. If his fellows in the enterprise had listened to his advice, all of them might have done much better. Smith pleaded that the new line be built, not on the barren north shore of Oneida Lake but up through busy, traffic-producing Syracuse, on its way to the lake port. His advice was disregarded. The enterprise became political. The Oswego Midland probably was the worst located railroad ever built upstate; and also the greatest failure. Oswego had one other almost like it, the ill-considered Lake Ontario Shore, built along the south bank of Ontario all the way to Niagara Falls. That ended it. The town was broke. It ceased to dream of commercial importance.

But neither bad judgment nor bad politics ever can rob Oswego of her strategic location. The time may come when she will resume much of her old-time importance. The federal authorities refuse to see the waterway problems of the pathway of empire with the eyes of Albany or of Buffalo. They see the pathway in the light of its national importance and value, and in that light, Oswego shines, brightly indeed. A federal canal plan undoubtedly will abandon the barge canal west of Three Rivers, or else reduce it to an unimportant lateral, and make Oswego, a fine harbor upon a great lake and nearest of all to metropolitan New York, the sole western terminal of a great new ship waterway. Oswego, once again on the direct pathway of empire! That is the present plan, and cool engineering brains probably will not depart far from it.

So Oswego still dreams on. She is a delightful old town, mounted upon both banks of the mouth of a swift-flowing, wide and powerful river. She, too, has magnificent trees, and in summer the breeze coming off old Ontario is a pleasant and a welcome thing indeed; in winter, not quite so pleasant. It has been said that the coldest place in the world (this side of Siberia) is the center of

Bridge Street Bridge (connecting one half of Oswego with the other) in mid-January or February.

Auburn may cherish no such grandiose hopes as these. She must be content to regard herself as a lovable town, with not only magnificent elms and maples but many handsome homes as well, of which, the most outstanding is the fine old house of William H. Seward (still occupied by his family). In this structure, the very bricks of which were laid by one Brigham Young, lived and died the great Secretary of the Lincoln cabinet; it is kept almost precisely as he, himself, left it. A loving tribute of the present to the past.

Auburn has Owasco Lake as her very own, and only a little way to the east are those of Skaneateles and Otisco. The lakes come pretty thickly in this part of Central New York. You can stand at one point, near Borodino, and from it see both Otisco and Skaneateles. And only eight miles west of Auburn is Cayuga, and that is a real lake—some forty miles in length and from two to three in width. Seneca, of similar size, is parallel and just beyond.

Two well-famed colleges are on the east bank of Cayuga and two, almost equally well-famed, on the west bank of Seneca; and perhaps this is as good a time as any other to speak of the cause of education upstate. It never has been neglected.

West of the Hudson there are many colleges of importance—Hamilton and Colgate for men, in the general vicinity of Utica; Syracuse University and Cornell, for men and women, and Wells, for women only; these last two on the border of Cayuga Lake. The two on Seneca Lake are ancient Hobart College (for men) and the comparatively new William Smith College (for women), both at Geneva. There is a sizable college at Keuka Lake, and the oldest of all women's colleges is at Elmira. Rochester and Buffalo both have their local universities; and both of these are important. There is a small college down in the southwestern corner of the state, at

Alfred, and a larger one in St. Lawrence University up in Canton, in the North Country. Some of these are very old; with the exception of William Smith, none of them is very new. Most of them average from seventy to eighty years in age—old enough to be well seasoned.

They are, in some cases, outgrowths of the excellent system of academies and seminaries that sprang up across the state almost as soon as the white man's form of civilization had taken root there. The academy at Cooperstown would match hands with that of Schoharie. The old-time Lutheran Seminary at Hartwick (six miles from Cooperstown, in the Susquehanna Valley) still stands. There were excellent academies all the way up the valleys of the Hudson and the Mohawk. A fine school at Fairfield in Herkimer County has long since been abandoned and left to its fate; you still can see its stone buildings ranged along the roadside. Utica had a famous academy of this sort and so did near-by Clinton. Cazenovia had another, and another was at near-by Manlius; there was also one at Homer and another at Cortland. I do not know what became of Manlius Academy, but the Cazenovia institution, after 110 years of steady Methodist progress, still thrives. Northern New York had its famous academies. In Jefferson County alone were the Union Academy at Belleville (still in operation), Ives Seminary at Antwerp, Hungerford Collegiate at Adams, and the Black River Literary Institute at Watertown—the last two long since merged into local high schools. That has been the fate of a good many of these once-important schools. Sometimes a better one awaits them. The huge Methodist University at Syracuse was an outgrowth, sixty years ago, of the old-time Genesee College over at Lima, which previously had been a seminary, and which, after it had shot its new roots over into Onondaga County, went back to the sensible job of being a seminary. It had a distinguished neighbor in Granger Place, a school for young women at Canandaigua which also still stands, even though it is years since feminine youth gathered under its room for admonition and for culture.

We begin with Cornell, not because it is the largest of the upstate colleges, but because it is conveniently at hand. And because Ithaca is so completely and inextricably mixed up with Cornell, it also comes in at just this time.

More than a hundred years ago, and half a century at least before its great university had even been dreamed of, Ithaca, at the head of Cayuga Lake, was an important commercial town, already of some two thousand population. Like towns upon the Hudson's banks, it was important chiefly because it served as a distributing point to a busy hinterland. Transport in York State a century ago was limited to highway and to waterway. The first Erie Canal was being completed, and by feeders it led into both Seneca and Cayuga lakes. So barges, of considerable burden, came easily to the wharves of Ithaca and there exchanged cargoes with freighting-wagons to and from the inland country. Lumber and grain were transported out from the hinterland and manufactured goods back into it. It was a brisk place indeed, this pioneer Central New York town that had been founded in 1789 by a group of immigrants from Kingston-on-Hudson, and that Simeon DeWitt, Surveyor-General of New York, following the whimsical habit of using classical names for new towns, called Ithaca (in 1808). It throbbed with life; then, suddenly, life all but stopped within it. Early Elmira had become jealous, jealously ambitious, and had raised the funds to dig a canal from the Susquehanna (near the present village of Waverly) past her own stores and streets and through to Seneca Lake. That was the Chemung Canal. And when it had been finished and put to work, poor Ithaca nearly died.

But not quite. There was something newer in transportation than these slow-moving, cumbrous and expensive canals. This was the railroad. And smart little Ithaca decided to have a railroad for herself. She built it, more or less paralleling her ancient and erstwhile busy turnpike, between her docks and the docks at Owego, on the then-navigable Susquehanna. As Ithaca is hemmed in by tremendous hills in every direction, she found the location of a railroad up and out of her waterfront a most difficult matter. It was

THE FINGER LAKES COUNTRY 139

only overcome by the construction of two long inclined-ways, whereon the cars were raised and lowered by cables worked, first, by horses and later by stationary engines.

In this way, and with horses as its motive-power for its entire length, the Ithaca & Owego Railroad was opened in 1828, and was an immediate success. After six years it discontinued using horses, and from that day to this has done very well with steam locomotives. After some years, the steep inclined-ways were discontinued and a curious switch-back device substituted. To this day the boys at Cornell can lie in bed and hear the morning train come in, with a tremendous racket of whistling, like a boy coming down a staircase. If you miss the train out at the station, you can take a cab and easily catch it at the upper level of the switchback. It takes the Lackawanna (present operators of the little line to Owego) some five miles to get out of Ithaca, even though the direct distance is hardly a mile.

This was the swiftly reviving Ithaca into which Ezra Cornell came, in 1828. He was a gawky youth of twenty-one, who had walked to town from DeRuyter, some thirty miles to the northeast, with fifteen dollars in his pocket and a spare suit of clothes in the pack upon his back. An ungainly sort of a Lincolnesque figure was he, tall, stern and determined, but, unfortunately, not possessed of the Lincoln humor or of the great, soft heart of the Emancipator. It was hardly a year before Ithaca knew that Ezra Cornell had arrived in its midst. He had an uncanny sense of the ingenious, which he put to work almost at once; he overhauled Beebe's flour and plaster mills at the foot of Fall Creek and then supervised the digging of a six hundred-foot tunnel (still in use) for the improvement of the water power in Fall Creek Gorge. Then, after twelve years, he left Ithaca and went down to Maine, where his curious mechanical ingenuity was of great help to a New England manufacturer of ploughs.

About that time a painter in New York City—by name S. F. B. Morse, and a very good portrait painter he was—had invented a device called the telegraph, and Congress had made a modest appropriation for a trial line between Washington and Baltimore. It was felt then that the telegraph line should be placed in a cable, and this was the reason Ezra Cornell soon found himself down in Maryland digging a trench and laying the cable between the tracks of the Baltimore & Ohio Railroad. That the cable did not work very well—insulation was not understood in those days—was not Cornell's fault. He had anticipated that; also some other things, with the result that soon he found himself a telegraph expert, instead of a plough one, and at last on a fair way to the success and the fortune for which he had so long striven.

Up in Rochester there was another hard-headed and successful business man, something of the Ezra Cornell type, although not in the least resembling him in appearance. This was Hiram Sibley, who before the middle of the last century had come to Monroe County from Western Massachusetts and within a few years had accumulated a fairish competence as a nurseryman. He then sought other fields of activity. He, too, hit upon the telegraph; and before he was done with it had become not merely a national but an international figure.

Up to the time of the active entrance of Cornell and Sibley into the telegraph field, Morse's invention was doing rather badly. Like a good many other inventors, he had not been able to make most effective commercial use of his device. His patents were contested. There were a number of telegraph companies in the field, all the way across the United States, even though all of them were weaklings. Hiram Sibley was the prime force in the organization of the Western Union Telegraph Company, in the old Reynolds Arcade, Rochester, in 1856, and Ezra Cornell and a Don Alonso Watson, were his chief aides. The new company, once it had got squarely upon its feet, became more and more dominant and powerful. It absorbed its rivals. And sometimes it crushed them. Sibley pushed its lines further and further into new territory. He was the man who first completed the transcontinental telegraph. And when it was said that the Indians would tear down the wires as fast as they were erected, Hiram Sibley only laughed. He went out into the plains, summoned the big chiefs to him, let them hear the clicking of the telegraph sounder and explained that the Great Spirit was within that single slender thread of copper wire and would not brook molestation. And it is a matter of record that from that day no Indian ever lifted his finger against the telegraph.

Sibley did more. Cyrus Field had stretched his first Atlantic cable, and it had been a miserable failure; had snapped asunder, only a few months after it first had been opened with much acclamation. It was nearly a decade thereafter before there was a working cable across the Atlantic. Before that, Hiram Sibley had planned to build a telegraph line all the way from the United States to Russia, with a short connecting cable under the Bering Strait. He went to St. Petersburg, was there received by the Czar, magnificently entertained, and his far-visioned plan endorsed.

It was at this time that the purchase of Alaska by the United States was first broached, during an interview that Sibley was having with Gortchakoff, the prime minister of the Russian Empire. The story of that interview has been told by Sibley's son (Hiram W.), as follows:

Mr. Sibley was asked how the American company proposed to acquire right-of-way across the territories of British America and the Hudson Bay Company. He replied that he thought there would be little difficulty . . . except in the case of the Hudson Bay Company, who did not welcome the proposition with enthusiasm and as a consequence he thought it might be necessary to acquire a considerable interest in the Hudson Bay Company.

The minister asked what would be the probable cost to the American company, to which Mr. Sibley replied, stating a considerable sum which drew from the minister the remark that it was not worth any such sum; that Russia would sell the whole of Alaska for a sum not much bigger. At the end of the interview Mr. Sibley asked the minister whether his remark in regard to Alaska was to be taken seriously and whether he might bring it to the attention of the United States Government. To which the minister replied that he was quite serious in his suggestion and had no objection to the suggestion being made to the United States Government. . . .

The result of all this was that the thing quickly was brought to the attention of Secretary of State Seward. The rest is history.

Returning to America, Sibley at once began the construction of his greatest telegraph enterprise. He placed hundreds of miles of poles across British Columbia. But just then the Atlantic cable was restored and the overland international telegraph abandoned. Sibley and his fellows then gave their attention to the intensive development of their successful Western Union, everywhere within the United States.

Cornell did not remain actively connected with Western Union in this latter-day development. Ithaca, its hopes and its aspirations, now claimed all his attention. With all the money in his pocket that he could well hope to have, the philanthropist was being born. He gave Ithaca one hundred thousand dollars for the first large free library in New York State, and the reception of this was such that he began to dream his great dream, the establishment of a real institution of advanced learning in the town that he had come to love so dearly.

In that day, early in the 'sixties, the cause of higher education upstate, after a beginning spurt, was not progressing very rapidly. There were several colleges, old and dignified, with their courses and professors alike generally as dry as dust. Eliphalet Nott still was president of Union College, but he was now a very old man, nearly come to the end of his life, and Union was slipping, and slipping fast. On the other hand, the colleges over in New England were rapidly forging ahead. Ezra Cornell saw all of this; more, too. New York State, with its wealth and its culture and its enterprise, must not be permitted to fall behind. In that day there was a curious form of federal aid being extended to various colleges: Washington was distributing large blocks of the public lands, one block to one institution of higher education in each state, which stood willing to comply with certain conditions, as to investment, endowment, military training and the like. Cornell knew of this and prepared to qualify his new college for the New York land grant. He incorporated his university, at once took definite steps toward that end, and ran into violent and unreasoning opposition.

There was in those days also a small college, known as the People's College, at the head of Seneca Lake, at Havana, near Watkins Glen, and this was preparing to take a large part, if not all, of the land grant. It ranged itself at once against the Ithaca plan. Small-town jealousy came into the picture. Genesee College, over at Lima, was another antagonist. And so was Syracuse (to which Genesee was afterwards moved, as Syracuse University), which dearly wanted a college of its own, up on one of its high hills. That powerful Syracusan, Andrew D. White, one of the ablest men who ever sat in the New York State Senate, and who was destined to become United States Ambassador at Berlin, was, at all times, most college-minded. He had already been on the faculty of the progressive young University of Michigan. He had traveled extensively abroad as a young man, had been an attaché of our embassy at St. Petersburg. From his boyhood days he had dreamed of the creation of a splendid new college in New York State, splendid in its idealism, in its teaching, in its architecture and in its setting. He groped for a "new deal" in education.

It was quite natural that Andrew D. White should have wanted this institution in Syracuse, upon the crest of that very hill upon which the present Syracuse University stands. He felt that Ithaca was inaccessible. And so it was then; relatively, anyway. That was long before the Lehigh Valley Railroad had extended itself across Western New York and had thrust one of its main stems right through Cornell's town. White knew Cornell (a fellow member of the New York Senate) well and appreciated him, particularly his generous gift of a library to Ithaca; yet for a time he was loath to come to the support of the Ithaca university. But when he came, he came in fine, full measure.

Cornell had his way. His determination and his resistless energy were almost bound to conquer. He was criticized, vilified, attacked in every way, openly and privately. He thrust his own fortune into the breach, risked every last dollar of it. But White was staunchly beside him all the while. The money was Cornell's, but the conception and the guiding intellectual force of the university that was to bear Cornell's name through the years, was almost exclusively that of the Syracusan. White became the first president of Cornell University, and a very famous one as well. Cornell got the federal land grant for the state; out of his own private purse he bought the scrip by which the state protected its million-acre gift, and then went himself out into the West to find the land, protect it, and, as necessity arose, to sell it. But he did not do this last too quickly. He only sold when serious necessity arose, and then at a comfortable advance over the price that he had paid the state. But this profit invariably went, to the last cent, into the coffers of the university.

Cornell owned a farm in a commanding location upon the crest of a high hill at the eastern edge of the village, and this was destined to become the campus of the new university. Upon it was begun the first structure actually built for the college, Morrill Hall, while near by there already was another stone building, Cascadilla Hall, destined to become its first dormitory. Neither of these was quite completed for the formal opening of the college, October 7, 1868, and so the opening exercises were held in the hall of the Cornell Library, downtown. It apparently was not a very auspicious beginning.

In his most interesting book, *Concerning Cornell,* Professor O. D. Von Engeln of the university faculty has written:

. . . The beautiful campus of today was for the most part a ragged cornfield, surrounded by rail fences. At the north end, where is now Sibley College, rickety barns and slovenly barnyards offended the senses. Between the Cascadilla building and the South University Building, as Morrill Hall was then called, were two deep unbridged ravines. . . . Not even a completed road connected the two. Aside from the unfinished Morrill Hall, the only other university structure was a temporary wooden campanile in which hung a chime of nine bells, the gift of Miss Jennie McGraw. . . .

The fact remains, however, that for the new college there were more students than ever before had attended the opening of such an institution. More than four hundred young men, one of whom was the late Senator Foraker of Ohio, came forward. Four of these wanted to be members of Cornell's first graduating class, '69, the following year. The new college was a success from the outset. It shattered traditions. It granted degrees as generously and readily to scientific students as to classical. It was completely undenominational. Chapel attendance was not compulsory, an unheard-of thing in the American college of that day. There was student self-government; faculty members were no longer policemen. Almost from the first it admitted women to its classes and its laboratories on the same footing as the men. This was an innovation in the college world, and one that did not go as easily as the chapel arrangement. Co-education was not particularly popular in the 'sixties and the 'seventies. Its adoption, even as late as 1890, threatened to wreck the long-established University of Rochester. Upstate *is* conservative after all. You may not fly lightly into the face of its traditions. Another powerful Ithacan, the late Henry W. Sage, built a residence college for the women students, but that did not solve the problem. For a long time the men at Cornell University continued to treat the women students in somewhat cavalier fashion.

Ezra Cornell, himself, had weightier problems than these to consider. No wonder that he did not live to any great age (he died in 1874). Always, as the university's chief backer and financier, he was hard pressed. Yet he never gave up control of the funds that the careful and conservative partial sale of the institution's grant lands brought it. It is a matter of record that this federal gift, originally expected to yield about forty thousand dollars a year, already has realized five million five hundred thousand dollars, and now brings in an annual income of over two hundred and fifty thousand dollars. Ezra Cornell wrought better than even he, himself, must ever have realized.

Cornell University has steadily continued to grow, until today it has a plant investment and endowment of sixty million dollars and some five thousand students, summer and winter. And this takes no account of the great Cornell Medical School operated in connection with New York Hospital at the foot of East 68th Street, in the city of New York, with three hundred more students, men and women, upon its roster.

There is a story, seemingly impossible to authenticate but persistent, that Hiram Sibley, up in Rochester, inspired by Ezra Cornell's generosity, sought to do something of the sort for the stout Baptist college in that town. He went to Dr. Martin B. Anderson, first president of the University of Rochester, and suggested that he give a college of engineering to it. Anderson hesitated. He finally said that he would "think it over," which a few days later brought a negative decision. He felt, apparently, that an engineering college was just the least bit under the dignity of Rochester University. But, if Mr. Sibley was willing . . . a new library and a geological collection would be much appreciated, while perhaps Mr. Sibley's friend down at Ithaca would like the engineering school for *his* new college.

Rochester got the library and the geological collection. And still has them. And Cornell University got the wonderful Sibley School of Engineering, which in many ways was the making of the parent institution. And still has it. The Sibley School foresaw the coming of the Electric Age to the United States and anticipated it by its teaching courses. Cornell is said to have had the first college campus ever lighted by electricity.

The years have not dimmed the beauty of that majestic place, only added to it, in fact, by the happy placing and the really fine design of most of the modern Cornell buildings. There is hardly one college in a thousand that has the advantages that nature has given high-placed Cornell on the hill. The sweep of the blue waters of Cayuga Lake, the vistas of distant hills, the deep gorges and the mountain streams and falls that rush through them, the glory of fine trees and broad lawns come to a dignified growth—these are the natural possessions of Cornell University, in which she revels.

Ithaca indeed may well be proud of her. She is, in fact, one of the tremendous assets of the entire state.

It is but fair to say that even if there had been no Cornell University, Ithaca still would have been a place of popular resort, though probably not as large nor as bustling as the big college with its five thousand students has made her; but her great natural charms and beauty, both within the town and just without, undoubtedly would have brought thousands of travelers to her each year. The great hills that hem her in, a vast amphitheater they are, stretching in every direction, except to the north, where Cayuga Lake glimmers its waters, are continually indented with deep ravines; and in almost every one of these there flows a lively stream with waterfalls. The Cascadilla Falls and the Ithaca Falls are right within the town; and just outside of it, Taughannock (the highest waterfall—215 feet—east of the Rockies), and Buttermilk and Enfield. These last three cataracts, with their glens and ravines, have been taken over by the state, placed in charge of its well-managed Conservation Commission and opened to the public as parks. A wiser step could not easily be imagined. It is one that is being followed in all the far corners of far-flung New York.

The effort has been in all these newer parks to conserve to the uttermost the natural contour and appearance. The temptation to "build things," particularly silly and needless things, within the parks has been, on the whole, nobly withstood. They have been left green and shady, very natural. There are facilities, properly placed, for picnickers and for campers. The parks are policed and kept neat and orderly. They form an asset to the state not easily to be estimated in dollars and cents. They, with the motor-car, are doing their large part in the transformation of America from an indoor to an outdoor nation. Perhaps some day we shall cease to be, as others know us, a people under glass.

The other college on the east bank of Cayuga Lake is at Aurora, thirty miles north of Ithaca. It is Wells College and it is exclusively for women. As such it has had a notable record for over sixty years. It is not a large college; in fact it has always been held to be a somewhat exclusive one. Its most famous graduate was perhaps Miss Frances Folsom, the beautiful wife of Grover Cleveland, whom he married rather late in his life, and who became one of the most gracious mistresses of the White House.

Aurora is a tiny village. So tiny is it that it almost seems that a stout wind might some day come up out of the east and blow it right out into the middle of the lake. Yet, like Ithaca, it is tremendously old—that is for Western New York, at least. It antedates Auburn, as the county-seat of Cayuga. And there still stands, upon its single main street, which follows the rim of the lake, the first Masonic Building in the state west of Albany. Farther up the road, a mile or two, is the town's great oddity, a fine California redwood, the only known one of its kind east of the Sierras. It was planted, in 1826, by one Peter Smith, and it has grown very well ever since. It now is a fine young sequoia. In the course of the next ten or twelve centuries, it ought to be a full grown tree and a matter of unusual interest to passing tourists.

Fine big houses, so characteristic of Central New York, line the quiet main street of Aurora Village. Perhaps the finest of these is the square stone residence in which Henry Wells lived, through the 'sixties and the 'seventies. The huge newel-post of the main stair has a silver plate which shows the name of the architect, that of the owner and the date of its construction (1852). Henry Wells always liked things that way.

With William G. Fargo, he is to be reckoned as one of the pioneers in the express business. Together they founded the famous American Express Company here in the East; and then they went out into the West and there founded an even more famous company to which they gave their names, Wells, Fargo & Company. Both of these enterprises prospered mightily, and Henry Wells and Fargo became very rich. The Fargoes lived, rather splendiferously, in Buffalo. But Henry Wells preferred the quiet village of Aurora. There he resided until shortly before his death (in Scotland, in 1878), and there he planned and built Wells College, around his fine house. The college has prospered and has shown a reasonable degree of steady growth.

These villages along the eastern rim of Cayuga Lake from Ithaca north are all very, very old. Aurora, Levanna and Union Springs are chief among them. A secondary paved road and a more-than-secondary branch railroad connect them. Formerly an old-fashioned side-wheeled steamboat, the *Frontenac,* also ran between them, and its loud whistle all summer long was a welcome sound to their residents. Then one summer night the *Frontenac* burned, with a considerable loss of life, and thereafter there was no steamboating upon the lake of Cayuga. The village of Cayuga stands as the outlet, at its north end. In olden days this place was famous as a staging stop upon the Great Western Turnpike (continuation of the Cherry Valley and the Genesee), which here crossed the outlet on a clumsily constructed, wooden-pile bridge, three wagons wide and a mile long, the property of the Manhattan Company, of New York City. The first of three bridges to occupy the site was built on mud-sills, cost one hundred fifty thousand dollars, and was opened in September 1800. It charged high tolls and was a constant scandal, politically and otherwise.

It is a good many years now since there was a highway bridge at this point (Routes 5 and 20, combined, cross the outlet, at a narrow point, three miles to the north), but the historic Auburn branch of the New York Central follows quite closely the route of the Manhattan Company bridge, famed for many years as "the longest bridge in the world"; and soon to be replaced by a fine steel structure, as a part of the improvement of the state's expanding highway system.

It is not twenty miles from Cayuga to Geneva upon the main highway or the railroad. On either you will pass through the thriving villages of Seneca Falls and Waterloo, and if you are driving you are sure to see the "scythe tree," just west of this last town.

This old settler stands near a farmhouse by the roadside, and the handle and part of the blade of an old-fashioned hand-scythe extend from its thick trunk. The legend, completely substantiated, is that when the first call came from Lincoln for recruits to save the Union, the boy of the house thrust his scythe into the young tree.

"There it will stay, until this war is over," he laughed, "and I come back to get it."

It still is there.

For many folk, Seneca Falls has a special measure of interest in the fact that it was here, that the great movement for the recognition of women's rights in America began. Into that small village had moved, in 1846, Henry B. Stanton and his wife, Elizabeth Cady, the latter a cousin of that same Gerrit Smith of Peterboro, who keeps popping into these pages. In Seneca Falls the young couple met two interesting local women, Susan B. Anthony and Antoinette Brown, the latter the first licensed woman preacher in the United States. Warm friendships began; many plans were made, of which the most definite were for the introduction of equal suffrage for women at the earliest possible moment.

But, alas, that earliest moment was not soon to arrive. Even Gerrit Smith, who, through the inducements of his distinguished cousin, was induced to contribute again and again to the cause, finally tired of it. He was an abolitionist, pure and simple, and finally found that he could not divide his energies in too many ways. He tired and grew cold. But the Seneca Falls women persisted. They spoke, they wrote, they wore the terrible bloomer costumes. They were laughed at, ridiculed, reviled, even persecuted and arrested and, eventually, it is needless to add, triumphant, although but few of them were alive to witness the final and complete triumph.

Central New York and the Finger Lakes County seem always to have been fertile soil for "movements" of almost every sort. It is only a few miles north from Seneca Falls and Geneva to Palmyra where the Mormons have just erected a tall marble shaft, topped by the figure of the Angel Moroni, upon the crest of the sentinel hill of Cumorrah, to honor the place where a little more than a hundred years ago, one Joseph Smith, printer of Elmyra, is supposed to have found the plates upon which were imprinted the faith and testament of Mormon faith.

Jemima Wilkinson, "the Universal Friend," once founded a Quakerish cult down near Penn Yan, while Rochester had the Fox Sisters, who were the pioneers, if not the actual founders, of Spiritualism, as well as Susan B. Anthony. There is something in the atmosphere of the region which seems to breed tolerance, to give welcome to new cults, new faiths, new mentalities; a fertile soil for this sort of thing, which neither New England nor Pennsylvania nor the South ever gave.

At Geneva you come upon something quite comparable in grace and beauty with Cooperstown or Ithaca. And that is saying much. The small city is set at the foot of Seneca Lake (largest and deepest —443 feet—of all the Finger Lakes; in all these years it has been known to freeze only four times), with the residence part of it elevated upon a wooded elevated plateau.

Geneva, as becomes its name and setting, has an oddly foreign look. It resembles in many ways some of the small towns in southern England; Cheltenham or Leamington, for instance. Its older houses, many of them, are of brick. They closely shoulder one another and face upon the lovely main street of the town or the curious square in its center. One row of these houses, while facing the street, gives to the rear upon the lake; and from their high-set verandas the view at all seasons of the year is entrancing. Halfway up that main street is Trinity Church, good ecclesiastical Gothic it is, designed by Upjohn and closely resembling his Trinity Church in lower Broadway, New York. Its stones have been whitened by the passage of nearly a hundred years. Recently its interior was seriously damaged by fire, but it now has been restored with great good taste and care. A little further up the street stands Hobart College, adding to the episcopacy of Washington Street, Geneva.

It is one of the older colleges of the state, having been founded in 1825, as an advanced school of the Protestant Episcopal Church, and as such it has always continued in piety and grace, and yet with a certain good-humored attitude toward modern life that makes its graduates revere it and young men come to it, in slightly increasing numbers, all the while. It has a gracious campus and a companion in its efforts and its joys in the near-by William Smith College (for women), which is not of many years as yet but doing its very best to make up for that.

Geneva shows its dignity and serenity in every way; and its beauty, too. Its houses, old and new, in their settings above the lake, are unusual. It has one of the handsomest modern Roman Catholic churches that ever I have seen. On an eminence three miles west of the small city stands a historic house (now an inn), behind a vast spreading tree, where Lafayette once tarried in his triumphal way across upstate. But the most historic tavern in the town still stands (no longer is it a tavern) facing the curious old-fashioned square within its heart. It began, years ago, as a hotel, and went through many vicissitudes as a sanitarium, a boarding-house and what not. But it was as a tavern that it achieved its largest reputation. Of it, in a far earlier phase, Captain John Maude, an English traveler, wrote, in 1800:

To give encouragement to this settlement, Captain Williamson (agent of the Pulteney Estate which laid out the town) built a very large and handsome hotel, and invited an Englishman of the name of Powell to take the superintendence of it. Captain Williamson has two rooms in this hotel appropriated to himself; and as he resides here the greater part of the year he takes care that Powell does justice to the establishment and to his guests. From this cause it is, that, as respects provisions, liquors, beds and stabling, there are few inns in America equal to the hotel at Geneva. That part of the town where the hotel is situated is intended for a public square. . . .

Technically and legally, Central New York ends and Western New York begins, just three miles west of Geneva at the Pre-emption Road, a cross-country highway running directly north and south. I shall refer to this again. But Canandaigua, fifteen miles westward, clamors for admission, here and now. She possesses one of the finest of the Finger Lakes, advertises herself rather prodigally as "the western gateway to the Finger Lake country" and is so much of a type with Geneva and Ithaca and Auburn that she deserves to be included in any classification with them. The other towns in the Genesee Country, of which she might fairly be called a part, are fairly new, particularly Rochester.

But Canandaigua is not new; not in any sense of the word. Those great elms upon that main street of hers, leading straight up from the outlet of her very own lake, have been growing a century and a half; the date plate upon her handsome old Congregational church reads, "1812"; her houses reflect the venerability of the place. You see her from a long way off, no matter from which direction you approach. The golden sheen of her courthouse dome, rising from the thick greenery, catches the sunlight and becomes a glittering beacon. A full century ago she already was a considerable town, county-seat of one of the earliest of the Western New York counties, and a place where the federal courts were, and still are, held. Her Red Jacket Inn was a tavern of more than local reputation. From it the Great Western Mail departed at midnight for Batavia and Buffalo, a nightly occurrence of much noise and confusion. The Western Mail long since ceased to rumble its clumsy way, from Canandaigua toward the valleys of the Genesee and the Niagara; the Red Jacket has ceased to offer its famed hospitality. It still stands, however, on one side of the Ontario County Courthouse. Upon the other is the more modern hotel of the town, no longer new, but pleasantly restored of late, in its fine park and overlooking the railroad station of which it once was part. In that day Canandaigua was, and in fact still is, an important rail junction; where passengers from Western New York changed to the through red trains of the Pennsylvania, bound south to Baltimore and to Washington. They have been doing that for a good many years now.

In the ancient jail of Ontario County at Canandaigua one still can see the place where hospitality—of a sort—was offered to one William Morgan, who, within a cell, was held in durance vile, while half the land was in wild turmoil.

Morgan was a tramp printer, who, more than a century ago, published a small volume which essayed to set forth the secrets of Free Masonry. Today, such a book would probably command but little general attention. But, back there in the third decade of the past century, there were not so many other important things to engross the public mind. And the Masons then were playing an undeniably large part in politics. Morgan's book was little less than the traditional bomb-shell. At any rate, it resulted in his arrest on some trumped-up charge and his incarceration in Canandaigua jail; from which he presently was abducted and, as far as testimony reads, not seen again alive by mortal man. Eventually his body was recovered and was buried under an imposing monument in Batavia cemetery. It may still be seen from the passing cars of the New York Central Railroad. Few journeymen printers ever would have aspired to such a noble shaft, or wanted it, under the circumstances that it came to William Morgan.

It was erected by popular subscription, in the wave of great popular indignation, not to say frenzy, which arose after his abduction. It was years before that feeling died away; and because of it many innocent men suffered grave persecutions. To this day, the exact fate of William Morgan remains a mystery.

Four small lakes lie west of Canandaigua Lake—Honeoye and Canadice and Hemlock and Conesus; just in that sequence. But they decidedly are part of the Genesee Country. Hemlock, long and narrow and wedged in between heavily wooded hills, rising abruptly from its deep waters, is by far the most beautiful of the quartet. It formerly was a place of much resort, summertimes, by Rochester folk. But now it is the chief source of the water supply of that important city and carefully guarded as such. Its summer folk now go to the shores of the lakes of Conesus and Canandaigua and there set up their small cottages. Canandaigua Lake, not particularly impressive at its northern end, becomes magnificently so at its southern one. If you will take the main road south from the town on the west side of the lake, you will find yourself completely losing sight

THE FINGER LAKES COUNTRY 155

of it, for fourteen or fifteen miles; then your car surmounts a particularly sharp grade, and suddenly you come upon another of those superb vistas with which upstate New York from time to time rewards its more diligent visitors. Again, California has no sight more beautiful than this gem of a lake, with its waters as deeply blue as those of the Mediterranean and directly across from you, Gonawandah, the sacred hill of the Iroquois.

The road leads on, over more high hills to the south and then to the west. The country is gloriously beautiful and inspiring. But it is a different principality. It is now the Genesee Country. And to the Genesee Country we are at this stage fairly come.

CHAPTER VII

The Genesee Flows Grandly to the North

Swift runs the noisy river,
The mad and merry Genesee,
Born of the mountains, bride of the sea.
A short life and a merry one.
Tumbling and tossing,
Reaching northward all the way.
Still moments in shady pools.
Rushing madly onward once again.
Plunging o'er great falls.
Losing itself in the mighty Ontario,
Far from the open sea.

The mad and merry Genesee,
Long since harnessed, tamed,
Enslaved to man's best efforts,
Still, in its sweet childhood,
A gentle river is,
Coming through green fields,
Twisting and turning its leisurely way,
Hurrying not.

This is the valley of peace and beauty,
This is the valley of understanding.

THE GENESEE FLOWS GRANDLY 157

Gentle indeed is this valley, save now and then, when in a wild moment of exhilaration, the Genesee suddenly finds itself tumbling over a succession of tremendous waterfalls. There are two series of these, like huge steps, one in the deep gorge at Portageville and the other, in a similar gorge, at Rochester. Between them the river is all serenity; indeed, a gentle and a sleepy sort of stream.

Once, some years ago, I rode on the cog railroad up Pike's Peak out in Colorado. Beside me sat a stranger. A very thin, sharp-visaged, rather uncouth-looking man was he, yet much absorbed by the magnificence of the scenery. Suddenly he turned to me.

"It's God's country," said he.

I took another look at the country roundabout, saw the majestic mountains, the clouds piling against their peaks, and thought that I understood.

"It is indeed, this mountain country," I replied. He turned upon me a look of great scorn.

"Oh, I don't mean this country," said he, decisively. "These lean, bare hills are beginning to get upon my nerves. I was thinking of the real God's country, back in Western New York, the valley of the Genesee, with the lazy river rolling down through the flats and the great green hills in the distance, on either side. That's God's country. Have you ever been in Livingston County?"

I murmured something about once having lived in Rochester.

"That's Monroe County," said he, rather sharply, then in a kinder tone, "That's good country, too. The Genesee gets pretty busy down there, tumbling over the high rocks and turning all the waterwheels. I know it there too, just as I know it at Portage, on the upper falls. She's a fine river, all the way from the Pennsylvania hills; she's the main stem, you know, of God's country."

For the moment I was tempted to play cynic and mutter something about "absentee landlordism," just for the sake of turning a smart remark; then desisted. I really understood. This man, like fifty thousand others in those altitudes of Colorado, was expatriate. Three days before, I had been seated in a small side-street restaurant in Denver, reading the old-fashioned newspaper from the New

York State town from which I originally came, when a waitress sidled across the room and asked if she might have the sheet when I was finished with it. The familiar first-page "masthead" of the Watertown *Daily Times* had attracted her attention. And when I had asked her of herself, the story was quickly told. Her sister and herself—the name showed that they came from a good old county family in our North Country—had been educated at the university upon the hill at Syracuse. They had hoped to be secretaries, at least stenographers. Fate had sent them hurrying out to high-set Denver, where there were more secretaries and stenographers than waitresses. They, too, were expatriates.

There is an indefinable something about upstate New York that seems to catch hold of its native-born and hold their affection and their loyalty throughout the rest of their lives, no matter where and how far they may wander away from it.

It is the Genesee that somehow seems most definitely to typify Western New York to the man or woman who is native to that country. With its source in the extreme northern hills of Pennsylvania, it stretches the greater part of its length through this state, running from south to north. It still is a small river when it comes into New York, and smallish villages begin to multiply along it.

Portage is the point that marks the separation between the upper and the lower valleys of the Genesee. The transition is sudden, startling, dramatic. In a short chasm, hardly a mile in length, the Genesee, now grown to be a river of real proportions, drops in three great falls, seven hundred feet. Westerners would call it a canyon—it is not inept even to compare it with the Grand Canyon of the Colorado—but Western New York seems content to know the gorge simply as the "high banks of the Genesee." The falls, themselves, are carefully protected by the state, through one of its larger parks, known as Letchworth, after the generous old-fashioned Buffalo physician who owned the property as a summer residence, and who, in the evening of his life, gave it to the public use. His large house is now an inn. There is a museum near by, devoting itself to the history of the place.

For Portage has its traditions, and rare traditions they are; running far back of the days of the coming of the white man. The Six Nations came to it for generations and for centuries, no man knows how long, to hold, in the grove beside the great falls, their deliberations, their councils, their formal festivities. And then came the white man; or rather, first, the white woman, in the person of Mary Jemison, who, in the passing of the years, has attained a somewhat saintlike status in the annals of the Genesee country.

She is supposed to have arrived in the region two decades before General Sullivan's ill-fated Revolutionary army ever saw it. The earliest settlers in the valley found her there. She had no home other than with the Indians. Long before, she had made herself one of them. You can see at Letchwork Park, near her statue, the house which she built for her daughter. The house is more interesting than the statue. She is said to have carried the planks for it, on her back, more than twenty miles. Each is of two-inch oak, a full six feet in length. There is indeed something in the romance of this "white daughter of the Senecas" which holds more than casual interest.

She was born on a sailing ship bound from Ireland to America and as a little child came to live in a small village in Pennsylvania. The settlement was sacked and most of its inhabitants killed. Mary Jemison was captured by the Senecas and adopted into their tribe, first as a slave in the cabin of her captors. This was in accord with the custom of the Iroquois. The women of their "long houses" were the dictators of life and death to the prisoners taken in raids and battles. Mary Jemison grew up among them, accepted their dress and manner of life, and became in almost all things, a Seneca woman. She took, as a mate, an Indian warrior, and her children lived in the Genesee valley long after her. She married twice after and in all had five children. A log cabin, built by one of her sons, is still standing on the Cuylerville road. Squawkie Hill, overlooking the lower valley near Mount Morris, was her home until the summer of 1831, when she sold her holdings in the Genesee country and moved to the Buffalo Creek Reservation, where she died two years later, at the ripe old age of ninety-one. So runs the simple story of the woman who was the aid and friend of the first white men who came to the valley, and whose descendants in this late day have given her the awkward tribute of a marble statue. Upon her heels there came the settlers, slowly in those first days after the Revolution, and then more and more rapidly as trails and roads became better marked and broken. Some of the soldiers of the Sullivan Expedition brought back stirring reports of the fertility of the soil of the country, of the grass in the lowlands of the Genesee growing so high that it all but completely hid the face of a man seated in his saddle.

There also stands near the Inn at Letchworth a rough-hewn cabin that once served as the council house of the Senecas. This cabin is believed to be one of the oldest buildings in the state. Originally it stood at Canadea, eighteen miles to the south (in the Indian "Go-a-ya-se-o," most southerly of the Seneca villages upon the Genesee). After they sold their lands in the valley, the Indians abandoned it and it fell into the hands of a small farmer. He later deserted it, and in 1871 it was moved to its present site.

One could spend a good deal of time studying history as it has unwound itself at the upper falls of the Genesee. My greatest interest is in the beauty of the place; its deep groves (if you are interested in statistics, please consider that there are now more than four hundred thousand trees, of fifty-five different varieties within them) with their game and their wild deer, the pleasantly old-fashioned inn, with the tall spray fountain in front, the deep gorge with its vistas, and, finally and grandest of all, the waterfalls, themselves. These are at their best in the spring and before the crowds of picnickers and campers and one-day tourists have thrust themselves upon the place. Then you find yourself practically alone within it. Its solitude, as well as its grandeur, impresses itself upon you. You can put yourself back a century or less and imagine once again the

In beauty and dignity few American colleges surpass those of New York state. One of the most ideally situated is Cornell University, at the near right. The ivy-covered building above it is part of Union College, Schenectady; the lovely building with the pointed tower is the chapel of St. Lawrence University at Canton; the chapel with the belfry and the clock belongs to Colgate University at Hamilton.

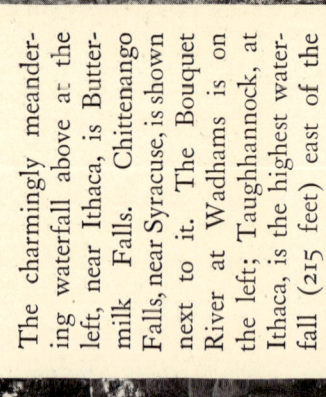

The charmingly meandering waterfall above at the left, near Ithaca, is Buttermilk Falls. Chittenango Falls, near Syracuse, is shown next to it. The Bouquet River at Wadhams is on the left; Taughhannock, at Ithaca, is the highest waterfall (215 feet) east of the Rocky Mountains.

old Genesee Valley canal passing through the gorge; the echoes of its boatmen calling to one another. This canal was an ambitious enterprise. That masterful early railroad builder and outstanding pioneer citizen of Rochester, Elisha Johnson, felt that he had worked out a solution for carrying the canal past the falls, by designing a tunnel, eleven hundred feet long, twenty feet wide and twenty feet high; for that day a tremendous engineering enterprise. He built for himself a huge residence on the site of the present park—*Hornby Lodge* he called it. It was four stories high, and here he frequently entertained, in royal fashion, as many as fifty guests at one time.

But when Elisha Johnson actually came to bore the canal tunnel, quicksand interfered, and he was compelled to substitute a deep cutting. The canal is gone, these many years. It was just another of the state's foolish investments. Never successful, it finally had to be abandoned. In much of its bed, all the way from Rochester up to Olean, on the Allegheny, now rest the rails of a branch line of the Pennsylvania, also not particularly profitable. A far more important rail line is the Buffalo main stem of the Erie, which is carried high above the uppermost falls upon Portage Bridge, once reckoned as one of the seven wonders of the world.

The original Portage Bridge, 234 feet above the water and about eight hundred feet in length, was indeed a tremendous construction. Silas Seymour designed it. An intricate trestle, it was, into whose fabrication went nearly two million feet of lumber, and which took nearly two years to build. Its opening (in 1852) was an event in Western New York, marked by a large celebration. For more than twenty years Portage Bridge stood, and then one night it burned; such a pyre as Western New York never before had seen and probably never again will see. After which there was no bridge, merely a deep chasm filled with charred timber and crews of tired and nervous men trying to replace it. Which they did, in forty-seven days and nights, with a spidery iron structure this time, that only recently has been replaced by an equally impressive bridge. But the feat of building the earlier one has never quite been equaled.

For years the development of the Genesee country, Western New York generally, was sadly halted and confused by great perplexities in the land titles. It seems that, away back in 1620, King James once granted the Plymouth Colony all the land reaching back of the New England sea frontage for an indefinite distance, rather a careless thing for King James to do. The Dutch, who had many claims in those days, also were granting titles, at times a little recklessly. The result was that eventually the land titles became most complicated and entangled. Lawsuits began to spring up, and it looked as if it would never really be settled.

In fact, it finally took a convention to settle the rival claims of Massachusetts and New York in the Genesee country, although litigation in the matter has existed up to within the last twenty years. This convention was held, in 1786, at Hartford, and its Solomon-like judgment was that the disputed country should have its sovereignty and jurisdiction vested in New York, but that Massachusetts, which had the prior royal grant, should have the actual ownership of the land. The decision covered all that part of New York, west of a line drawn north and south, three miles west of Geneva. Which, in turn, explains the quaint name of Pre-emption Road, which has come down to this very day.

Massachusetts, being in need of ready cash, promptly sold its New York State holdings, most of them east of the Genesee, to two shrewd Yankees, Phelps and Gorham. They, in turn, sold some of them to the Pulteney Estate; and the land west of the river, with the exception of a narrow tract along the Niagara, was sold to Robert Morris, the Philadelphia banker of Revolutionary repute, from whose hands it went to the Holland Land Company. It is only within the last half-century that the Holland company resold its final holdings, and then it was that its snug little office in the main street of Batavia became one of the entertaining museums of the state.

Phelps and Gorham proceeded at once to the disposal of their holdings. They were sharp real estate operators, not too scrupulous, predecessors of a generation which, a full century later, was to speculate in city lots and country estates. They succeeded in inducing many long-visioned New England farmers, discouraged at the faint prospect of ever attaining agricultural success on the hard hillsides of their native terrain, to move into what was then the newest West. So to the Genesee country came many fine settlers, and not the least of all these, James and William Wadsworth, nephews of a successful Connecticut miller, one Jeremiah Wadsworth, of Durham.

The Wadsworths came to the Genesee country to see, to conquer and to remain. Today they are, almost without exception, the only family in the region which for more than a century has retained its traditions. In all that time, none other than a Wadsworth has dwelt beneath the roofs of the manorial homes at Geneseo. The full record of this fine American family easily would run to great lengths. It includes a devotion to the cause of education, which resulted in one of the earliest normal schools in the state being established and maintained at Geneseo, and a patriotic fealty to the nation, which gave the life of one of the most beloved sons of the family in the Civil War, and which, for generation after generation, has presented an unbroken record of public service, in Livingston County, at Albany and at Washington.

And yet, if you were to ask the Wadsworths what they were, they would reply simply, "just farmers." Tradition says that an earlier generation of the family could ride in its saddles all the way from Geneseo to the outskirts of Rochester, some twenty-nine miles distant, and never leave the land to which they hold title. However, this is another of the cases where tradition errs. But the fact remains that the family still owns and farms more than thirty-five thousand acres of the finest land that God ever put into any of His country. It is not all continuous or contiguous. Some of it has been in the hands of the family for more than a century, while other acres are of recent acquisition. For the Wadsworths are good traders, as well as farmers.

For the so-called tenant system, they have the utmost contempt. Knowing farming from A to Izzard, they are quite happy in operating their broad acres, themselves. And quite successful they are, too. Yet success, in their case, has only meant the upkeeping of as simple a democracy as one may find today in the whole length and breadth of the country. Even the Hunt, so famed a feature of the Genesee Valley, has been operated upon a thoroughly democratic principle. The wealthy, horsey crowds of both Rochester and Buffalo have aligned themselves more or less with it, but its strength and control always has been that it was in the hands of the Livingston County farmers, with whom the Wadsworths are proud to be enlisted.

In that hour that Philip Church and the Wadsworths were working their way through forests and hardships into the fair promise of the Genesee country, three southern gentlemen of means and taste and distinction, were listening with great attention to every report that came out of it. Nathaniel Rochester and James Fitzhugh and Charles Carroll, all of Maryland, were more than slightly interested in prospects at the lower falls of the Genesee, where the river takes its final leaps, before burying itself in Lake Ontario, but seven miles distant. Their increasing interest finally led them across the wilderness to those falls; there to purchase a townsite and to lay out a milling community, with power in plenty to drive its wheels. The choice of a name for the nascent town having come to lot, Rochester's was chosen. And he it was who was to become most closely identified with its future. He supervised the preparation of a town plan, with a decent space reserved for a school, a church and a possible future courthouse, and saw to it that important streets were named after Fitzhugh and Carroll.

So was born the future metropolis of the Genesee country. To that country Colonel Rochester had finally brought his family, servants and slaves. But they did not come at once to Rochester. The site of the future metropolis was swampy, malarial, unhealthy. The "Genesee fever" was famous. The Rochesters tarried for a few years at Dansville and at Bloomfield, some miles to the south. In 1818 they moved to the brisk young village, that had been incorporated as Rochesterville, and took up residence in Spring Street; and there remained the rest of their lives.

The town forged ahead. A bridge was thrust across the Genesee above the falls; at the precise point where the town's Main Street still crosses the river, although the casual visitor does not realize it, because the stores on either side are carried across with it, after the fashion of ancient London Bridge. Further down the stream, where the lowest falls discharge the river into a deep gorge, a huge wooden-arch bridge (325 feet high) was next built. It was first regarded as an engineering triumph, but proved to be something less; for after about a year of use it fell, of its own weight, and with a mighty clatter.

All this was merely incidental to the swift development of the new town, which adopted cityhood in 1834 and hardly more than a score of years after its founding boasted some twenty-five thousand souls resident within it. Highway traffic across the state began to desert Avon and to favor the crossing of the Genesee at Rochesterville. Coaches and post-chaises and wagons and men on foot and on horseback choked the roads with traffic. Most of them were bound for Buffalo and the boats up the Lakes to the western country, but some liked Rochester so well that there they tarried; and finally settled within its precincts.

The comments of a chance traveler, a Philadelphia gentleman who came through Western New York on his way to Niagara in 1829, and whose letters afterwards were privately printed, are interesting. Of Rochester he wrote:

> After breakfast I spent several hours in rambling through and about this town of rapid growth. There is no great beauty about it and I consider it a dirty place. All the streets are filled with mud and rubbish. Building is the order of the day, but there are few houses in the place that can be called handsome; and even the best are nothing to what I have seen in the other towns. Yet, when its natural advantages are considered, I know no place which can compare with it. Paterson and Brandywine are very far behind it. It is calculated for as many mills as there are spots to place them, and the water can be used five or six times

within the distance of a mile. Water seems to be made to do everything here. The blacksmiths have become so lazy that they even make it blow their bellows. There is an oil-mill (flour-mill) at this place, calculated for sixteen runs of stones, eight of which are now in operation; with many others having six, seven and eight, all in complete operation. Several manufactures and mills for different purposes are now building; and I have no hesitation in saying, that although Rochester can never be a handsome town, owing primarily to its low situation, yet I believe it will see the time, perhaps very soon, when no place in the Union will exceed it, in point and variety of manufactures. . . .

The Philadelphian was partially accurate. He forecast correctly the future manufacturing prowess of the new town; yet he did not foresee that, within a very few years, it would become known for its beauty as well.

Another picture of the early Rochester is from the pen of Captain Basil Hall, the distinguished English traveler, who came through at about the same time as the Philadelphia gentleman and who wrote of it, after this fashion:

Everything in this bustling place appeared to be in motion. The very streets seemed to be starting up of their own accord, ready made and looking as fresh and new, as if they had been turned out of the workmen's hands but an hour before, or that a great boxful of new houses had been sent by stream from New York and tumbled out on the half-cleared land. The canal banks were at some places still unturfed; the lime seemed hardly dry in the masonry of the aqueduct, in the bridges and in the numberless great saw-mills and manufactures. In many of these buildings the people were at work below stairs, while at the tops the carpenters were busy nailing on the planks of the roof. Some dwellings were half-painted, while the foundations of others, within five yards distance, were only beginning. I cannot say how many churches, court houses, jails and hotels, I counted creeping upwards. Several streets were nearly finished, but had not as yet received their names, and many others were in the reverse predicament, being named but not commenced. . . . Here and there we saw great warehouses without window-sashes but half filled with goods and furnished with hoisting-cranes, ready to fish up the huge pyramids of flour-barrels, bales and boxes, lying in the

THE GENESEE FLOWS GRANDLY 167

streets. In the center of the town the spire of a Presbyterian church rose to a great height, and on each side of the supporting tower was to be seen the dial-plate of a clock, of which the machinery in a hurry-scurry had been left in New York. I need not say that these half-finished, whole-finished, and embryo streets were crowded with people, carts, stages, cattle, pigs, far beyond the reach of numbers and as all these were lifting up their voices together, in keeping with the clatter of hammers, the ringing of axes and the creaking of machinery, there was a fine concert.

Captain Hall makes reference to the aqueduct of the Erie Canal, also to be regarded as one of the "seven wonders of the world." (They seemed to be a little careless with the use of that phrase in those days.) The Rochester aqueduct was indeed a notable piece of early engineering, eight hundred feet in length and solidly constructed of New Jersey red sandstone. The canal had not hesitated between Rochester and Avon, even though it would have been far easier to have crossed the Genesee at the latter place. It was out to seek traffic for itself, and this new "Lion of the West" promised plenty of it. So the canal's engineers devised the aqueduct and a few years later, it being too small in girth for the traffic, tore it down and replaced it by the present splendid bridge of granite, still in use, although no longer as an aqueduct.

Rochester by 1840 had climbed to a population of over thirty thousand persons. There were not less than thirty-five flouring-mills in the place, standing in a row on the west bank of the Genesee gorge, just below the upper falls, and grinding a vast output. The town quickly became known the country over as the Flour City. Monroe and Livingston counties had soil well adapted to the growing of wheat, and night and day the wagons filled high with it rolled into the town and up to the doors of its mills. The canal and railroad vied with one another for the outbound transport of the flour. It all came to be a considerable enterprise. Other manufacturing industry followed in its wake; foundries and wood-working shops and others incidental to the conduct of a prosperous and swiftly growing town. One was different from those of other York

State towns—the nurseries. Rochester soil and climate seemed particularly well adapted to the propagation of young growing things. The nurserymen of Rochester soon attained a wide reputation for their products. That shrewd Rochesterian to whom we already have referred, Hiram Sibley, made the first of his fortunes in this business.

For half a century more the town continued its steady, impressive growth. It had long since lost the swift onrush of the boom days of its first two decades; folk no longer referred to it, rather grandiloquently, as the "Young Lion of the West," but people as a whole had a good deal of respect for Rochester. It had solved many problems which worried it at the outset. It finally had managed to bridge successfully the river at various places; and by reaching to a lovely high-set lake forty miles to the south (Hemlock Lake), to secure what then seemed to be an inexhaustible supply of the purest water. A system of high-pressure steam-pumps was installed at the edge of the river so that in case of a severe conflagration the Hemlock Lake supply could be augmented almost instantly. The town used to have some terrific fires. I think that perhaps the worst of these was the evening the lantern works burned. It was a tall brick factory that stood at the very brink of the upper falls. The fire swept madly through the lower floors and imprisoned the operatives, some of whom, in desperation, leaped from the upper floors. In all some thirty-four lives were lost, and for many a day thereafter the town was most depressed. The only disaster that could compare with it was the burning of the orphan asylum, in the middle of a bitterly cold winter night.

My own acquaintance with Rochester dates back nearly half a century. I was a cub reporter on the old *Herald* there, and I came to know the town quite thoroughly. In the late 'eighties it had acquired a settled and substantial look. The Genesee cut it squarely in two, but the river was so well bridged that you hardly were aware of it. The West Side and the East vied in strength and in popularity. The West Side had most of the public buildings of the town, D. W. Powers' semi-public ones and most of the churches. It also possessed in the aristocratic Third Ward, just south of the old canal, a sort of local Boulevard St. Germain. The best families of Rochester had lived there, ever since Colonel Rochester built his fine old house in Spring Street, almost within stone-throw of the canal. They held themselves a bit aloof, as if constrained to uphold the social dignity of the town.

But the East Side was looking up. It had the nicer retail shops and one or two good hotels, the old Cook Opera House, the fine new Lyceum Theater and the University. It also had succeeded, after a bitter battle, in wresting the main railroad station of the town away from the West Side, where it had stood since the cars first began running in and out of Rochester.

But, best of all, it had East Avenue, a superb residential street. And if the Third Warders now and then were inclined to be a bit snooty and lift their eyebrows at East Avenue and even whisper that raw French word, *nouveau,* the East Avenue folks would call attention to the fact that four of the oldest and finest houses of Rochester were ranged along *their* street; the two clans of Sibleys, the Perkins and the Powers, dwelt in state within them. And by a gracious fate, these houses still stand and are maintained in all the elegance with which they were inaugurated more than a century ago.

So it was quits, then and for a time thereafter. The Four Corners were within the purlieus of the West Side, and they were then regarded as one of the busiest street corners in all America. From them the street cars departed for every part of the city. The last cars went at midnight, although it nearly always was at least ten minutes after the hour before the starter's shrill whistle blew and the hurrying and scurrying of late wayfarers to catch them (and perhaps also a drink at the Silver Dollar Saloon near by) came to an end. There were herdic cabs in East Avenue, but these had gone to sleep at a much more decent hour. . . . If you missed that last trolley you were almost completely out of luck, unless you had the stiff price for one of the old cabs ranged in front of the Court House a block away. If it was winter, and you finally succeeded in waking the driver, you found that he had the comfortable solace of hot bricks within his vehicle.

At the Four Corners stood the Powers Buildings; and at one time they were the wonder and the glory of Western New York. Daniel W. Powers was another self-made man of the town. He had come out of some little town along the canal to the west and become an outstanding figure of the place, albeit a little Barnumesque in spots. It became his whimsy to build. And so, at the Four Corners, he began, over sixty years ago, to erect a home for his banking business. In that era, when calamitous fires were shaking the land, Powers gave attention to the possibilities of fireproofing his buildings. He became proud of them; and continually was adding to them, until (with his adjoining hotel) they covered an entire block frontage upon Main Street and had a tower that reached fourteen stories above the pavement, an unheard-of thing in the America of that day. And once, when Rochester poohpoohed at Dan Powers and his claims of a fireproof building, he caused the rooms of the tower to be cleared of their fittings and started simultaneously a bonfire in each of them. The tower blazed into flame, like a funeral pyre of the ancients, and lit up Rochester and the country roundabout for miles. When they had all burned themselves out and the building was unharmed, save for a little scorching, Rochester was convinced.

The god of publicity had lit upon Daniel W. Powers as one of his very own. He liked the experience. There was a portico in front of Powers Hotel, and upon its roof he was wont of Saturday evenings in summer to place the 54th Regiment Band, while all Rochester came with camp chairs and sat in the roped-off street and listened to the music.

This dalliance with the muses so pleased Powers that presently he did more; he created for the town upon two of the upper floors of his office building an art gallery, which was a little bit more than New York had ever seen before outside of its largest city. He had marbles by Story and paintings by most of the good modern artists and by some that were not so good. But Rochester was proud of it. The town's formal receptions to its more distinguished visitors were held within it, and no stranger was permitted to remain long without being hauled upstairs on the new fast hydraulic elevators to Powers' Art Gallery.

In later years the Powers' Art Gallery was closed, dismantled. It has been replaced by a fine modern gallery, in an exquisite housing, on the old campus of the University.

There was another banker in Rochester in those days, but people did not pay much attention to him—not then, at any rate. He was a clerk in the old savings bank across from the Court House in Main Street, a smallish fellow who had come from Waterville over in Oneida County; by name, George Eastman. Eastman had a hobby, a black box of a camera, with which he was forever experimenting. So much so that after a time the president of the savings bank called young George to him and suggested that perhaps it would be better if he did not let his banking duties interfere so much with his camera. Eastman took the hint and quit the bank. He induced his boarding-house keeper to take all his savings out of the bank and invest them with him. They rented a small factory in State Street, hung out a sign, Eastman Kodak Company, and went to work. But no one paid much attention to that in those days.

It was much more fun to live the pleasant everyday life of Rochester. All summer long there were the joys of the countryside; Hemlock and Conesus and Canandaigua lakes up in the hills to the south; and only seven miles to the north, the fine sandy, rocky shore of the big lake, Ontario. Irondequoit Bay was also near at hand. For many years Rochester, with a strong German element in its population, enjoyed its beer gardens in and about the town; the most famous of these were Falls Field, close to the river, and Fred Cook's Bartholomy Brewery. Then some one developed Ontario Beach at the very mouth of the Genesee, and overnight it became the rage. You could go down to it on any one of the many local trains of the Central branch and, soon after the trolley had displaced the horsecar across the land, by fast electric car as well. Ontario Beach became to upstate about the same as Manhattan Beach was to down. It had a big hotel, and excursion trains, twelve, fourteen, sixteen crowded cars on each of them, came up to its very doors, sometimes from as far as two hundred miles away. There were band-concerts and bathing and eating and drinking and rollercoasters and rides—all the spending knick-knacks that seem to attach themselves to such a place.

The vast success of Ontario Beach brought others along the lake rim and the Bay. Little local railroads, on some of which long strings of open cross-bench cars were hauled briskly by small locomotives, reached them from the town, and to a degree at least, these shared the prosperity of a larger place. And in the fall when one began to tire a bit of the Lake and the Bay, and the September winds across it from Canada began to get chill indeed, there was the Monroe County Fair and the Grand Circuit races under the trees at the Driving Park, much nearer town. To this day, Rochester has hardly forgotten the thrill it had when William H. Vanderbilt's "Maud S" broke the world's trotting record—a mile in 2.08—on the home-town track. It nearly burst with pride that day.

In winter we had all the ordinary entertainments incidental to a brisk and forward-looking town of a couple of hundred thousand folk; and very good theater. It seems as if Rochester has always had good theater. When I first went to work there, the town's famous old Corinthian Hall still stood, although it had fallen from its high estate and gave itself to rather cheap forms of melodrama and burlesque. It was a quaint, old-fashioned theater, which one reached through one of Rochester's most historic passageways, the Reynolds Arcade, a fine old structure which only a year or two ago was torn down and replaced by a hideous modern one. Corinthian Hall was up a flight of stairs and was a fire-trap; and the town breathed a sigh of relief when it finally burned, two or three hours after the close of an evening performance, with no one left in the place.

We generally had three nights (and a matinée) of a play in the Rochester of the 'nineties, and most of them did very well. The town progressed from sharing week-stands with Buffalo and Syracuse to week-stands upon its own account. The new Lyceum over on the East Side was a handsome and roomy theater, with one of the largest stages in America, and Rochester really felt very badly when last fall it was torn down for taxes, after nearly half a century of usefulness. It had begun to look a little antiquated, out-moded; but it stood for a something that seems to have gone, all but completely, for the present-day America, the glories of "the road." Rochester was a town for "tryouts" of important productions. The actors liked it, and it liked the actors and extended to them the warmest and truest of welcomes—substantial patronage.

That was the Rochester of the 'nineties. The Rochester to which I returned thirty years later was a changed place.

The change had been a long time coming. Yet one could easily sense it, even before the World War. Physically, it had some curious and not entirely agreeable manifestations. The trend of growth from the West Side had become much more markedly pronounced. The Erie Canal, which once had formed a sort of protective boundary for the aristocratic Third Ward, had disappeared. No longer was life on the West Side interrupted by the risings of the lifebridges with their clamor of bells. The bridges had gone with the old canal. In its place was a wide paved thoroughfare, under which ran a four-track subway from end to end of the city. The purpose of this was to provide rapid transit for Rochester as well as an entrance to the town for the interurban trolleys. But about the time the elaborate subway was finished, the interurbans folded up and went out of business; there has never been much rapid transit service in it, anyway. The thing is a good deal of a failure. So, too, is the elaborate inner harbor of the Barge Canal system, for which the state expended some two or three millions of dollars, and which is formed by a movable dam in the bed of the Genesee just above the old aqueduct (now used by the new subway and the street above it). In all the years that I have watched it, I never have seen but one boat in it, and that was a dilapidated-looking old Erie barge.

The elaborate warehouse upon its quay serves as a garage for the port employees, of whom there seem to be quite a number.

The West Side looked pretty badly. State Street, which thirty years ago still held its head pretty high, despite the bitter loss of the Central Station, had long rows of empty or half-empty buildings, whose faces needed washing. There is only a shadow of the former great activity at Rochester Four Corners. It would seem even more tragic if this were not also the bitter experience of many and many another American town. Buffalo, for instance, is having the same desperate time with her lower Main Street, New York with mid-Broadway, Chicago with her South Side. Rochester cannot be charged with neglect in the question of her badly-raped West Side. When the East Side gained a fine new hotel and a fine new department store as well, a gentleman sought to offset these with a new hotel, a new department store and a new theater on the West. His sentiment was better than his judgment. He could not stem the tide. It's a way that American cities seem to have—just picking up and emptying still valuable real estate, in order that new may be created. Put it down, if you will, as another one of our inexplicable national tendencies.

But the trek toward the east, just like that of so many thousands of ants, was not merely to be expressed in physical and outward values. Social forces also moved. East Avenue, never neglected, came into absolute social dominance. It gained much for itself. And not the least of it is the elaborate residence of George Eastman, millionaire manufacturer of cameras and films. Kodak had prospered beyond all dreams of its founder. The boarding-house keeper who had backed the savings-bank clerk found himself possessed of millions of dollars. There was a new crop of millionaires in the town; and it felt the onrush of great wealth, showing it in its fine new houses, in its smart new specialty shops, its clubs and restaurants, in the long line of sleek and aristocratic motor-cars of quality that purred their way up and down East Avenue.

George Eastman had not alone done well by himself and his associates, but he had saved Rochester commercially. Some of the old industries had not been successful; a few of them had ceased, others were on ragged edge. Kodak, of itself no small enterprise, with its fourteen thousand employees in its various plants throughout the town, had become the inspiration for the creation or upbuilding of other industries, either related or of similar type, such as the development of the Bausch & Lomb company, today the largest optical works in America and maker of most of the Kodak lenses. Bausch & Lomb far antedates Eastman. Away back in 1853, in the old Reynolds Arcade, John Bausch, formerly an itinerant seller of ready-made spectacles, began to grind spectacle lenses—the first time that it had been done in the United States—and the fine business that he there founded has grown steadily to magnificent proportions.

Kodak was possibly the inspiration for the creation of other works in Rochester whose output requires rather high technical skill on the part of the workers: thermometers and scientific instruments, delicate electrical equipment for motor-cars, gear-cutting machinery, check protectors and other office devices. The list runs to considerable length. To these specialized forms of Rochester industry, may be added the uninterrupted development of some of the older ones. Clothing is one instance. The city still is an industrial power. It has gone through the recent years of depression without a single bank failure, and that is almost a record among the larger cities of the land.

Rochester never has exactly lacked culture. Always she has had a taste for lectures, books, music of a high order; and, as we have just seen, good theater.

But upon her was to be made an experiment in advanced culture, without a precedent or parallel in the land.

The bachelor, George Eastman, sitting in his great house and beginning to enjoy a little leisure in the latter years of his life, had created for his own pleasure, and that of his coterie of friends, a string quartet of exceptional merit. These four men came to the Eastman house Sunday evenings and there entertained the supper guests with a program of chamber music, carefully selected and well played. The manufacturer seemingly had real pleasure in music. He made almost a rite of it with his breakfast, an organist of quality playing a huge pipe organ as he went to his coffee each morning.

One night, the story goes, Eastman called the leader of this quartet to him. The man was Herman Dossenbach, and for years he had struggled, with little material success, to provide Rochester with better music. He and his fellows had a small music conservatory in Prince Street, and it was a struggle to keep it going and both ends met—until George Eastman came along.

Eastman, the story continues, asked Dossenbach if he were given plenty of money, what he most would like.

The musician was not slow to answer. He visioned a school of music, right in Rochester, something after the fashion of the conservatories of Paris or Berlin or Vienna. With it there would be a fine theater and a real opera house, producing real opera. But it all would cost money, much money. His eyes glistened in his enthusiasm.

Eastman smiled upon him. Although the world did not then know it, he already had made a large contribution to education, giving the extensive new buildings of the Massachusetts Institute of Technology, just across the River Charles from Boston. He closed his eyes for a moment, then asked if such an enterprise could be made into a glorified film house—an academy of music, of the motion picture, as it were, which would give the finest music in connection with the finest films. Dossenbach saw the point. He said that it could, very readily.

The tired old eyes closed again. When they opened, the man spoke definitely, as was ever his way:

"Very well, when this war is over, we shall try and build that theater."

Which was George Eastman's way of signing his name to a promissory note.

Covered bridges were used extensively in New York state until modern engineering came along. The two bridges shown above span the Delaware River; the one with the warning signs is near Delphi, the other near Walton.

Historically-minded individuals have formed covered bridge organizations in recent years to fight for the preservation of such picturesque structures as shown below. The bridge with the wooden lacework is at Cook's Fall, the other at Jay.

When you are hunting for the most charming bit of architecture in a New York state village you look for its church. The stern-looking edifice with the pointed steeple and the clock, at Pompey Hill, is typical. A less common specimen is Clement Church at Cooperstown, at its left. The one below, resembling a Belgian chapel, is on the river road to Nyack. The Dutch Reformed Church at Tappan is of interest for it was here that Major André was tried and sentenced.

So came the Eastman Theater into existence, thirteen years ago.

That it is one of the handsomest theaters in the world, no one doubts after he has had but a single good look at it. All that good taste and good architecture, and plenty of money, could bring forth have been poured into it. There are defects in its location and some details of its arrangement, but these perhaps are quite natural to so large an enterprise, and they are quickly overlooked. The house charms by its very simplicity. In its broad main floor, its mezzanine and its great gallery, it seats more than thirty-three hundred persons, comfortably and in great luxury. No comfort detail has been omitted, and because it was Eastman's whim that it should be a democratic theater, in the fullest sense of the word, the last seat in the last row of the gallery is of the same quality as the best of the orchestra chairs.

With the theater is the school of music, handsomely built, with a very beautiful small hall and many studios equipped with pipe organs and pianos and other essential equipment. There is a complete music library and classrooms and all the rest of it. A fine school it is indeed.

When the entire building, with its annexes and workshops, had been completed, Rochester wondered what it had all cost. Eastman, as was his way, was reticent. Finally he told me: He had put eight and a half million dollars into building and equipping it, in addition to a four-million-dollar endowment fund.

"But the theater must stand upon its own feet," he warned. "I am not putting up an endowment to give Rochester society the elegance of a symphony orchestra. It will have to pay its own way always. So will all the other entertainment that is produced within this theater."

He was sound. He nearly always was. He had a definite plan. He nearly always did. For six days of the week the house would be run upon a strictly commercial basis, as a "movie theater." It would show the best films, with ballet and other incidental entertainment, and would have also a sixty-piece orchestra of merit. The "movie house" would earn enough profit to pay the deficit of a hundred-piece symphony orchestra, which, with certain forms of traveling musical entertainment, would occupy it on the seventh day of the week (at certain seasons of the year). The "movie orchestra" would train its men for the larger symphony one. The endowment was for the school of music, alone. The entire enterprise Eastman placed in the hands of the long-established University of Rochester. He wished to keep it out of the hands of any future politics at the City Hall. He was sound every step of the way.

So began the Rochester Experiment.

Good music for a good town. Good music for the men and women in the Kodak works. Good music for the men who ran the trolleys and the buses. Good music for the girls in the Sibley store. Good music for the "university crowd." Good music for Joseph Street. Good music for East Avenue. Good music for every one. A swell idea, and perhaps some day—ten years, twenty years, fifty years off—Rochester would awake to find that it had a really musical soul.

It was like giving a town culture by hypodermic injection. Eastman, himself, took the needle and jabbed it in, clear under Rochester's skin. And Rochester slightly reeled, with the delirium of the affair.

Now, after thirteen or fourteen years, the inevitable question—how has it all worked?

For a time it went quite easily. The idea was new, the theater so wondrously beautiful, the entertainment that it offered so unusual, that Rochester took to it—like a bear to molasses. It drank it all in hungrily. Of course there were mistakes, the inevitable conflicts of judgment, due, in part at least, to the size of the experiment and to the fact that it was sailing entirely uncharted seas. For a time the visits of outside orchestras were encouraged, then they were shut off, abruptly, and Rochester used its own good orchestra, one of the thirteen major symphony orchestras in the country. It was, almost uniformly, well supported. The larger opera companies all came and all did well, in this most unusual setting. It was only the film end of the enterprise that proved entirely perplexing.

The Hollywood magnates from the first had viewed the Rochester Experiment, presenting high-grade films in a high-grade manner, with distrust. If it succeeded, it would show them up, in a ridiculous way; if it failed, it would be bad for the film industry, as a whole. Therefore they gave little help to it. Moreover, they were beginning to form chains of picture-houses across the country, to standardize the showing of films, as they had standardized their production. The Eastman Theater stood as a stumbling block in the way of their plans. Rochester was a forbidden land to them. Eastman's agents had seen to it that before the new house opened, the former chief houses of the place had come into their hands. And no outsider had the audacity to attempt to build a new one, in contrast to the gorgeous new temple of music in East Main Street.

The University, to which Eastman had entrusted the ownership and management of the theater and its school of music, was most perplexed of all.

For eighty years now the University of Rochester has gone the even tenor of its pleasant way. It has had no great high lights, neither has it had any sorrowful depths. In all those eighty years it has had, practically, but three presidents, another unusual record. Dr. Rush Rhees, who relinquished the reins of its control last June, after thirty-five years of most successful work, was a former Baptist minister, who became a wise educator, with a shrewd and kindly business head upon his shoulders.

Rhees must have been pretty perplexed at times with the problem of the theater. With its Sunday performances and its ballet, both of them requested by Eastman, it must have been something of a load for an institution which was pretty Baptist; in its beginnings, at any rate. But Rhees accepted all of this. It brought his institution, of which he was undyingly proud, for the first time into an intimate connection with Eastman. It was a connection which a little later, when the University was to help create a fine medical school and hospital as a part of its work and a brand-new liberal arts college for men on the bank of the river above the town, was to prove of very great practical value. Curiously enough, up to the coming of the school of music the University had been that in name only; merely a good college of liberal arts which, until 1890, had been restricted to men. The most outstanding woman of Rochester's history, the late Susan B. Anthony, had forced the college finally to accept women, somewhat to its own discomfiture.

Slowly but surely the distant opponents of the Eastman Theater closed in upon it, as before they had helped close the legitimate theaters of a good part of the country. It became increasingly difficult for the Eastman, like the other "independents," to get the important new films. And the producing industry finally dared to invade Rochester. A big, gaudy, new house was built in South Clinton Street, with all the gilt and plaster and clashing color that the American movie industry can devise when at its best—or its worst. It installed a cheap orchestra, specializing in jazz.

Now what was the reaction of Rochester to this newest house?

All too typical of its fellows, I am afraid: It deserted the splendid theater into which all possible good taste and the good architecture had been woven and flocked to the newcomer. The movie boys took heart. Rochester was vulnerable, after all. They built another big theater in Clinton Street—this one, however, much handsomer and more appropriate than its immediate predecessor. The doom of the Eastman, as a movie-house, was sealed. Its owners, almost in desperation, rented it for a term of years to a third producing chain out of Hollywood, which immediately started to cheapen it and to deface it as far as it dared; all in the name of "showmanship." The house went very jazz, indeed.

And, again, what the reaction? How was Rochester's own "noble experiment" working?

Apparently there was something in that injection after all. Rochester was enraged. It considered its temple of music to have been defiled. It refused to patronize the house under its new policies and management. In less than three years the movie-chain came to the

University on bended knee and begged to be released, paying handsomely for the privilege. And the Eastman Theater at last arrived at its proper *métier,* a sort of glorified Carnegie Hall and Metropolitan Opera House all in one.

Today it holds to its final rôle—handsomely. Eastman is gone. A lonely and distrustful old man, he shot himself in his lonely house, chiefly because, as he himself said in a farewell note, his "work was done" and he faced increasing loneliness and incurable disease. But other forces have acted to support his theory of community culture; the Hochstein School over in the Jewish section of the town has done some educational things in music that the Eastman institution had found difficult, if not impossible. A community theater has sprung up in another quarter, which has met with more than a moderate degree of success. The town has held to its fine symphony orchestra; has supported it, even in these hard years of depression. It gives its concerts frequently and steadily through the winter. Many opera companies, including the Metropolitan, come to the Eastman Theater each winter. And the successful School of Music produces grand and light opera and other forms of high-grade music and does it very well indeed. It would not be fair to say that the experiment is a failure. It may yet work. Rochester may yet find itself an American Milan.

And always it will find itself at least a fine American city. Its business district is a bit disappointing. It is ringed about with parking stations, very necessary these days, but not adding to the neatness or the compact appearance of the town. And what might have become one of its noblest vistas, looking down East Avenue, has been utterly spoiled by the erection of a high yellow brick building, absolutely plain and devoid of any architectural ornament or effect whatsoever.

But Rochester makes up in the lush beauty of its residential districts and its abundant parks, what it has lost, perhaps not irrevocably, in its business center. Almost the entire town is, in effect, a huge park. Its chief club, the Genesee Valley, is not excelled in any other city of the land. With real acumen, some years ago, this club secured one of that quartet of fine old East Avenue houses (with six acres surrounding), even though this involved giving up a most comfortable and well-located clubhouse further downtown, and made it, in no small sense of the word, a community center of the highest type. While in these days a good many old-fashioned clubs have languished, and some of them have died, the Genesee Valley, by broadening its privileges, extending its clubhouse and adding to it squash courts, basketball, open-air swimming pool and what-will-you, has enjoyed a new burst of prosperity. To my mind, its loveliest feature is the row of Lombardy poplars that borders the pool. Long ago, I named them, in my own mind. The loveliest of them all is the Empress, and the most lordly the King, of Prussia. You really should see for yourself the King bow to the Empress and the Empress, in gentle breeze, nod back to the King.

Ontario Beach and its big hotel are long since gone; they have been replaced by one of the city parks, and a most modern bathing establishment. (The town really is more than proud of its extensive park system, stretching roundabout it in all directions.) The rim of Ontario for twenty miles is lined with the handsome homes of Rochesterians, some of which are occupied the year round. But the simple glories of some of the older places, such as the lovely New-Port House on Irondequoit Bay, remain and are much patronized.

In every direction the big three-hundred-thousand-soul modern city extends itself. It reaches up the Buffalo Road and the Ridge Road for nearly a dozen miles, an almost continuous community. It is the sort of thing that alarms England today—"ribbon development" she calls it—and that she is trying to handle by parliamentary legislation. The Englishman seems to be much more apprehensive about preserving the inherent beauty of his land than we are.

The original builders of the Erie Canal found water level for their pathway wherever possible; which meant that its route, east of the Genesee at least, was well to the north of the main highway across the state. That earlier highway seemed to court hills rather than to avoid them. But the canal followed the pathway of the Indians and the early white traders—the water-level route, the natural pathway of empire across the state. When it finally turned from the upper Mohawk River, it began to find its way along the easy plateau-land, parallel to Lake Ontario and from ten to twelve miles south of it. And so it continued, all the way to the Niagara Frontier.

Few of the early established towns across the western part of the state were upon its banks. Instead, it created a new chain of communities, such as Weedsport and Port Byron and Clyde and Lyons and, west of Rochester, a whole list of "ports"—Spencerport, Brockport, Middleport, Centerport, Gasport and Lockport; this last is a dramatically situated place where, in a precipitous gorge, the canal-boats, old and young, have made their way these many years up and down the stairlike flights of locks. The old canal took five locks, hand-operated, to make the climb. The new one does it in but two, operated swiftly and mechanically by electric power, generated by the gravity flow of the canal waters from the upper levels to the lower.

When the railroad came, following a little laggardly upon the heels of the first canal, it paralleled the Erie, more or less closely, east of Rochester. At that point, however, the main stem of the Central swerved off to the southwest, on its way to Buffalo. The "ports" west of Rochester were left to their own devices and the services of a secondary line of rails. Left to their own devices, they seem to have chosen a sleepy path of comfortable prosperity. They are, for the most part, agricultural communities, of some wealth and much comfort. A few quarries, some modest factories and the finest orchards in God's County are the foundations of their prosperity.

For God seems to have designated the south shore of Lake Ontario, all the way from Oswego at its foot to the Canadian Hamilton at its head, as a natural growing ground for the richest of His fruits—the pear, the plum, the peach, the grape, the big red apple. The hard winters of the Western New York country seemingly are tempered along the lake shore district, even though it faces squarely to the north. There is a something in its slopes, moreover, that seems to spell good drainage; and that, with a natural fertility of soil, makes the orchards thrive most bountifully for over 150 miles. We have heard a good deal in recent years about the apples of Oregon and of Washington. The Western New York growers must be modest men indeed, for the fact remains that, from half a dozen comparatively small railroad stations, northwest of Rochester, enough apples are shipped in the course of an average year to more than equal the entire annual output of these two noisily prolific states of the West Coast. These are but a few of nearly a hundred shipping stations whose extensive canneries and storage-warehouses proclaim the fullness of the fruit of the orchards that they serve.

The fine highroad through this part of New York bespeaks attention. No description of the territory could claim completeness if it omitted mention of the Ridge Road, which stretches straight east from the falls of Niagara, to and through Rochester and for miles beyond. It is a natural highway. No better description has ever come to me of it than in those same letters of a "Philadelphia gentleman" that I have already quoted. Of it he wrote, on the 14th day of May, 1829:

I was called up early (at Niagara) to take stage for Rochester, distant eighty miles, fare $3.25. We started at five o'clock, six of us, and arrived at the wonderful Mushroom of the West at five in the afternoon, over the great Ridge Road, the finest I have ever traveled. This road is truly remarkable. It seems to me that when old mother Nature, after having perfected the cataract, originally begun at Lewiston, was so tickled and delighted with her production, that she resolved to make a pathway for the children of men to come and see her prodigy—accordingly she went to work and made this beautiful turnpike of from eight to twelve rods wide, of hard gravel and sand . . . and said to the children of men: "Travel, behold and wonder!" But, to speak seriously on the subject, I should say that when the falls were at Lewiston, this remarkable turnpike was the shore and beach of Ontario, as the whole of the land, lying between it and the lake is low and swampy. Its direction is in the form of a curve and parallel to the lake shore. . . . Its elevation above the land on either side is from ten to thirty feet, and it is perfectly hard and free from stones or ruts. . . .

The road intersects few sizable towns; the ones that line it are small and far between. But it does present at least one feature of passing interest, the "cobblestone houses" that seem to exist through a small part of Western and Central New York and nowhere else. They are fabricated of neat rows of varicolored stones, that once lay upon the beach of old Ontario and that long ago were washed to ineffable smoothness by its waves. It must have been a neat trick of construction to arrange these in rows and sink them into home-made cement. At any rate, they once had a great vogue, just as it was the fashion to build houses and barns of octagonal shape, a building fad which seventy-five years ago swept all the way across the state.

Today the Ridge Road is perfectly paved, its entire length; an important link in the New York highway system, used by the motorists of forty-seven other states as well (to say nothing of the near-by Canadians). Not all the cars that come gallivanting over its polished surface are those of aliens. The Western New York country possesses a tremendous number of its own. There is not a farmer in all of this prosperous district who does not own his automobile, generally a motor-truck or two in addition, and invariably of good make and cost. I have gone to a fruit-growers' meeting in Orleans County and thought myself at an open-air automobile show. An afternoon's callers will sometimes choke the front yard with expensive cars.

These farmers of Western New York frequently are hard workers; in their short harvest seasons, feverish ones. Yet they make their brains work, as well as their hands. I have known a pear-grower on the Ridge Road, a man with three hundred acres of as magnificent trees as one might wish to see, after a hard day's work in the orchard, to ride down to Charlotte at night, there to inspect the railroad yards and see for himself where the fruit was going. If most of the white "refrigerators" were destined toward the New York and Philadelphia markets, he quickly billed his output to Boston; yet if the Boston market looked as if it might be drugged two days later, he quickly reshipped to Philadelphia or to New York. He told me that such tactics might make him upwards of ten thousand dollars in a single season.

There are the big annual fairs at Rochester and Syracuse and Toronto, but to see the real Western New York folk one should find his way to the county fairs at Canandaigua or Caledonia or Batavia or Brockport or Albion or Lockport. There the horse-trots are genuine affairs, the drivers local talent, the two-year-olds within the sulky shafts probably raised on the blue-grass of the Genesee flats. If one scorns the racing—but who of Western New York ever does?—there are the products of the home in Farm Hall or the automobiles and the tractors in Machinery Hall, or the ladies of the First Methodist Episcopal Church setting up a dinner in a widespread tent for seventy-five cents that couldn't be equaled in town for twice that sum.

When winter comes, the upper Genesee at last is solidly frozen, and the hills which line the valley are so blanketed in white that the bare trees and the barns and the crazy fences stand out more clearly than at any other time of year. When, by day, the smoke ascends straight upwards from the farmhouse chimneys and men's shoes crunching through the crusts betray zero temperature; and night brings the stars and the crescent moon a little nearer mother earth than at any other season—even then the Western New York folk refuse to be discomfited. A few of them may hie themselves off to Florida or to California. But these are merely to be classed as weaklings. The real Western New Yorker still owns horses, gets out the old pung-sleigh that great-grandfather first owned, hitches the brown mare into the offset thills and packs to town. In the dusk he drives home again; the mare ambling briskly in the sleigh-runs, with thoughts of the warm stall just ahead; and the man ruminating upon the goodness of just being alive, in a land which knows nothing of fuel famines or food shortages or subway crushes or picketing or red flags (save those on the cabooses at the rear ends of the freight trains); which interprets life with an exquisite simplicity and definiteness; which considers itself extremely remote from internationalism and those puzzling, intricate things for which internationalism stands; and which prefers to regard itself merely as a segment of the old-fashioned America, the America which was good enough for its fathers and its grandfathers.

CHAPTER VIII

Sentinel Stands the Western Gateway

THE state of empire begins, abruptly, at Montauk Point, sticking its high-set nose far out into the Atlantic; and ends, with equal abruptness, at the deeply cut gash of the Niagara. The pathway of empire begins at the imperial city of New York; and it may be assumed to end at Buffalo, which, if not exactly an imperial city, is, nevertheless, a very handsome and important one. It came into existence more than a century and a quarter ago, and it has thrived steadily ever since, until it now has come to be a community of close to six hundred thousand souls, the second city in population in the state and the thirteenth in the Union.

For the first fifteen or twenty years of its existence, the small lake port at the foot of Lake Erie, at almost the very point where it begins to be the turbulent straits of the Niagara River, struggled bitterly for existence, against its rival, the earlier village of Black Rock, three miles further down the river. For a time this fight was so bitter that it threatened the total extinction of one village or the other. Eventually the more southerly one, at the mouth of the Buffalo Creek, won; by having itself designated as the official terminal of the new Erie Canal. It was not so many years afterwards that Buffalo, as the terminal town was called, completely absorbed

Black Rock, name and all. The Holland Land Company's agent, Joseph Ellicott, saw to that.

This seems to be about as good a place as any to tell of the Holland Land Company or, as it sometimes was called, just the Holland Company. As a matter of fact, it was really not a "company" at all, at least not in the sense of our modern incorporations. A group of prosperous merchants in old Amsterdam, seeking new investments for their earnings, decided upon westernmost New York as an advantageous possibility. As Hollanders they felt that they might have difficulties in acquiring and holding titles to American lands. Therefore they worked at first through friends and relatives, in New York City and roundabout. Still there was no incorporation. It was quite a voluntary company, and the wonder is that it stood so well for so many years. It is quite a tribute to Dutch integrity.

One Wilhelm Willink, of old Amsterdam, was the head of this organization. With him were eleven of his fellow townsmen. They took a mortgage upon a huge area in Western New York, owned by Robert Morris, of Philadelphia, extending from the Genesee through to within a mile of the Niagara frontier. Morris was unable to carry this tract, and the Holland Land Company foreclosed and became the proprietors. They at once opened an office at Batavia and despatched one Theophilus Cazenove to America, as their agent. Cazenove had other tracts to engage his attention, one in Pennsylvania and another around the present village of Holland Patent, near Utica. He therefore employed Joseph Ellicott as the company's agent in Western New York, and Ellicott came to real glory and achievement as the founder of Buffalo.

Ellicott was a man of talent and of taste. His brother, Andrew, was Surveyor-General of the United States; and the two men had worked with Major Charles L'Enfant, in the production of the magnificent city-plan of the national capital. Joseph Ellicott became enthusiastic about city-planning. When he went up into Western New York to lay out hundreds of square miles for the Holland Company, he carried in the back of his head a dream of creating a splendid city for it. He made his way through the forests and mapped out the entire area; it was cut into ranges, six miles in width and extending from the Pennsylvania line north to Lake Ontario, and these into six-mile squares—now the townships of that terrain. This done, he went to the site of the present city of Buffalo, stood upon a slight plateau overlooking the waters of Erie for many miles to the west and said:

"This is the place. Here we shall build our city."

And immediately suited action to thought. It mattered not to him that much of the land for the site of the future metropolis was low and swampy, that less than four miles away was the "long house" and headquarters of the powerful and unfriendly Seneca Indians, that already there was an enterprising and ambitious young village down at Black Rock (*not* on Holland Company land); Ellicott was determined to have his way, and have his way, he did. He at once produced an elaborate plan for the new Buffalo. L'Enfant had influenced it. There was a rectangular pattern of streets as a foundation; upon this, fine avenues radiating from central points, squares, and traffic circles. In the heart of the future town and upon its main street, then named after Wilhelm Willink, facing two of the finest radial avenues, Ellicott reserved a hundred acres for the great house that he was to build for himself. He even bowed its frontage into the main street. In those days a good many other grandiose cities were being planned upon the shores of the Great Lakes, most of which came to nothing. But none of them had a more fascinating city-plan than this one, which actually came into being. And in its entire development the inspired plan of its founder was followed closely. For a century or more of its development, like Washington, Buffalo has not only proved the great efficiency of the European method of laying out a city, even against the tremendous traffic necessities of the present day, but its sheer beauty, as well.

He never built his palatial house there in the very center of the town, as he had originally planned it. Instead he erected a much more modest one, of brick, covered with clapboards, in Main Street (the former Willink) at High. It was a big house and a handsome one, with its six great pillars, each the trunk of a primeval tree, cut from the Indian lands along Buffalo Creek. High locusts grew roundabout it, and there in Main Street it stood for many years, until the city had grown to be too close and noisy a neighbor, and then it was taken out to the Amherst suburb, where it still stands. Ellicott never lived in it. The Second War with England broke, and the untrained American forces along the frontier did not do well. To make matters worse they made a sortie across the Niagara and burned a helpless Canadian village. After which the British troops (aided by the still unfriendly Indians) burned both Black Rock and Buffalo. It was soon after the end of that war that Joseph Ellicott built his house. But before it was finished, his health failed and he had to leave Buffalo and go to New York—there to die, neglected and forlorn, in the old Bloomingdale Asylum.

But the city that he had brought into being continued. The war over and peace declared again, the Niagara frontier shot into new prosperity and growth. Buffalo went on apace. The great roads that connected her with the East at last were finished, and tremendous arteries of traffic they were. It was said that there was not a mile along them that one could not see at least one stage-coach or heavily laden freight-wagon; generally several. There were many taverns in Buffalo and all of them did a thriving business; chance travelers, arriving late at night, were fortunate to get a bed. From early spring to late autumn there was tremendous traffic upon the Lakes as well. Buffalo had a port of swift-growing importance, vessels coming and going at all hours, new vessels being built by the dozens in her shipyards, and finally there being excavated the terminal basin of the wonderful new Erie Canal which was to give her a continuous waterway through to the Hudson and the Atlantic. Even before she gave serious thought to the coming of the railroad, she was a powerful commercial town. Her first railroad did not come until 1836, and then it was merely a local line, reaching down to Niagara Falls, twenty-five miles away. It was six years later before she had through rail connection with the East. She did not dream in those days that she was to become one of the greatest railroad centers in the world.

Already she was a great lake port and passing proud of that, alone. She was a growing town too; by 1845 there were thirty thousand folk residing within her limits and more coming all the while.

To this Buffalo there came in those formative years a trend of population bound to be of great effect upon her future life and prosperity. These were the Germans. Most of them came as individuals, but some of them were in the form of definite immigrant organizations; such as, for instance, the Ebenezer Society, which settled in the flats of Cazenove Creek, not a dozen miles from Joseph Ellicott's fine house and within half a dozen of that East Aurora, which in a far later day, one Elbert Hubbard was to bring to fame. The Ebenezer Society, which arrived just prior to 1850, worked gangs of men and women together in the fat fields and sent out shepherds (and little portable houses, in which they lived) with their itinerant flocks. In this way not one spear of grass was lost. The farmers roundabout stood aghast. It all was so very new to them. After a while (some twelve or fifteen years) the Ebenezer Society folded its tents (and its little portable houses) and moved further toward the West. But in that time it had left a definite impress upon Erie County. And other Germans were following, from Erfurt and Mecklenberg and Alsace.

The Germans who came to Buffalo found a comfortable town already awaiting them; Ellicott had done his work well. As far back as 1840, it was a brisk city, feeling its oats. A description of it, written that year, says that it already had two thousand houses, 18,041 residents and thirteen churches, a "literary and scientific academy," three banks and seven newspapers, of which two were dailies, "many hotels and taverns required for the great concourse of strangers," and then goes on to say:

> . . . The buildings, public and private, are generally good, many of them four stories high, among which are fine specimens of architecture. An enterprising citizen, Mr. Rathbun, during the year 1835 erected ninety-nine buildings, at an aggregate cost of about $500,000; of these, fifty-two were stores of the first class, thirty-two dwellings, a theater, etc. . . .

Afterwards Mr. Rathbun collapsed. His real estate speculations proved most unfortunate, not only to him but to a large number of investors, and he was sent to prison.

Among those earlier builders of Buffalo was its first bishop, the remarkable Reverend Father John Timon. Bishop Timon, who came to the place toward the end of the first half of the nineteenth century, decided that it must have a cathedral, and that, at once. He blazed with enthusiasm at the idea, and very soon he was on his way to Rome, to secure approval for it. That quickly was done, the Pope having contributed two thousand dollars out of his private purse to start a building fund. Bishop Timon then went all over Europe, soliciting funds from the crowned heads for the new cathedral in Buffalo. They were pleased and amused at his importunities, most of them not even knowing where Buffalo was; it might have been in Timbuctoo. But they gave, and gave generously, and Bishop Timon returned and began construction of St. Joseph's Cathedral. A Brooklyn architect was called, and gradually there was produced, down near the Terrace, a splendid great church of stone, with a rarely beautiful Gothic interior. It is a curious commentary that when a score of years ago it was determined that Buffalo should have a new cathedral, up on its magnificent Delaware Avenue, it was designed by an Italian architect, to be fabricated of marble, like the churches of Florence or Pisa. This Italian never had been in America and he did not have the slightest idea of its terrific winters, especially those roundabout Buffalo. As a result, the fine church that he planned was utterly unfit to withstand the heavy frosts and extreme cold. And, after it was completed, much of its façade had to be taken down and rebuilt. But the old cathedral, which is still in use, has never required more than a minimum of attention.

For it, Bishop Timon, as one of the final acts of his life, secured the first carillon ever to be brought into Western New York. This chime of forty-three bells was cast in Paris and was first shown there at the Exposition of 1867; after which it was shipped to Buffalo; and from time to time still sends its sweet message out over the town. In later years a shepherd of the flock, Father Nelson Baker, equal in energy and vigor to its first great bishop, erected in suburban Lackawanna, a tremendous monument.

As you go in or out of Buffalo from the south you will see, outlined upon a low ridge of hills, the dome of a mighty church that, if ever you have been to Rome, will startle you, so great is its likeness in setting to St. Peter's. That is the Basilica—the great Shrine of Our Lady of Victory—that a simple parish priest, located in a small steel manufacturing community, succeeded, through his own efforts alone, in building and in consecrating. This glorious church has cost some two millions of dollars. It is decidedly one of the outstanding features of a city which has many. And it is more than well worth a visit from any casual visitor.

Another churchly effort in Buffalo deserves mention. When the Holland Land Company instructed Joseph Ellicott to lay out its city at the foot of Lake Erie (at one time it was planned to call it New Amsterdam), it also authorized him to set aside free sites for churches and for schools. Three of these were directly opposite the bowed front of his future palace (that remained unbuilt), and one of them was immediately taken by the St. Paul's Society of the Protestant Episcopal faith; and from that day to this, St. Paul's has stood in the heart of Buffalo.

There are many fine churches in Buffalo—Protestant and Catholic—and a further listing of them would be invidious. One of the finest of them, architecturally, is the Church of St. Louis, also in Main Street, and this brings us back to the Germans, who, despite its name, were chiefly responsible for its creation. Originally they had combined forces with some old French families of the town in building this imposing fortress of the Lord. But as Buffalo grew the French element in it all but disappeared, and St. Louis church has been thoroughly Germanic these many years.

The Germans prospered in the town and roundabout it. Gradually, in a quiet but unmistakable fashion, they became dominant. They ruled its politics and directed its business policies. Even today, when every third person in the city is a Pole, they still are a strong factor in its workaday life. Polish and Irish strains have grown to great strengths, but never to dominating ones, politically or otherwise. There is something in the German idealism, as well as conservatism, that has been of great help to Buffalo, as it also has greatly helped the civic progress of both Cincinnati and Milwaukee. It led to the building, many years ago, of almost the first extensive public library of any of the larger cities of the land; and also of the huge Music Hall (now the Teck Theater), modeled upon similar institutions in Leipzig and in Dresden. It is only in recent years that the great theater has fallen into comparative disuse.

The conservative Buffalo of the 'fifties became the outstanding Buffalo of the 'seventies. When 1929 came and the bottom dropped out of many things, Buffalo stood staunch. Banks in Cleveland and Toledo and Detroit and Chicago reeled and fell by the dozens. In Buffalo, one or two minor ones collapsed, but ninety-seven per cent of all deposits remained intact.

Conservatism is a mantle that the town always has been most loath to drop. Instead of being primarily, if not exclusively a point for the interchange of water traffic, the railroad gradually came into the picture. New lines found their ways to her terminals, until there were not less than a dozen important individual companies, striving for traffic. Their vast and murky yards, Saharas in summer and Greenlands in the winter, stretched for many miles in all directions. They marked, with their docks and elevators and coal-storage facilities, the development of one of the greatest rail centers in the universe. Their passenger traffic did not lag. Gloomy old Exchange Street Station always was one of the busiest in the land. A little way west of it, the New York Central had another busy passenger station for its trains to Niagara Falls and their connections to the West. If it wished to send a train from that station to Exchange Street (less than four blocks distant), it had to go by way of Rochester, nearly two hundred miles. Through passengers crossed from the one station to the other by omnibus or hack, sometimes afoot. If one went afoot on a bad night in the 'seventies he literally took his life in hand. There were many murders on the Buffalo waterfront in the early days.

Buffalo folk (as well as the New York Central) were much relieved when the city finally gave permission to the railroad to bridge that gap, by laying tracks through Joseph Ellicott's Terrace and across Main Street, in exchange for a belt line and rapid transit service around outlying sections of the town. Thereafter, for many years, the passenger business of the road was concentrated at Exchange Street, and travelers, too, breathed a sigh of relief, for conditions along the waterfront did not clear up rapidly.

I have known Buffalo a good many years. I recall it in the 'nineties as an extremely well-finished and important-looking city, as compared at least with most others upstate. At Ellicott Square (then called Shelton, but afterwards renamed for the man who had planned to place his palace there) there stood (still stands) the lovely old St. Paul's and the fortress-looking Erie County Savings Bank; just across from them, and much newer, is an office building, covering an entire city square, which Buffalo proudly referred to as "the biggest office building in the world." A stone's throw away was the Iroquois Hotel, than which there never was any better tavern anywhere. The handsome Public Library faced the near-by Lafayette Square; the solid stone Court House and City Hall was two blocks distant, in the other direction. Somehow it all looked like a big city, and a thrilling one, to boot.

It still looks like a big city, a really big city. The well-famed Iroquois Hotel has been supplanted by an even larger house, and across from it is a new City Hall and Court House, thirty-two stories high with a smoking chimney in its very center, a sort of man-made Popocatepetl. There are other unmistakeable evidences of progress. Old Exchange Street Station is gone—without its unceasing activity lower Main Street looks pretty dead—and has been replaced by a very elaborate structure at the eastern edge of the town. But the Michigan Central and Niagara Falls trains still pause at the Terrace, and that little station ranks with the old Erie one, not far distant, as an interesting bit of railroad memorabilia.

The Terrace always fascinates me, with St. Joseph's Cathedral and the old Court House (where once I saw a cringing bit of human flesh on trial for the assassination of a President) and the jail where Czolgosz was incarcerated, awaiting his trial and execution for the cold-blooded murder of President McKinley, and the little stands where they sell fresh clams. Not long ago I drove into the town and past one of these emporiums. Clams, in such a place—impossible! But the thought *was* beguiling. And after a block or two, I turned the car back and indulged in a whole dozen Little Necks—and never ate better. Buffalo is a place of strange contrasts. You will see in her heart, great retail markets with widespread sheds, like those of Charleston or Savannah or New Orleans, and they are entrancing places; but, seemingly, not of the North.

Politically, it has been conservative, and politically it always has loomed large. Its history has been mixed up with four Presidents of the United States. The first of these was Millard Fillmore, a New York State boy born in Moravia, not far from Auburn, who went to Buffalo to make his fortune, and made it. They thought a good deal of Millard Fillmore in the town, and they made him Chancellor of the University of Buffalo, which really was not a university at all, but a corking good old-fashioned school of medicine. However, it was about the best honor that Buffalo had to give, and it gladly gave it to Millard Fillmore. And the city filled with pride when he became President of the United States. He had a way with him—polished orator, *raconteur,* good-fellow all around. His quaint old-fashioned house of many gables stood until a few years ago on Niagara Square. Then they tore it down and put up the big Hotel Statler on the site (E. M. Statler also was one of its products, and Buffalo always reciprocated the faith and the pride that he put in it), but the older Buffalo that is passing always will think of it as Fillmore's home site.

When Millard Fillmore came back from the White House, they had to think up new honors for him. During those four years in Washington, he had not resigned the chancellorship of the university, so something else just had to be produced. At about that time the newly created Buffalo Club came into existence, so Millard

Fillmore became its first president. It still is housed in its venerable residence in lower Delaware Avenue, with its nth degree Victorian magnificence.

There came the day when the memory of Millard Fillmore was overshadowed.

Another ambitious young man came to the town, first to study law and then to intermingle with its politics. His name was Grover Cleveland, and he was a Presbyterian minister's son from down in New Jersey. He was a quiet fellow, thickset, a tremendous worker. It was not very long after he had arrived, before Buffalo was aware of his presence. He became assistant district attorney of Erie County, then sheriff, then mayor of Buffalo. And then it was that the town definitely realized that he was there. Its local politics had sunk to a low estate; there was a good deal of corruption within earshot of the City Hall, and Grover Cleveland was not slow to realize it. When he was powerful enough so to do, he struck at it, with deadly and unerring force. Men, powerful men in the town, went down, and the incorruptible Cleveland went up. A term in the office of the Governor in the new Albany Capitol and then the White House. Two terms in the White House. The dramatic history of Grover Cleveland does not have to be told in these pages.

Curious how a city can entwine itself with presidential history.

The turn of the century came, and Buffalo, feeling its pride and energy, its great wealth and its growth, decided to take a tremendous plunge and indulge in a world's fair. I say "indulge" advisedly. It is a pretty courageous sort of a town that can take a fling at an extravagance of this sort, and stand the after effects. Buffalo did not hesitate. She raised the money and she found a site (at the north end of her principal park) and there she constructed, just prior to 1901, the Pan-American Exposition, one of the handsomest fairs that America ever had seen. Since the Chicago Fair, eight years before, there had come tremendous advances in the use of electricity, especially in lighting. The proximity of Niagara Falls and its great generating stations, gave Buffalo large opportunity to capitalize this. The Pan-American, with its Court of Honor dominated by a high and exquisite tower, its lovely coloring by day (in contrast to Chicago's "White City"), its tremendous effects in lighting, set a new note in expositions; it has not been surpassed from that day to this in its showmanship or its beauty. For here it was that Fred Thompson and Skip Dundy, mere youngsters they were then, produced their *Trip to the Moon,* which set a new note in side-shows and became the foundations for their sweeping successes elsewhere, particularly at the New York Hippodrome and at Luna Park, Coney Island. Luna Parks sprang up all over the world, and the Buffalo exposition of 1901 was the beginning of all of it.

Too bad that such a brilliant beginning should have had such a tragic ending.

From rather slow business at the outset, the accepted fate of most exhibitions of this sort, the charm and attractiveness of the fair was building a steadily increasing attendance—until that autumn day when it was honored by the presence of the President of the United States, his family and his staff. It was a gala day in Buffalo. And then, by a pistol shot, a laughing crowd was instantly transformed into a panic-stricken one. Men, like hyenas, tried to fight their way to the miserable human being who had fired that shot. If they could have had him, they would have rent him, limb from limb, Roman fashion.

There followed hard days indeed. President McKinley became a fearfully sick man in the Milburn house (since torn down) in Buffalo's charmed Delaware Avenue. Then came the almost inevitable end to the chapter, the death of McKinley, the man who, seemingly, could not have had it in his heart or mind to harm any other man in the world. When the news was sent out from the house that the President was better, that he actually had sat up in bed and smoked a cigar, the older medical men of Buffalo shook their heads, gravely. They knew that if there had been any chance of saving his life he never would have been permitted that indulgence.

They were right. That reassuring message had hardly gone out to the nation before a tragic one followed it. The pavement of Delaware Avenue resounded to the hoof-falls of a Paul Revere rider who shouted the tidings to the town, at the top of his voice. The hundred telegraph keys in the newspaper tents that had spread about the Milburn house, relayed the bad news to the whole world. In the deep depths of the Adirondacks, a hunter was summoned by woodsmen and driven, like mad, to the little North Creek station and a waiting special train. The train, with rights over everything else upon the rails, raced down to Schenectady and over to Buffalo at better than mile-a-minute speed. The hunter, grave and subdued, hurried in a cab from the railroad yards to the old-fashioned Wilcox residence, also in Delaware Avenue, there to be greeted after midnight by a little group of not more than fifty men.

"Are you ready, Mr. Roosevelt?" said Judge John R. Hazel to this newcomer, and then administered the oath of office to the newest President of the United States, Theodore Roosevelt.

It must be added that the assassin's shot also was fatal to the Pan-American. It never recovered from it; and a few weeks later was glad to close its doors for the last time. Buffalo still shudders when it thinks of those September days of 1901, and that was more than a third of a century ago.

It is pleasanter by far to think of her steady progress all these decades.

Until comparatively recent times she has not been a manufacturing city; not primarily at any rate. It has suited her convenience—and her innate conservatism—to be toll-keeper at a tremendous gate, the western gateway to the pathway of empire. As long as freight had to break bulk within her harbor, she could collect the toll, small in amount but large in volume. An eighth of a cent a bushel on grain seems little enough, but when there are many millions of bushels in the course of a single season, it comes to a very pretty penny indeed. That is why Buffalo always has so zealously opposed any change in the main inland waterway route to Oswego or down the St. Lawrence, any enlargement of the main stream of New

York's canal to accommodate lake craft and so avoid breaking bulk in her harbor. That harbor is her bread and butter, and that bread and butter is the solid fare upon which she lives and thrives.

In more recent years she has gone more extensively into manufacturing; with great annual steel output in normal years, a sizable one of high grade motor-cars and of airplanes. She has many other industries, including flouring and an extensive meat-packing plant. In developing these she has entrenched herself against a possible day when traffic halting at her harbor might come to low ebb, her giant elevators become all but empty. . . . She is forward-looking in this. Being a toll-keeper is good, when there are any tolls to collect; a sort of safe and sure kind of business. But when there are no tolls!

And she also has broadened her cultural activities. Lacking a George Eastman, to give the benefit both of money and brains, she has done well nevertheless, with an art gallery, originally built by John J. Albright for the Pan-American Exposition and then deeded by him to the city; an industrial museum; an orchestra of growing importance in the musical world; and the University of Buffalo. No Ezra Cornell in wealth, Walter P. Cooke did pretty well with the limited resources at his command. At least he made the University, in the fullest sense of the word, a community affair. Starting with the old-time and well-established college of medicine (and its allied dental college) it took over the old county-house property, well out on Main Street, and there it now is, developing into a most creditable institution, well rounded as to its university activities and well housed in substantial and dignified new buildings. But the chief pride of the new University of Buffalo is that the five million dollars subscribed in the home town for its reincarnation came from the pockets of exactly 26,628 individual donors. Community effort with a successful vengeance!

The state of New York reaches some sixty miles west and southwest of Buffalo, and this interesting district, including the well-famed Chautauqua, we shall consider when we arrive at the Southern Tier. For the moment, we turn to face toward the north. The Niagara River starts under the new International Peace Bridge on its passage to Lake Ontario; it is hardly forty miles all told. But in those forty miles the Niagara races a mad and turbulent course. The first ten or twelve of them are quiet enough, and so are the final eight or ten. But in between it becomes one of the fiercest rivers in all creation. It is possessed of a million devils, dropping, dropping, plunging over the crest of the world's greatest waterfall, tearing and tormenting itself fearfully and frightfully, then becoming serene and navigable once again, passing between gentle banks and losing itself in Lake Ontario. For its entire length it is international boundary; and along that boundary has been some of the fiercest and least fruitful of all fighting in the history of the nation. If the old white stone building, with many chimneys, that marks the passage and the obliteration of the Niagara into Lake Ontario, only could be given a tongue it would have a rare story indeed to tell.

In September 1934, I attended in the near-by American city of Niagara Falls (there also is a Canadian one of the same name) a mighty pageant, which commemorated the four hundredth anniversary of the first visit of that dashing French cavalier, Jacques Cartier, to America. In a brief three hours there was depicted much of the history of the Chimney House and of the fort which has sheltered it these many years. Fort Niagara, which stands at the extreme northwestern point of New York, with one bastioned edge upon the river and its broad parade looking out upon the waters of the lake, was built by the French, 210 years ago. Even before that there had been crude defense on the spot. La Salle had enclosed it with a stockade, in 1679. Fort Conty, that crude wooden fortress, had been reduced and destroyed, and then the present fort, with the Chimney House, had been built by the Marquis de Denonville, Governor of Canada, for King Louis XIV. Denonville's agent in the transaction was one Louis de Joincaire, French trader, who had, for some reason, succeeded in having himself adopted by the Senecas. With them he bargained, adroitly, for the construction of the chimneyed building, which soon became known as "the castle."

For, in truth, that it was. De Joincaire had asked his Indian associates for permission to build a *house*—not a fort, *nothing* of that sort! They were astounded at the solidity of the "house" that he built there upon the point. French military engineers, at that time the best in all the world, designed and built it, of thick-walled, cannon-defying stone, instead of the wooden structure that the simple-minded Senecas had anticipated. Underneath it were dim and fearsome dungeons. A real fortress it was, whose grim secrets never will be known. So does the white brother sometimes get out of hand!

This staunch outpost stood guardian of the west frontier for thirty-four years. It was the final objective toward which the British Braddock aimed, when he met his crushing defeat at Fort Duquesne, at the head of the Ohio. The doughty Sir William Johnson avenged that defeat. Coming across the pathway of empire in 1759, he routed out the French defenders of Fort Niagara, tore down the Fleur-de-lys and put the British ensign at the masthead of the fortress in its stead. For the next thirty-seven years Fort Niagara and Chimney House were British. In the last thirteen years of that time the Union Jack legally was as alien as the French ensign might have been. In the press of other matters, the British did not deliver the fortress to the new United States, until more than a dozen years after the close of the Revolution. They hated to let it go. It had been not only an outpost but a base in their hopeless struggle against the colonies. From it their armed expeditions went forth to war, and to it came, in increasing numbers, scared Tories, fearful of the future and seeking refuge under the king's flag and the king's stout cannon.

But the British were to occupy it again. The state of New York, which had been convulsed and overridden in the first war with England, went through a similar experience in the second war. In the first case, it was the easterly edge of the state that became the Belgium of the conflict; in the second, it was the northerly and western rims that caught the brunt of the fighting; particularly, the Niagara frontier. Moreover, the Second War was to be a conflict, for the most part carried on by the state of New York, almost unaided by the federal government. When Washington lent aid, it generally was of most unsatisfactory character. It was New York, herself, who (as far back as 1807 and 1808) built stout arsenals of brick and stone all through her North Country and her West and filled them, at great expense and against terrific odds of transport, with powder and ball and stands of arms. It was New York who prepared a militia army of nearly one hundred thousand men, who although poorly trained and incompetent, were at least a hundred thousand men, brave and fearless and anxious to fight. And if New York furnished such unsuccessful generals as Stephen Van Rennselear and Alexander Smythe, she more than compensated for them with that brilliant North Countryman, Jacob Brown, of Brownville, a sheer military genius and nowadays recognized as such.

The British, as we have seen, had a grand time with us during part of the War of 1812, burning and sacking Black Rock and Buffalo, repulsing our attempts to cross to their side of the Niagara chasm, playing with us at Sackets Harbor and at Plattsburg (as we shall see, in due time) and then, as a crowning insult, taking over Fort Niagara. This was the final humiliation, but it was not to be for long this time. Peace came, and the international boundary, save for ordinary commercial and political purposes, was all but obliterated. There did come a time, at the beginning of the Civil War, when the attitude of Great Britain seemed a bit uncertain, and then it was that Fort Niagara was greatly enlarged and rebuilt. You can see the tremendous brick-and-earth bastions and gunports to this day. It all was needless expense.

As part of a military reservation along the frontier the old fort never has been permitted to deteriorate. It has been maintained, as has the similar Fort Ontario, at Oswego, a hundred miles to the east. But a few years ago a definite move to rebuild and restore it to the appearance of earlier days took headway. The Old Fort Niagara Association was formed, and with generous co-operation on the part of both the state and federal governments, the Chimney House, one of the oldest bits of masonry west of the Hudson, has been completely restored and refurnished, after the fashion of the days of its most glowing importance. In the entire state of New York there is not a historic shrine more worth a visit; in this it ranks with the also restored Fort Ticonderoga at the easterly edge of the state. To which we shall presently come.

Fort Niagara stands at the foot of the lower navigable section of the river—about eight miles, all told. Lewiston is at its head and Lewiston is hardly less interesting. It is at the extreme west end of the Ridge Road, and its ambitious street plan and some of its older buildings show that once it, too, had dreams of metropolitan importance. It might have taken the rôle that great Buffalo now fills. Once it vied with Buffalo in size and in commercial importance. The old Frontier House, which still stands, is one of the historic taverns of the state. If it had tongue, it, too, could tell many weird tales. Once upon a time there were many warehouses upon its docks and a constant line of freighting-wagons and stage-coaches coming up the Ridge Road to them. Now it is all but forgotten. Buffalo got the Erie Canal and its terminal and then, a little later, the railroads; and what Buffalo did not get, the village of Niagara Falls was glad to receive, railroads and fine bridges over the deep and rushing Niagara. It is only within the past score of years that Lewiston again has had a bridge. Before that you took the ferry across to Queenston, as unspoilt a British town as you might expect to find in England, Ireland, Scotland or Wales. Of course, even before that, there was a bridge, and Lewiston hoped against hope. . . .

Forty years ago you still could see the ghostly remnants of the first suspension bridge at Lewiston, the undaunted cables of steel and fragments of the light superstructure of what had once been a busy crossing. It first had been built in 1851. For thirteen years it stood, and then an odd combination of circumstances ended its career. An ice-jam in the river caught against the footings of the stays that stiffened it against the wind, and rather than lose the bridge, it was thought advisable to release these. A fatal mistake. Hardly had this been done, before the wind rose again, violently, and the framework of the entire cobwebby structure was demolished. It was cheaper to leave the cables than to attempt to remove them, and there is a thrilling saga at Lewiston of smugglers who risked life and limb to crawl across them in the dead and dark of night. When the new suspension bridge was built in the same location, some twenty years ago, the old cables were of some use in the placing of the new.

Less dramatic, but far more satisfactory, is the story of the suspension bridge three miles further up the river, at the lower end of the village of Niagara Falls (then called Manchester) and within plain sight of the great cataract.

It is with this bridge that the name of the late John A. Roebling, who afterwards was to design the world-famous Brooklyn Bridge, over the East River, is connected. But Roebling, who already had completed a fine suspension bridge across the Monongahela at Pittsburgh, was not with the Niagara enterprise at the outset. It was first entrusted to Charles Ellet, also a distinguished engineer, who had completed in 1849 the suspension structure (still standing) which carried the national Highway over the Ohio, at Wheeling, in a single graceful span of 1010 feet, then reputed to be the longest in the world. Ellet, at the outset, succeeded in winning the Niagara Falls job from Roebling, much to the latter's discomfiture. For it was a most unusual problem. Not only was the new bridge to carry a tremendously busy highway traffic, but also a railroad track connecting the New York Central (just coming into existence at that time) with the Great Western Railway of Canada (now a part of the Canadian National system). The span was to be slightly over 800 feet and the superstructure to carry both highway and railway would have to be very strong and rigid. But the most serious part of the problem at Niagara was the fact that the river lay far below, in its deep gorge, and was at all times so turbulent that men hesitated to cross even in the staunchest small boats. It was a different problem indeed that confronted Ellet from that of the Ohio at

Wheeling, where in the summer that stream is so low that a man might almost wade across it. Yet he did not flinch.

In the New York *Courier and Enquirer* of eighty-seven years ago, one finds a correspondent telling of Ellet's shrewd device in sending a kite across the Niagara chasm and using the twine attached to it to draw, successively, heavier and still heavier cords across from the United States to Canada. He quotes Ellet, after this fashion:

. . . I raised my little wire on Saturday and anchored it securely, both in Canada and New York, today (March 13, 1848). I tightened it up and suspended below it an iron basket which I had prepared for the purpose and which is attached to pullies along the cable.

On this little machine, I crossed over to Canada, exchanged salutations with our friends there, and returned again, all in fifteen minutes. The wind was high and the weather cold, yet the trip was very interesting to me—up as I was, 240 feet above the rapids, and viewing as I did, from the center of the river, one of the most sublime prospects which nature has prepared on this earth of ours.

The machinery did not work as smoothly as I wished, but in the course of this week I will have it adjusted so that anybody may cross in safety. . . .

Ellet quickly followed this rough device with a footbridge, as a preliminary to the larger. But the larger bridge he never built. He became involved in a controversy with the men who were promoting it and, in 1849, withdrew from the work. Roebling then was called into it. He revised the plans, making the structure double-decked and then coolly abandoning some of the traditions that the best of British engineers had used in the fabrication of their suspension bridges. He began work in September 1852, and finished the job two years later, at a cost of some $400,000. That Roebling knew his business, is evidenced by the fact that his bridge stood to its steadily increasing task for forty-two years. When it was torn down and replaced by the present modern steel arch, it was not that it had worn out; it merely had grown too light for the heavier rail equipment that was coming into use everywhere upon the North American Continent.

Once the railroad had been completed to the Falls, almost an even century ago, it quickly became the accepted mode of transport to them. The swift new line from Rochester, generally paralleling the canal and the Ridge Road, came into the small village of Niagara Falls from the north. A mile before the train finally entered the arches of the stone "passenger house" in the village and came to its final stop, it passed close to the east rim of the gorge and gave then, as now, a fine vista of the cataract. To quote an old-time writer (in *A Jaunt to the Falls of Niagara*—1841):

The travelers that are the *dramatis personae* of this jaunt, are seated in the Lockport and Niagara Falls railroad cars. They have arrived within two miles of the object of their visit, and the exclamation is heard—"the Falls! the Falls!" An imposing scene has, indeed, broke upon them, and a general move takes place to catch a glimpse of the mighty cataract. Those seated at the right side of the cars have a full and direct view in front, and of the Niagara River, which, by their side, flows far beneath. On the very verge of its banks, at a dizzy height, they are whirling at the rapid rate of eighteen miles an hour. On looking below, some passengers hold their breath in amazement; others have been known to express their astonishment by a low protracted whistle, until the supposed danger was past. . . . In a few minutes after the Falls are first beheld, the cars have rolled on; have passed through the main street of the village and have stopped at the upper end. . . .

The *Jaunt,* while admitting that "the aid of a guide is indispensable, to point out the different views and to impart a full knowledge of all the localities," does take the trouble to suggest a little caution to the traveler, in resisting the importunities of the hotel porters and self-appointed guides. That was a prime trouble for years at Niagara. Bad on both sides of the river; a little the worst upon ours. Guides, porters, hackmen, became insufferable pests. The place was honeycombed with graft. So much so, that it all began to react, seriously, against its tourist business. From time to time efforts would be made to wipe out the abuses, but invariably these came to nothing. It was not until 1885 that the state of New York (under the leadership of Governor Grover Cleveland) gave heed to the constant protests of folk who had been fleeced at Niagara Falls, and ended most of the system of irritating small charges by purchasing Goat Island (formerly Iris Island, a much more attractive name), dividing the American and the Canadian (Horseshoe) falls, together with the small Prospect Park on the American side of the cataract. All this area was placed in the hands of a capable commission, which at once began to clean up the entire area, making a splendid park, absolutely free to the public. This really was the beginning of the state's present conservation and park policy, and it resulted immediately in a new flow of patronage to the place. Three fine old hotels had survived, the International and the Cataract upon the American side and the Clifton upon the Canadian. Two of these since have burned; but others, more modern, have come to replace them. The old Cataract remains in a good deal of its pristine pride—with much éclat they will show you the name of "A. Lincoln and family" upon its faded register; there are other names, hardly less distinguished. The public park system, upon both sides of the river, has been vastly extended. The Canadians have vied with us to make the surroundings of the great cataract in every way beautiful and attractive. New York State also has created small parks below the main falls, a plot of fifty-seven acres at the elbow in which is situated the deadly and terrible Whirlpool; and below this the Devil's Hole, whose uncanny contribution to history is the recorded fact that in 1763, a small force of 350 British soldiers were suddenly attacked by Indians, the survivors of their fire being herded together into the "hole" and gradually forced over the precipice, with many casualties.

Niagara has held uncanny fascination for jumpers, either those seeking to end their lives, or else, in this unerring fashion, to court the great god, publicity. One of the first class was the melancholy Francis Abbott, expatriate Englishman of rank, who came to the

Falls in 1827, made but few friends or acquaintances, lived for twenty months alone upon Iris Island, played late at night (sometimes all night) upon his guitar, to the unceasing accompaniment of the cataract; then finally plunged himself into it. Less melancholy was the fate of Sam Patch.

Patch was a curious fellow; a New Englander, who had made no small fame for himself by leaping into the falls of the Passaic, at Paterson, New Jersey. Puffed up by his prowess there, he went up to the western end of York State, accompanied by a rabble troop of equestrians and acrobats and musicians. The hotel-keepers received him with acclaim.

He was accorded the freedom of the Falls. They all but gave Goat Island to him. But finally he thought better of the idea of leaping from above the precipice and into it, and went down to the foot and there built a small tower, from eighty to one hundred feet in height; and on October 17th (1829) he made his leap, successfully, amidst the applause of a huge crowd that had assembled. Later he was not so fortunate. He journeyed east to Rochester and there jumped twice into the falls of the Genesee. Upon the second occasion he lost his life, and a protest went up across the country against further exhibitions of this sort. It was a long time thereafter before any one made a boastful leap into the Niagara, although along in the 'sixties, the Frenchman, Blondin, created a sensation by stretching a tight wire across the gorge and going across it with a balancing stick and a man mounted on his shoulders.

In my father's hotel up in Watertown, half a century ago, there was a young man who blacked boots and made himself generally useful about the place. His name was Bobby Leach, and he was forever bragging to me that some day he was going over the falls of the Niagara. Eventually he did it in a barrel, much padded. He had his brief hour of fame. Afterwards he went to New Zealand, slipped on a banana peel, and was instantly killed.

There is no question but that the mighty and constant onrush of Niagara does catch hold of men, tempting them to daring and to fate. No one knows the number of folk that have yielded to this impulse. The place is tragic with its memories. One of the most fascinating of all these is the fate of the small steamer *Caroline* which, at the very end of December 1837, slipped quietly down the river from Buffalo and became hopelessly embroiled in the so-called Patriots' War, an almost farcical, yet tragic, conflict that waged for a time along the entire Canadian border. A little group of Americans, misguided and misled, sought to enable similar groups to accomplish the independence of Canada, a deliverance which most of the Canadians did not themselves wish. The *Caroline* late that December night had been moored to a wharf at Schlossers Landing. In the near-by tavern there was much drink and brawling. A watchman remained awake on the steamboat; a number of the party slept within. The watchman saw in the half-dark a group of men in a small boat cross from the Canadian shore, come under the lee of the steamboat, cut the hawsers, then watch it drift to its certain doom. To make the matter the more certain, they set fire to it. A few on the *Caroline* escaped by jumping into the shallow rapids above the Horseshoe; the others went with the blazing boat, over the rim of the cataract and into the depths below. Then all was dark again. It was a sight for the Walpurgian gods. The following morning they found the charred remnants of the small steamer floating in the currents and the eddies far below the base of the falls.

The industrial development of Niagara Falls that completely transformed the town and at one time threatened entirely to destroy it as a tourist resort, began about the middle of the 'nineties. George Westinghouse, perhaps as much as any other one man, was responsible for it. The power possibilities at Niagara as a potentiality had been obvious for many years. It was Westinghouse who found the way of changing them from potentiality into actuality; of bringing a part of the six million horsepower of energy into strands of copper wire and carrying it over the surrounding country, for more than a hundred miles in every direction. He it was who wrought the miracle of the Electric Age at Niagara Falls.

Actual beginnings of power development at the Falls go as far back as 1852, when a hydraulic canal was begun from a point on the American side just above the head of the rapids above the cataract and carried across in a tangent to the edge of the gorge about a mile below. The Porter family, which has been connected with the Falls ever since there was the first village there, made a donation of the right-of-way for the ditch. But despite this, it was nine years in building, and when it was completed the stagnation of industry, due to the Civil War, was in full force, and for some years more it was unused, spilling its waters into the river far below. Then entered that shrewd Buffalo German, Jacob F. Schoellkopf, who with his associates bought the stagnant canal enterprise in 1877 and used it to drive the runs of a large flouring-mill. Other factories followed, all located right on the banks of the canal, together with a small electric station for the lighting of the near-by Prospect Park.

Then it all languished.

Ten years later discussion of the larger power possibilities of the Niagara became rife. Two engineers, Thomas Evershed and Edward Atkinson, went into the thing. Various plans were suggested; all of them chimerical. It was proposed, for instance, to take the water from Lake Erie right at Buffalo, and there drop shafts 150 feet to an outlet tunnel, which would be carried, at a tremendous depth, to a point well below the cataract. The result of it all was to accomplish nothing, except a badly upset state of the public mind. Distinguished journals, such as *The Nation,* foresaw the possible ruination of one of America's greatest scenic spots. And it began to make bitter protest.

The thing did not move quickly. Not so much because of the protests, as because the men who wished to develop the power upon a sizable scale and perhaps carry it considerable distances did not know just how to go about it. Even George Westinghouse, when finally he was brought into it by the newly organized Niagara Falls Power Company, was much perplexed. He conferred with Edward D. Adams, its president, and he then went overseas to study similar projects in Europe. It was suggested to him that the Niagara power, once generated, might be carried considerable distances by the use of wire or manila cables. A transmission system of this sort had been in use at the power development on the upper Rhine at Schaffhausen since 1867 and operated mills a mile away from the falls. The hydraulic systems of Turrettini in Geneva and the compressed-air system at Bellevue on the outskirts of Paris, also came into Westinghouse's ken. He rejected them all.

He felt that alternating-current electricity was the one and only solution. A 16-mile transmission line of this type in Italy, between Rome and Tivoli, had been in successful operation since 1884, and this became the inspiration of the Westinghouse electrical venture at Niagara. Adams and his fellows bade him go ahead. And the result was that the long low granite building (just above the city) that now bears the name of Edward D. Adams, carved over its door, began (in 1895) to send out the energy of old Niagara to a far-flung countryside. Soon it was lighting the streets and houses and shops and driving the trolley-cars, not merely of Buffalo and the big towns grouped roundabout it, but of Rochester and Syracuse and Hamilton and Toronto, and the many, many places in between, while the defection of the water from the cataract was—even to the folk who for years had dwelt close to it—barely perceptible ... Still further use of the seemingly inexhaustible power was urged. Yet the men who were back of the enterprise urged caution. They laughed at the idea that they might dam the Niagara and so (at different seasons or even hours) regulate its waters against the varying needs for it.

"To dam the Niagara River and so regulate its flow through our wheels and penstocks is impossible," they said, definitely. "We must use the power as it comes to us, each hour of the twenty-four. But lighting is a seasonable thing each day; a matter of peak load and of minimum. And so, to a large degree, is the operation of trolley-cars. What we really need at Niagara for the greatest effective use of our current is industry which demands an evenly sustained volume of great power, twenty-four hours out of the twenty-four, seven days out of the week."

And this was the thing that came to pass. For while the light and power requirements of a wide territory, with Niagara as its center, have continued to receive the energy of the cataract in generous measure, the greater part of that energy now goes into a type of industry that cannot live without it; chiefly the manufacture of aluminum, of carborundum, of calcium carbide and other commercial chemicals, as well as of their alloys and by-products. It has been said that there could have been no Detroit of today, no vast automobile industry here in the United States, without the developed power of Niagara to make them possible, by bringing forth at low cost some of the greatest essentials to motor-car and motor-truck production. It also has been said that, if for any reason it ever became necessary to shut off the Niagara power for as short a period as even sixty days, every manufacturing industry in America would feel it; many of them would be compelled to shut down.

And still the cataract roars on, unsullied and unspoiled. Motor-cars come from every part of the Union and park beside it; long trains and trolley-cars pull into the stations in the twin cities on their respective sides of the river; folks put on rubber slickers and hats and go down the elevators and out to the misty Cave of the Winds, close to the Horseshoe Falls, as they have been doing for nearly three-quarters of a century past; the doughty little *Maid of the Mist* plies aimlessly about the giant pool of unknown depth at the base of the cataract. Folk by the hundreds of thousands go annually to Niagara Falls to be awed and charmed by the place and to enjoy it to the uttermost. It would be a pity if ever it were otherwise. It is one of the pet playgrounds of a nation, and it has been so for so many years that their reckoning has all but been lost.

And finally—Grand Island.

Grand Island, twelve miles long and seven wide, lies in the middle of the Niagara, not more than two miles above the falls, and just below Tonawanda. It is surrounded by great activity and population; yet, until now it has been, seemingly, as remote as the

Hebrides. A broad level space with rich soil and quiet farms, it was once a dense forest of white oaks, which, when the Erie Canal had been completed, were cut down and sent to the seaboard for the building of ships. One of the finest of the clippers was the *Niagara,* wrought of Grand Island oak. . . . The state of New York has just completed two huge bridges, which will link the island to the main shore, on the American side. It seems to be a little of a pity that they had to be built. It would have been far nicer to have left Grand Island the unspoiled place it was until but yesterday. Mr. Rockefeller might have wished to restore it as a bit of the early-day America, like his Williamsburgh, Virginia. He could have made no better use of his money. A Grand Island of the 'seventies or the 'eighties—no telephones, no electric lights, no radios, no movies, no paved roads, no automobiles—would have been an interesting thing; if for no other reason than for comparison with our headlong progress of the past half century.

It is the motor-car that has transformed Niagara Falls; to no small degree, it has helped save it. A good many folk still come by railroad or by steamboat. There is an excellent service across the head of Ontario from Toronto to Lewiston, and the high-speed electric line from Buffalo to Niagara Falls hangs on tenaciously, as does the similar line down through the gorge below the cataract. But there also are the paved roads; and three highway bridges between the Falls and Lewiston as well as the new one right at Buffalo. There is abundant parking space everywhere. This is the day of the motor-car, and the man who drives it is king. All bow to serve him. The Canadian government gives him warm greeting. Customs formalities at Niagara Falls are little more than formalities. On the Canadian side of the border, and within easy reaching distance, are many fascinating drives. . . . The old city of St. Catherines might easily have been stolen out of Surrey, so sweet and placid and English is it. I always get a thrill watching the ships bound overseas from Chicago or Duluth sail through the Welland Canal, and in realizing that this waterway has been more than a century in the making and is one of the busiest in the world. The south shore of Ontario all the way to Hamilton is filled with surprises and with charm, and Hamilton, itself, has no small portion of natural loveliness.

So sweeps the Niagara and its wonderful frontier, for forty brief miles from Lake Erie and the waterfront of the second city of the state, down to the lonely Ontario—the mightiest of all cataracts and the swiftest of all rapids. As the sentinel of the western gate of the pathway of empire, it concedes nothing whatsoever to the eastern one.

CHAPTER IX

Southern Tier

THE entire Southern Tier is a sort of Cinderella of New York State. Always she has hoped for something that seemingly she never could receive. The pathway of empire passed her by. She had dreamed it otherwise. Back in 1829 William C. Redfield, of Brooklyn, had stirred her immensely with his project for a railroad, which was to start at the west bank of the Hudson, somewhere near New York City, and to continue through the southern part of New York State, not touching Lake Erie however, and by long stages through to Council Bluffs, upon the Missouri, the eastern terminal of the projected railroad to the Pacific. Remarkable as was this proposal, it fell flat. It was many years ahead of its time. In 1829 canals were the chief vogue. Even the hilly Southern Tier gave ear to them. The Erie Canal had proved itself a glowing success. Canals were springing up everywhere. Yet, when it all was done, there was to be no canal. Nature, herself, ruled otherwise; she had flung her great hills into the Southern Tier, as if defying the puny efforts of man to conquer them with his curious artificial waterways, even with such devices as his long strings of locks or inclined cableways as against sharp ascents or descents.

And even when the men of the Southern Tier finally turned

toward the canal's noisy rival, the young railroad, it still seemed as if those selfsame hills might prove to be barriers, all too difficult to overcome. But man has a way of persevering, and in the case of a railroad, the engineering difficulties were not as grave as those of canal construction. Even so, the Erie Railroad, the Southern Tier's retort to the challenge of the canal and the railroads across the center of the Empire State, when it finally was put through, encountered terrific obstacles and took eighteen years in the building. And once or twice it had to dip into Pennsylvania to get through, even though the legislature of the state of New York specifically had forbidden that very thing. Still, charters are not impossible of changing, legislatures *sometimes* are amenable to common sense, and the point of all this is that the Erie *was* built and opened all the way through from Piermont-on-Hudson to Dunkirk on Lake Erie. That was in 1851, and a special train was run for the opening, all the way from Piermont to Dunkirk, with Daniel Webster as its guest of honor and chief figure. In order that he might the better see the country, Mr. Webster had ridden in a rocking-chair on a flat car, and in order that Mr. Webster might not rock himself off into the country, the rocking-chair had been firmly affixed to the flat car. At any rate it was a pretty auspicious sort of an opening, and folk everywhere along the Southern Tier were mighty glad that the Erie finally had been completed. It had been a pretty slow sort of business. There is a monument along the right-of-way near Deposit that marks the breaking of ground for the new railroad, away back in 1835. That is about all that was done for a considerable time. The promoters of the new road seemed to have a fearful time of it, what with unfriendly legislatures and captious and difficult bankers and the claims of many anxious and rival communities. But they persevered, and presently the New York & Erie Railroad reached all the way across Orange County, from the Hudson to the Delaware; and in so doing tapped a very rich and prosperous farming country.

But Orange County is not the Southern Tier. The Southern Tier reaches no farther east than Port Jervis, at that sharp bend of the Delaware to the south where it ceases to be the boundary between New York and Pennsylvania and for the rest of its existence becomes the border line between Pennsylvania and New Jersey. And once the young Erie finally had put its track down the steep breast of the Shawangunk mountains into Port Jervis (named after that distinguished engineer, John B. Jervis, who had located the Delaware & Hudson Canal to and through it), it found that its troubles had only begun. The Delaware & Hudson had pre-empted the New York bank of the river for many miles, and there was nothing to it but that the Erie folk must coax the New York legislature to let it cross into Pennsylvania for a considerable number of miles and then convince the Pennsylvania legislature that it was not going to be a bad piece of business to admit to the state a railroad which obviously was going to cart folk and freight right out of it and to a seaport, sharp rival to its own Philadelphia. Not an easy thing to do.

But the Erie promoters did it, and so successfully that once again, a hundred miles farther west, they dipped the new road into Pennsylvania, both to follow the course of the Susquehanna River and then, when the New York tax situation seemed to be a little appalling, to build its chief shops in the alien state. But by that time the Erie folk were nearly desperate. Those mountainous hills along the Southern Tier were infinitely worse for railroad building than they had imagined. They conquered them only by feats of engineering really superb for that day, as when they were confronted by the deep gully of Starrucca Creek (just south of the New York State line) which just had to be bridged and at a high level. James P. Kirkwood built the Starrucca Viaduct; built it of solid masonry, 110 feet high and 1200 feet long (eighteen great arches in all); and charged the Erie some $320,000 for the job, which was a lot of money for 1848 and today would be considered a low figure indeed for a bridge which has stood undaunted for nearly ninety years already, and which, designed for 20-ton locomotives, stands nobly to the pounding of 400-ton ones and 100-car, 6000-ton trains. Once when first they began to increase the size and weight of rail equipment, the engineers of the road became alarmed and cut the two tracks upon its deck down to but one; but they gained courage again, and it has carried a double-track ever since.

With the Starrucca Viaduct finished, the trains could reach the thriving town of Binghamton, at the confluence of the Susquehanna and the Chenango rivers, and this they did on Christmas eve, 1848. The eve of the great holiday was made one of especial rejoicing, with the townsfolk gathering by the uncompleted depot and with blazing pine-knots welcoming the first iron horse to poke his nose into Broome County. A few months later he was finding his way to Owego, then to Waverly, both farther down the Susquehanna, and finally to Elmira, which was not on the Susquehanna at all, but on the Chemung. Elmira was then, and for a good many years thereafter, the chief city of the Southern Tier. It was pretty much wilderness all the way through to Lake Erie. The new railroad made its own towns as it found its way to the west, and some of them, such as Hornellsville and Olean and Salamanca, became substantial and permanent towns. But after it had finally reached navigable water at Dunkirk it found that it had made the wrong port. Fortune was favoring Buffalo. To get the big business one had to go to Buffalo. So presently the Erie was building branches from its main line up to Buffalo (also to Rochester), and one of these was the railroad that crossed the upper falls of the Genesee on the enormously high wooden bridge at Portage.

All that was right for the west end of the road. But a problem worse than Dunkirk confronted it at its eastern terminus. In order to keep within the limits set by the New York legislature, it finally had decided upon a point on the west bank of the Hudson, some thirty miles from New York City. Here it built a long pier, and if you go to Piermont today you still will see that long pier—it serves as a very convenient landing-place for the Irvington ferry. Between that pier and downtown New York the Erie ran two steamboats a day, in connection with its trains. In pleasant weather this was a rather agreeable service for travelers, but at other times it was not so good. So eventually it was compelled to change this plan, too. It secured rights over a new railroad running from Suffern through Paterson to Jersey City; and eventually this became the Erie's main line, and the Piermont one was all but abandoned.

Poor old Erie, it was always changing things. And then, just as it had them all nicely settled, along came the slick young peddler from Vermont, Jim Fisk, and that canny young man from the East Branch of the Delaware, Jay Gould, and old Daniel Drew, of Carmel, and what they did to Erie hardly could be told within the pages of this book. It was the biggest business scandal of all time here in America. But Erie always bobs up serenely. And after it had gotten itself out of the clutches of Fisk and Gould and Drew, oil was being found over at the west end of the Southern Tier. Wellsville and Olean and Salamanca were mad with prosperity, and so were their neighbors just across the Pennsylvania line. It seemed as if the Erie could not get enough engines and tank cars to handle the traffic. Fortunately it had changed its track gauge from an absurd six feet to the standard gauge of its fellow roads so it was able to handle most of the traffic that was offered it, and it was a lot. Then, just as it was nicely settled down to the new prosperity, the oil people found that they could send the larger portion of their product to the seaboard much more cheaply by pipe line, and there was grief for the Erie once again. And then the Lackawanna and the Lehigh Valley built their parallel competing lines to Buffalo.

Erie never gave up. It underwent receiverships and reorganizations, until you almost lost count, but it hung gamely on. And today the old Erie is a spicker and spanner railroad and doing a larger business than some of its more showy competitors. Its stations and its bridges all are neatly painted, and its locomotives are, most of them, bright and shiny. It narrowly escapes being a model railroad.

As it rose and fell, the fortunes of the Southern Tier towns along its main stem rose and fell. Take Elmira for instance. Its fortunes almost always were to be measured by those of the Erie—once the road had been completed through to it in the late autumn of 1849.

Elmira has had a curiously interesting career. Although in recent years a little outrun in population by Binghamton, she has held to the title of the Queen of the Southern Tier with pertinacity. If the Tier is to be regarded as Cinderella, she is perhaps the Cinderella of Cinderellas. Yet she is as interesting, as she is old-fashioned. So many interesting things have happened to her, and so many interesting people have come to her. She is redolent with memories; and most of them are fascinating memories.

She began, as so many other towns have begun, by playing the rôle of *entrepôt,* at a point where water transport ended and inland transport began. The momentous tour of General John Sullivan across the Southern Tier and into the Genesee Country had just ended. If you remember your Revolutionary history you will recall that Tories, Canadian Rangers, Indians—renegade enemies of every sort—had used the bend of the Tioga River (now the Chemung) as a rendezvous for raids against the Continental Army. It was there (close to the site of the present Elmira) that the evil expedition that led to the brutal Wyoming Valley massacre was prepared. Finally Washington had determined to clean out that whole gang in Southern New York. He sent General John Sullivan to do the job; Sullivan was assisted by General James Clinton (brother of the George Clinton, who was the first State Governor of New York, and father of the redoubtable DeWitt Clinton). They came up into the wilderness country, fought a nasty but victorious battle at Newtown on the Tioga and then marched, undisputed but triumphant, through to Seneca Lake and the Genesee Country. After that there was nothing but peace and quiet in the heart of the Southern Tier, and before the Revolution really was over, immigration was in full sway into it.

The old Pennsylvania city of Wilkes-Barre, on the Susquehanna, was godmother to Elmira. Men and goods moved slowly but with comparative ease up the river, from the old town to the new. They poled their barges against the current, up the Susquehanna to Athens, close to the state line, and then up the Chemung to the new settlement, which, for lack of a better name, first was called Newtown. It was not until 1829 that Elmira was chosen as a designation for the place. Colonel Nathan Teall, one of its earliest settlers, had a lovely daughter named Elmira; moreover you could translate the word into the Spanish *El Mira,* meaning "fair outlook," and the new town of Elmira had more than a fair outlook with its broad river and broader valley and the high hills encompassing both. As the town prospered and swiftly shot ahead of all its rivals in the Southern Tier, the new name sat very prettily indeed upon its rounded green shoulders.

For a considerable time Elmira continued to pay both homage and tribute to its godmother, situated more than a hundred miles down the valley of the Susquehanna. Gradually, however, it began to loosen these ties. Highroads were built to it across its native state of New York, and its allegiance to Pennsylvania lessened. But highroads and freighting-wagons and stage-coaches were not enough; Elmira, in her new prosperity heard of canals and of railroads and hankered for them.

The canal came first; or rather, John Arnot came first. John Arnot was a hard-headed, hard-fisted, honest Scot, like so many others that came to this land more than a century ago and laid the solid foundations of commercial success. Mercantile adventuring had sent him into the new and swiftly developing Chemung Valley, as early as 1819. Eight or ten merchants were already in its chief town; but in ten years John Arnot was the chief merchant and business man of Elmira, making more money than all of them combined. He worked against tremendous odds. Twice a year his goods came through from the city of New York; by boat up the Hudson River and through the Erie Canal and Seneca Lake, and then by wagons for the twenty-two remaining miles from Watkins (at the head of Seneca) down to Elmira. The nearest bank was in Ithaca, more than thirty miles away. But John Arnot merely set his Scotch jaws the more closely together and decided to remedy the transport and the banking obstacles.

He did both. Before he was done, Elmira had its own canal, the Chemung, and its own banking institution, the Chemung Canal

Bank. The Canal prospered very well, thank you, as a water carrier across the portage between the Chemung River and Seneca Lake (it also had a well-patronized branch from Horseheads across to Corning, fifteen miles), and the Chemung Canal Bank slowly became, and for many years remained, the richest and most powerful bank in all upstate New York. The Chemung Canal has long since finished its work (forty-five years of it), but the Chemung Canal Bank (under a slightly altered name) continues—after 103 years of active service.

The Chemung Canal Bank is the Arnot family; it always has been. The original John Arnot long since departed this earth; before he went, however, he had identified himself with nearly every large enterprise in Elmira and in the Southern Tier, one might say, not only in merchandising or transportation (in 1829 alone, he ran nineteen great arks, each loaded with 1800 bushels of wheat down the river to Wilkes-Barre) or banking or railroading (he was the contractor who built the central section of the Erie), but in almost numberless other things, as well. There was hardly a successful thing in Elmira, in which the hand of John Arnot was not to be found.

His sons continued his activities. By a curious series of fatalities, two of the three lost their lives at a comparatively young age; the youngest son, Matthias, and the daughter, who married William B. Ogden, first mayor of Chicago and the great moving spirit of the building of the Chicago & North Western Railway, continued to live to good ages. It is only a quarter of a century ago that Matthias Arnot died. He lived in the fine old house in Lake Street, surrounded by his possessions, the chief of which was the superb collection of paintings that Lord Hamilton had collected so many years ago. And when he died, the old house and the old paintings went to the town, and Elmira found herself in the possession of such an art gallery as few large cities might even hope to possess. And a splendid modern hospital, founded by his largess, and that of his sister, was added to the town's assets. Elmira seems to have been Cinderella, in the largest sense of the word.

But, like the storied Cinderella, she has had her adversities, and they have not been small ones.

The Erie Railroad, after much difficulty in building its line over the flats of the Susquehanna (at one time they tried putting the tracks on tall wooden stilts, which for years afterwards remained, unused, across the swamps), finally got into the town late in December 1849. By that time Elmira already had a railroad of her own—the Chemung, extending up to Watkins at the head of Seneca Lake, and ready to operate twelve months of the year, as against the brief seven of the canal. The Erie took the Chemung road as its own, and its through trains from New York (Piermont) presently were operating right through to Watkins. The following spring they began connecting there with the swift steamer *Ben Loder* (named after an early president of the Erie Railroad), which ran down Seneca Lake to Geneva, where there were connections with the trains all the way across Central New York. Never was there a finer and a swifter lake steamboat than the *Ben Loder,* and she continued in service for a considerable time. But the Erie finished its road through to Dunkirk on Lake Erie, and that was bigger game; and the Chemung Railroad (afterwards called the Jefferson Railroad) was relegated to the business of being a branch line, until a few years later when the Northern Central (up from Baltimore, and now a part of the Pennsylvania) took it over, extended it to Canandaigua, and so made a through route of it, on to Rochester and to Niagara Falls.

Those were busy years for young Elmira; the pumpkin coach and the cream-white horses all revolved pretty rapidly. There were tragedies as well as triumphs. The town's famed Eagle Hotel burned just as the Erie was completed through to it, and the many passengers who arrived on the train each night were hard put to it, before continuing west by stage, until the new Rathbun House was built, a year or two later; and it has been doing business ever since. It was at about that time that Miss Clarissa Thurston was beginning her female seminary in the village, conducting it with such success that presently she was enthused with the idea of starting a college for women, which should award the same degrees as the men's colleges. This idea, somewhat radical for the middle of the past century, Clarissa Thurston succeeded in putting into effect; with the result that the first woman's college in the world, the Elmira College for Women, opened its doors in 1855 and has kept them open ever since, with an increasing degree of success. Its quaint main building, with its high octagonal tower rising above thick foliage, long has been a landmark of the town.

A mile or so farther out College Avenue and nestled against the side of a hill is another Elmira landmark of a far different sort. This is the equally famed Elmira Reformatory, also a needed force in the land. A few years ago this venerable institution came to a questionable sort of fame, through the somewhat scandalous performances of its superintendent. Since then, however, it has been reformed and modernized and brought to a high degree of usefulness. It exerts a peculiar sort of fascination for a good many tourists, who are received cordially and shown the workings of the institution.

Of great interest to many tourists is Quarry Farm, situated at the top of a high ridge, just to the east of the brisk small city. (This ridge, incidentally, has been used of late for the remarkable feats of the gliders, those super-airmen who persist in riding in planes without any sort of motive power. Elmira seems to be an ideal location both in topography and climate for this sort of flying.) In case your memory needs refreshing, Quarry Farm is the place where Mark Twain went, summer after summer, to rest mind and soul and there to do some of his best and most vigorous writing. Eighteen years in succession (beginning in 1871) he went there; and even after that he returned to it, time and time again. He had married in town, and loved everything about it. And when, in the early 'seventies, his sister-in-law, Susan Langhorne Crane, built as a surprise for him, a studio on a peak seven hundred feet above the town and overlooking both it and its superb valley, Mark Twain's cup of happiness was filled almost to overflowing. Of this small structure, he was to write:

... It is the loveliest studio you ever saw. It is octagonal, with a peaked roof, each face filled with a spacious window and it sits perched in complete isolation on the very top of an elevation that commands leagues of valley and city and retreating ranges of distant blue hills. It is a cosy nest and just room for a sofa, table and three or four chairs and when the storms sweep down the remote valley and the lightning flashes behind the hills beyond and the rain beats upon the roof over my head, imagine the luxury of it. ...

The present occupants, Mr. and Mrs. Jervis Langdon (that same nephew, Jervis Langdon, to whom Mark Twain so confidently bestowed his body in his latter years), maintain Quarry Farm in a loving and complete impeccability. They care for the drinking-fountains, one named after each of his children, on the long, steep road up to the farm. The small studio is kept as a shrine to the immortal humorist; locked, and exhibited only to such folk who show themselves quite capable of full appreciation of it. They are privileged, indeed. In its single small room, not ten feet across is it, are his table and chairs (the sofa went years ago) painted in red, which was always his favorite color, a few pictures of the man at his work, and that is all. The place charms by its simplicity.

Mark Twain is buried in Woodlawn Cemetery on the far side of the town. And again his simplicity shows itself. There is nothing to distinguish his headstone from its fellows in the Langdon burial plot, save its lettering and a tiny American flag upon the grave.

Not far away is a section of the cemetery reserved for a burial plot which always must have been of greatest interest to him. Long neglected, it is now a national shrine, exquisitely kept, and back of it all lies a story:

Elmira, in the spring of 1864, achieved the not altogether pleasant distinction of being chosen as the location of a Federal prison camp. For this purpose the town had many advantages. Not only was it a very healthy place and far removed from the theater of war, but it also was an important railroad center; four-square was it in this regard with lines reaching south and east to Washington, Philadelphia and New York, and northland west to Rochester, Buffalo and Niagara Falls. So it was chosen, quite logically. A large plot of land on the river bank was secured, and a stout wooden high fence built around the land sides of it. Batteries of guns commanded it, against any wholesale attempt at a delivery.

Into this pen 11,916 men came in 1864 alone. Some of the prisoners never even reached Elmira. They died of their wounds or disease en route; and upon one occasion an Erie train ran off the track and into the Delaware near Shohola, and sixty-four prisoners and sixteen of their guards were killed. They were buried near-by, then the bodies brought to Elmira for final interment. It was one of the worst railroad wrecks on record.

Nor did death overlook the camp itself. There is no evidence of sickness or death due to neglect or to bad food. Elmira was not to become a second Andersonville. Yet her record is not entirely clean. She made something of a circus of the entire affair. Peanut and soft-drink stands sprang up around the outside of the enclosure; and one citizen, more enterprising than the rest, erected a tower close to one of its corners, and for a small fee one might ascend to the top and through spy-glasses watch human misery at its worst.

For there was a great deal of misery that summer and fall of '64 and in the early spring of '65 there beside the Chemung. Death stalked the place. The river rose suddenly in the middle of the night, and men were drowned seeking to escape. A small-pox epidemic broke out and claimed between three hundred and four hundred lives. In all 2988 prisoners, most of them North Carolina boys, died in the Elmira prison camp. They were taken out to the town's then-new cemetery, and there were buried somewhat indiscriminately. An escaped slave, John W. Jones, who had become a parson and sexton of the cemetery, made it his business to make a careful record of the name and company of each man as he was buried. Many years afterwards, when the men had lain in their unmarked graves for decades in the corner of Woodlawn Cemetery, a tardy Federal government made an American Belleau Wood of it, erecting neat stones at each grave, and it was the negro sexton's carefully compiled records that made this possible. Today it is immaculately kept, its row upon row of small white headstones telling of a gruesome and unhappy chapter in Elmira's fanciful history.

For years she reigned quite supreme, as Queen of the Valley and of the Southern Tier. Cinderella came into her own. She was the largest city in the Southern Tier and passing proud of that. Her bar was filled with men of unusual distinction, such as David Bennett Hill and J. Sloat Fassett and John B. Stanchfield. There were few more famous preachers in the land—more progressive, more forward-looking—than Thomas K. Beecher (brother of the illustrious Henry Ward and of Harriet Beecher Stowe). For education there was the College for Women, and for literature, Mark Twain up at Quarry Farm. What town might ask for a more brilliant galaxy than this? She was proud, too, of her industrial position. The development of large coal and iron mines just across the Pennsylvania line to the immediate south had been of large benefit to her. She was an iron-mongering town. She had made many bridges, forged the long and snakelike structure of the Sixth Avenue Elevated in the city of New York, just as in later years she was to produce the steel-work for the adjoining Radio City. She made carriages, and when the motor-car era came, she manufactured (for a long time) automobiles in great quantities.

Cinderella indeed!

Yes the day was to come when she was to reassume something of the Cinderella rôle. Her larger industries, many of them, ceased to prosper; some of them closed. A tremendous shoe manufactory sprang up in her neighboring and rival city of Binghamton, and Binghamton swept ahead of Elmira in population, to Elmira's great discomfiture. She lost heart a bit, and settled, quite naturally and easily, into an old lady's rôle—a mature sort of Cinderella she was. Today she is beginning to emerge from that staid rôle. But she still is a comfortable, old-fashioned town. More ambitious towns of the Southern Tier, such as Binghamton and Olean and even near-by Ithaca, have banished trolley-cars in toto from their streets, in favor of motor-cars and somewhat stodgy-looking little buses, but Elmira clings to her trolleys, even though these no longer venture all the way up to Watkins Glen and Seneca Lake as they once did. She looks at the world serenely and bids it go its way. She'll go hers. No mistaking that.

A fine, hard road now makes its way from Elmira up to Watkins; and an occasional through train as well reaches that interesting place. There is no telling just how long people have been going to Watkins Glen. Certain it is that the Indians loved it; it was one of their earliest places of sojourn. While as an early resort for their successors, it ranked with Saratoga and Niagara and Trenton Falls. The deep and narrow glen, with its slender stream, dropping in two miles more than seven hundred feet in almost innumerable waterfalls, long since has been a favorite with the upstaters and with those from many other states. A quarter of a century ago it became one of the earliest of the splendid system of state parks, which keep showing themselves within these pages. A good deal of money has been expended in making the place more accessible to visitors; there now is an elaborate system of pathways and stairs and shelters, almost too elaborate in fact. The best way to see the Glen, if you do not have a car with you, is to take a taxi from the main street of the village up to the top of the ravine, dismiss it there and walk slowly down. If you try it the other way, you are apt to regret it; that is, unless you are a pretty well-trained athlete. It is rigorous climbing.

Of recent years Watkins has undergone a transformation; and it now has become a health resort—the American Nauheim, its promoters like to call it. This transformation came about, almost by accident.

Health resorts were extremely popular in the America of fifty or sixty or even more years ago. There was, of course, no motor-car, and Americans had not developed their present-day restlessness. They were content to go to some good place and there to stay, reasonably put, for weeks or even months. In addition to the better-known spas across New York State, Saratoga and Lebanon and Sharon and Richfield and Avon, there were lesser ones, developed primarily as health places rather than ones of showy and idle resort. The lack of open or athletic life in the America of that day, as well as somewhat consistent overeating and drinking, rendered these sanitariums necessary. There were at least three pretty well-famed ones in upstate New York; at Dansville, close to the valley of the Genesee; at Clifton Springs, near Geneva; and at Glen Haven, at the upper end of Skaneateles Lake. The Glen Haven resort disappeared years ago, when Syracuse appropriated the entire lake for its water supply; but Dansville and Clifton Springs have continued on bravely against varying fortunes. The latter has become very prosperous of late years, and it boasts a record of eighty-five years of continuous activity.

In the days of the top prosperity of Glen Haven, two young men of the near-by village of Aurora, Dr. E. D. Leffingwell and his brother, William M. Leffingwell, had become associated with it. After it was demolished, W. M. Leffingwell went over to Dansville and for some years was connected with the famed Jackson Sanitarium. But he was not content there; and one day, chance gave him the opportunity that he desired.

Fifty years ago when the oil and gas craze swept madly all the way across the Southern Tier, one or two promoters had tried sinking a well, in a deep pine grove, close by the Watkins Glen. They were not successful. Instead of the magic oily fluid there came a briny water. "No good," said the promoters, and went to more promising fields. Some one, however, picked up a sample of the water and sent it up to that brilliant chemist, Samuel A. Lattimore, at the University of Rochester. Dr. Lattimore analyzed it and said of it:

"This brine differs from all I have ever analyzed and also I think from nearly all whose analyses have been reported, in the very large percentage of calcium chloride."

This analysis caught the eyes of the Leffingwells. Here was a saline water almost precisely like, if not superior, to those of the famed Bad Nauheim in Germany. They moved promptly. Fortunately there stood in that same pine grove, not a hundred feet from the unsuccessful oil well, a stoutly constructed brick building, which had been operated for some years (with varying success) as a summer hotel and then had closed. This building, the well and several hundreds of acres were bought by the Leffingwells—and the Glen Springs Hotel and Sanitarium, situated high upon a hillside and commanding a remarkable prospect of Seneca Lake and the great hills which hem it in, began its remarkably successful career. To it, in a little less than half a century, have come most of the great and the near-great of America. Its waters and its cure are efficacious in many human ills, particularly cardiac ailments. But even folk not ailing in body or mind like to come to the place. It is, perhaps, the nearest approach to one of the German cures that we have as yet attained in this country, although Saratoga is rapidly progressing. And there are so many short side trips out from Watkins Glen—to sweet old Elmira, to Ithaca, to Geneva, to Keuka Lake, to Corning and the glass works there.

Which brings us, rather quickly and definitely, to Corning and its glass works.

For a good many years, Corning, seventeen miles to the west of Elmira, was content to be a sort of poor relation to her; Cinderella to a Cinderella, as it were. She was the terminus of a busy end of the Y-shaped Chemung Canal, for forty-five years feeding it coal from her own railroad (the prosperous Fall Brook) which ran down into the Pennsylvania coal fields; a town of some three thousand folk, not looking for a much larger place in the world.

At that time there was a skilful family over in Massachusetts, by name Houghton, who had engaged themselves, with a moderate degree of success, in the manufacture of glass. The Houghtons sought a new location and found it in Corning, with cheap coal and good sand at hand. But they were not successful there in the manufacture of ordinary commercial glass. Pittsburgh was too hard a competitor. And the local coal was not quite suited to their needs. They all but gave up the ship. Then a new idea came to them. Why not specialize in glass products? The answer is the immensely successful Corning Glass Works of today, still in the hands of the Houghton family, and now employing pretty nearly as many folk as lived in all Corning in the year of its foundation, 1868.

This well-developed enterprise came to international attention a year or so ago, when it succeeded in pouring a gigantic mirror-disc (one piece of glass, two hundred inches in diameter and weighing twenty tons) for a new observatory out in California. It was a colossal task to undertake, something quite without precedent, and the wonder was that the plant was even able to undertake the thing, let alone make a success of it.

That success, however, was built upon years of preparation. Since well before the War, the company had been assembling at Corning a highly skilled technical staff, similar in style and scope to that of General Electric at Schenectady, and this made the spectacular effort a great success. Corning's work, incidentally, had tied in, quite closely, with that of the electric company. For, long before, Thomas A. Edison had come to Charles Houghton of Corning and had told him just what sort of glass bulb he would need for his forthcoming incandescent lamp. That was in 1878. Edison had asked Houghton if he could possibly make the glass bubble for the new light. And Houghton had replied that he would try. The first attempts were ridiculous, the bulb being entirely too heavy. Edison shook his head sadly. It would never, never do. With the patience that was so characteristic of him he sat down and made a little sketch of the precise bulb that he needed. And practical Joe Baxter of the Corning works took that sketch and from it blew the bubble; blew it, as Edison wished it. It was the beginning of tens of millions of others; and now an offshoot plant of the main concern just over the state line, at Wellsboro, gives its entire attention to that one task.

The fact that the coal so near to Corning finally was proved to be quite unfit for the manufacture of fine glass was overcome by fate. Hardly had it failed the test, before natural gas in great abundance was discovered in the immediate neighborhood, and it has been this abundant fuel that has been one of the greatest factors in the upbuilding of the entire enterprise. It now has dozens of chimneys, hundreds of forges, and a mass of intricate special machinery for a vastly varied output; which runs from ruby and green lenses for traffic lights and railroads to fine etched table glass; to say nothing of two hundred-inch reflectors, which take but a few hours to pour and many months completely to cool. It is one of the most unusual enterprises of a state that is filled with unusual enterprises.

In the long, pleasant summertime, these bustling, busy cities of Elmira and Corning find their recreation close at hand, either up at Watkins and other points on Seneca Lake, or else over at Keuka Lake, which runs parallel to Seneca and empties its waters into it. Just why they used to call Keuka, Crooked Lake, is a little hard to discover. For really it is not the least bit crooked, simply Y-shaped, with a great tongue of high land, four or five miles long and coming to be over two in width, stretching between two lovely bays, or "branches," as the natives prefer to designate them. The quiet old county-seat town of Penn Yan is at the head of one of the branches. Its unusual name is a concoction of Pennsylvania and Yankee (original founders of the town).

A state road (and then a county one) leads from Penn Yan along the cottaged edge of the lake, and finally comes to the tip of the tongue, which rises some eight hundred feet above the waters of Keuka (which are, in turn, 720 feet above the level of the sea). A fine old stone house (built much more than a century ago) stands at the top of the hill, and at the foot there is a fine modern one, the home of one of the prominent wine-growers of the region. A few years ago the young son of this house died, and his memory now is kept green by a really exquisite Gothic stone chapel, halfway up the steep mountainside. This is the famed Little Chapel on the Mount, and to it each year come, in increasing numbers, thousands of pilgrims from every corner of the Union. Throughout the night its electric beacon glimmers steadily and may be seen for many miles up and down the lake. So does the memory of one boy live.

There is an enterprising school (Keuka College) partly down the point, and there are all sorts of birthplaces, almost within walking distance of Penn Yan: Robert G. Ingersoll's (whose own memory is kept alive by making his house in the neighboring village of Dresden into a museum); that of Marcus Whitman, a somewhat different sort of man, missionary and explorer to the Pacific Northwest; of Red Jacket, most intelligent and belligerent of Iroquois chieftains; and of Jemima Wilkinson, a curious religionist, who started an early and worldly "New Jerusalem" on the shores of near-by Keuka Lake. There are a lot of other lakes in the neighborhood, the very names of which you probably have not heard before, such as Wayne and Lamunka, just to take two sizable and beautiful instances.

But Penn Yan's chief interest to most folk is that it shares prominence with Hammondsport (at the far end of Keuka) as the center of the wine-making industry of the East, a long-established business, which after several heart-rending years, finally has begun to come into its own once again.

The soil, drainage and climate of the steep slopes of Lake Keuka seem to render them ideal for the culture of wine grapes. That fact was not discovered yesterday. It is on the same line of latitude as the French Rheims, and that is why the American Rheims (two miles south of Hammondsport) seems to be the only place in North America where wine of the champagne type can be successfully produced; and annually is again produced in large volume.

A clergyman, the Reverend William Bostwick, founder of St. James Episcopal Church in the tiny village of Hammondsport, seems to have been responsible for the development of the now widespread wine industry of the Finger Lakes country; he sensed its fitness for viticulture. As long ago as 1829 he sent over to the Hudson Valley and obtained slips of the vines of the Isabella and Catawba grapes, and these he planted in the grounds of the rectory at Hammondsport. They thrived and they grew in the saintly soil, and pretty soon the parish of St. James had as nice and as flourishing a vineyard as any of its compeers across the Atlantic. It is the parent of all the other Keuka vineyards—with some twenty thousand acres of trellised grape under cultivation, before the blow of Volstead, when the production dropped to less than twelve thousand acres. Now it is on the upgrade once again. But the industry had a hard time of it for fourteen dark years.

Once, in one of them, I drove into Hammondsport, from its larger neighbor, the Bath that is county-seat of Steuben. The highroad (and the all but abandoned branch railroad, that once ran its six well-filled passenger trains each day) led through a terrain between hills, aptly designated as Pleasant Valley. As we neared Keuka and Hammondsport, the grapes grew the more thickly together, the stout stone wineries set into the hillside multiplied. It all gave one a mighty thirsty feeling. That much I confessed to the hotel-keeper of Hammondsport.

"Too bad," I murmured. "Prohibition and all those empty warehouses."

"Who told you they were empty?" said he.

"So I surmised," said I.

"You've surmised wrong," said he. "They're filled, chock-a-block."

"For what?"

"For export," said the doughty keeper of the tavern with a smile, and added: "For export—and Hammondsport."

And I was right in Hammondsport!

Champagne-making (to be correct, one should say the making of wine of champagne type) did not begin until about eighty years ago. At that time, one Charles Davenport Champlin started his Pleasant Valley Wine Company, and the post-office at Rheims, New York, came into existence. Both of the last have continued in existence, and the clan Champlin has continued at the helm. That's the way we do business in upstate New York.

Charles Davenport Champlin, the founder (there's a present one, of the same name, conducting the business) knew little or nothing about the difficult business of making a sparkling wine. So he did the next best thing: He imported a skilled Frenchman, one Jules Masson from Burgundy, who had learned the precious secrets of blending and fermenting in the bottle from the masters of his native land; and ever since then there has been a Masson, as well as a Champlin, at Hammondsport. Plenty of other wineries have sprung up roundabout; even so far off as Penn Yan and at Naples (at the head of Canandaigua Lake), but it is at Hammondsport, or rather Rheims, that the business of making the sparkling wine has centered. The great caves go into the rocky hillsides for hundreds and hundreds of feet. They are filled with long racks in which rest the bottles in the four-year period of fermentation. Weekly every one of the five hundred thousand bottles is turned—it takes more than three hundred separate operations to produce a bottle of champagne—and finally they are "shot" with a dash of brandy, permanently corked, labeled and sent off to market. Almost every detail of the process is done by hand; the machinery of the winery is quaint and French and old-fashioned. Yet the wines that it has produced have more than once gone to Paris and there received high acclaims; also gold medals and highest awards, at one exposition after another. Reverend Mr. Bostwick, planting his slips in the rectory grounds of old St. James more than a century ago, wrought more than he possibly might have reckoned. The industry to which he gave birth now represents a capital investment of upwards of fifty million dollars and employs thousands of men and women, almost the whole year round.

It is but a short ten miles after all from Hammondsport to Bath and, to a real antiquarian, Bath, the county-seat of Steuben, ought to be worth at least a passing visit. Not only is it one of the very oldest towns in Western and Southern New York (having first been settled in 1792), but it remains a most interesting and pleasant village; a bit redolent of its crinoline past, but sufficiently up-to-date to suit, at least its residents, and to tempt the passing traveler.

That same Captain Williamson, whom we saw up in Geneva,

and who was the agent of a wealthy resident of the English Bath, Sir William Pulteney, is largely responsible, for the neat appearance of the American Bath of today—its orderly plan, its broad, radiating streets; all the rest of it. Williamson saw to it that the new town had schools, churches, saw-mills, a grist-mill, newspaper offices, even a theater. For a short time the place was not self-supporting; its food had to be shipped up the Susquehanna to it, from the fat fields of Pennsylvania. But Williamson soon had it standing firmly upon its feet; gristing its own wheat, doing its own spinning and knitting. In every way it became a self-sustaining community. The energetic Captain Maude, who came to it in 1800, wrote of it in this way:

. . . Steuben County contains at present about three hundred families. On the first settlement of the country these mountainous districts were thought so unfavorably of, when compared with the rich flats of Ontario County (or the Genesee country), that none of the settlers could be prevailed upon to establish themselves here till Captain Williamson himself set the example, saying "As Nature has done so much for the northern plains, I will do something for these southern mountains," though the truth of the case was that Captain Williamson saw very clearly on his first visit to the country that the Susquehanna and not the Mohawk would be its best friend. . . .

The original hope for the town was that it some day would develop into a considerable city; the amplitude of its planning shows that. This it failed to become. For many years marooned on a small branch of the Erie (it was not until a half-century ago that the Lackawanna finally came through it with its main line), it lacked transport to make it an industrial center, while the hillside country surrounding it (as the Englishman aptly put it) is not, by nature, highly productive. The real wonder is that the town has come through as well as it has. It is no small compliment to the energy and to the loyalty of its inhabitants.

If you follow the Southern Tier for its entire length—that is from Port Jervis to Jamestown—you will find yourself in for a trip of rare and constantly changing interest; as well as one of most unusual beauty. A good way to see it, if you have not a car available, is to take one of the excellent day trains of the rejuvenated Erie Railroad (incidentally, the Lackawanna also threads it, from a point just east of Binghamton to Elmira and up the Cohocton Valley toward Dansville). The train slips down the long thirteen-mile grade off the Shawangunk Mountains into Port Jervis and presently begins the ascent of the Delaware Valley, as old-fashioned, unspoiled and changeless a country as we have in the entire East. The Erie Limited slips in and out of New York and of Pennsylvania with equal facility; at Deposit it says good-by to the Delaware, climbs over a respectable mountain range and drops down into the equally lovely valley of the Susquehanna, which it follows in turn for the better part of a hundred miles. It crosses over the great Starrucca Viaduct, halts at Binghamton, at Owego (pleasant riverside town where still stands Glen Mary, once the residence of the writer, N. P. Willis, but now given over to a private sanitarium), at Waverly (which is so close to Pennsylvania that the state line runs through the center of an ice-cream parlor in the village), at Elmira, at Corning.

The valley of the Susquehanna now is left far behind, and the train is forever crossing high chains of hills. It hesitates, invariably for a considerable time, at the busy junction town of Hornell and then resumes its way, across the mountainous ranges of southwestern New York. At Wellsboro (a famous and a busy place in oil boom days) it crosses the Genesee, follows it for a few miles, and somewhere east of Olean (also an oil boom town) it enters the valley of the Alleghany. Salamanca, another busy junction town, is also the gateway for the great Alleghany State Park (of sixty-five thousand acres) which the Erie runs beside for a number of miles. Jamestown is the final principal stop for the train (within the limits of the Empire State).

Jamestown is a busy and a pretty place, chiefly devoted to the manufacturing of furniture. It is close by Chautauqua Lake, and no one who has devoted any time or thought to the progress of the sacred cause of education in America has to be told what Chautauqua is. It is a remarkable sort of a place, and it has played no small part in American education and amusement. I went to it years ago. I recall that I had to buy an admission ticket (it all was surrounded by a high and unscalable fence) for fifty cents, and numerous signs gave me solemn warning that if I lost my ticket I would be assessed for a full season's entrance fee of ten dollars. I never have hung on to a piece of pasteboard so tightly as that, or with such an uncomfortable feeling.

Chautauqua really is a very interesting sort of educational experiment. I went back there the other day and found it vastly improved. They had torn down the ugly old fence, and warm welcome awaited any stranger. You could drive in and through the narrow streets of the community for a small two-bits and were privileged to remain an hour, and I do not think that the young men at the gate would have been very fussy about the precise moment of one's leaving.

For sixty years Americans honestly desirous of bettering their intelligence and understanding of things have been finding their way to Chautauqua pretty religiously. The best teaching brains of the land are at their service; curricula and courses of study are carefully planned and organized and carried through. There is plenty of fine music, both in teaching and in rendition, and lectures of every sort as well. There is no Commencement, but a Recognition Day that serves much the same purpose.

The place is pretty Methodist but not entirely so. Once card-playing and dancing were frowned upon, and now they are not encouraged. But even in that early day roller-skating was permitted. Nowadays you can buy cigarettes, but no liquors, in the stores of the big community, and the young girls from Buffalo and Cleveland and Pittsburgh, to whom Chautauqua is a cool and welcome haven, always, look as natty in their smart bathing suits, as those along the Long Island or the Jersey coasts. Chautauqua has broadened. Or, shall we say, grown more mellow? Drama in the old days never, never would have been permitted; now there come the

Coburns or Little Theater groups from Buffalo or Cleveland and the fine opera company from Rochester. There is something always a bit pathetic in the place—a sort of hungriness for knowledge lined in the faces of older folk who were denied it in their youth, as if they feared now that there would not be time; a haste to end the days well educated. That's Chautauqua. No, that's more than Chautauqua—that's America.

If you do have a motor-car available and are ready for a quest, you still will find the run through the Southern Tier of intense interest. As yet the paved road does not follow the Delaware nearly as closely as the railroad, although this is to be remedied; apparently the poor old railroad is to be left no terrain of its very own. But from Hancock on, the through motor highway (Route 17), which has climbed over some pretty stiff hills all the way from the Hudson, finally comes to the valley and follows the West Branch closely for twenty miles, on to Deposit. Then it takes to the hills again, crosses the Susquehanna at sleepy, old, tree-filled Windsor, bends over another great hill and rejoins the river near Binghamton.

There is hardly a mile of this run that is not filled with great beauty; and with white farmhouses, with two-story Colonial pillars; there must be, literally, thousands of these houses in Central and Southern New York. It will be hard to resist turning north to Ithaca at Owego, and north to Watkins at Elmira, but Route 17 persists in sticking rather closely to the state line. It climbs hills and drops down over them, and once, when you least expect it, somewhere east of Wellsville, you will find yourself confronted by a large sign, which informs you that you are at the highest point (2306 feet above sea level) on the state's astounding highway system. (This of course does not include the ascent up Whiteface Mountain in the Adirondacks, which is a toll road and so not a part of the free highway system.) It all has been done so easily, that you are not conscious of having come to so high a point in the great Allegheny chain.

At Wellsville you will have the choice of two routes on to Olean;

the one very close to the state line through the still-busy oil town of Bolivar, where the little pumps are everlastingly at it bringing up the thick black fluid from the bowels of the earth; or the other, more northerly, through the quiet old town of Cuba, where New York State oil first was discovered. In fact there are alternate routes all through this portion of the Southern Tier. I rather like the one through Hornell and Belmont and Cuba. You find at the bottom of one very steep hill a little town whose ancient houses are all skittishly hatted with red tile roofs, and this should tell you that you are coming into Alfred, where they make tiles and where there is a state college of ceramics. Still, if you take the southernmost road, you will miss Portville and it would be a shame to miss Portville. Some day I want to go back there and lunch again in one of its several good eating-places.

All this while and hardly more than a passing reference to largest and perhaps the handsomest of Southern Tier towns—Binghamton. Purposely have I saved one of the best for the last. Binghamton likes to call herself the Parlor City, and smack her lips over the phrase. It is not inept. Situated as she is at the confluence of the Susquehanna and the tributary Chenango rivers, she has made good use of her unusual location and her several miles of waterfront. She has beautified most of it. She is a modern town, the county-seat of the rich county of Broome. Motor highways radiate out from her in every direction (including the famed Lackawanna Trail, over an abandoned roadbed of that railroad, south to Scranton), and she is a railroad center quite equal in importance to Elmira.

She came to her industrial distinction within recent years, however. The failure of a shoe factory, run upon old lines, in one of her suburban villages, gave a brilliant American opportunity to show his sheer genius as an industrialist. His name is George F. Johnson. He still is very much alive, and he it is who has now made Binghamton and its immediately surrounding communities of Johnson City and Endicott, the chief shoe-producing center of the universe. The shoe consumption of the United States is some three hundred million pairs annually, which seems like a pretty big figure, until you bring into consideration the fact that this is a pretty big country, and it actually means a little less than three pairs a year to the average American.

Of all these shoes, Binghamton and its immediately surrounding communities turn out one hundred seventy-five thousand pairs each working day, or something more than one-sixth of the national output. Yet it is not the fact that a pair of shoes is turned out in each of these three allied towns every few seconds that renders their huge factories of greatest interest to the average man. It is the vastly human quality back of the entire enterprise. Today "George F.," as Johnson is known from one end of Broome County to the other, is head of a forty-million-dollar corporation, with twenty-nine factories; but when he came to Binghamton, in 1884, he was a twenty-seven-year-old bootmaker, out of Massachusetts, with but eight cents in his pocket and an indomitable courage. Ten years later he bought a half interest from his employer, Henry B. Endicott, in the Lestershire shoe factory, which was having hard sledding, giving his note for the entire amount and then borrowing one hundred and fifty dollars from Endicott to pay the tax on the note. Lestershire is now Johnson City, and the town of Endicott a little farther down the Susquehanna valley, when Johnson first came to Binghamton, was a two-hundred-acre farm.

There are few more fascinating romances in the history of all American industry than this one. George F. Johnson should be an immensely rich man by this time, but I doubt if he is. He has given away several considerable fortunes in his lifetime, for parks, playgrounds, hospitals, swimming pools, co-operative markets. (No wonder that Binghamton loves and appreciates him.) Nor have his private benefactions been small. He gives away from forty to sixty fine motor-cars each year to people who he feels would appreciate them, and who can not afford them. He is a pretty human sort of an industrialist.

But, best of all, he has brought content and peace into an industry which formerly was terribly rocked by labor troubles and strife of every sort. If you are really interested in knowing how a great industry can iron out its troubles with its thousands of workers, apparently definitely and permanently, I recommend to you the reading of *George F. Johnson and His Industrial Democracy*, by William Inglis. Inglis has done a good job. And his book is well worth the reading, even by folk who are not ordinarily interested in industrial relationships, but who, in passing through Binghamton and her sister shoe-making towns just to the west, more than vaguely realize that here something rather unusual in factory and community life is coming to pass. Here are nineteen thousand men and women living and working in great amity, not only with one another but with their employer, who has really ceased to be their employer (in any ordinary sense of the word) to become their friend and advisor. In other words, George F. Johnson, having convinced himself that he has made all the money that any man should possess, and having no great flair for museums or opera houses or colleges or any other educational institutions of that sort, has set his mind to work, devising means for a reasonable division of the profits of the highly profitable enterprise which Endicott and he founded. Which is a book in itself. And Bill Inglis has done the book.

CHAPTER X

North Country

THE Watertown that once I lived in as a boy and knew so well indeed, then as now, was a charming town and the center of that upland area of the state long since known as the North Country. A really vast domain this. Six great counties comprise it—St. Lawrence, the largest of all the counties of New York, Jefferson, Lewis, Franklin, Clinton and Essex. The larger portion of the huge and desolate Hamilton may be included in the domain, and possibly parts of Warren and of Oswego as well; there are no definite boundaries to the North Country, save the St. Lawrence and Canada line to the north, Lake Champlain to the east and the foot of Ontario to the west. It has no large cities, few even sizable towns. Watertown, its metropolis, never has reached a population of thirty-five thousand persons. There are few towns and few closely settled districts. It is a great barren area, with flat acres, many of them sterile, with swift-running and power-giving rivers, and with some of the vastest forest areas in the entire northwestern United States. There are tracts mountainous and beautiful, such as the well-famed Adirondacks, and some mere wilderness, unprofitable and unbeautiful, such as the forlorn region between the Black River valley and the east shore of Lake Ontario, known for eighty years and upwards as "the Borderlands," unpenetrated by motor roads and to this day peopled with bear and other sizable game.

One used to take Train Three out of Watertown about nine o'clock in the evening, ride north, hour after hour, and some time after midnight, if luck was with you, Number Three would pull up at Norwood station, and you would find your way across the street to Sid Phelps' famous old hotel; and perhaps still find the genial Sid sitting there back of the bar to greet you. Four hours, or less, in bed and then back to the selfsame little depot, to take a 5 A.M. train on the Ogdensburgh road off to the east. If fortune favored you still, you were in Malone by nine o'clock and Rouses Point by noon, and then you had crossed the North Country. That is as well as you might hope to cross it before the coming of the motor roads. You really only had slipped along its northerly edge. And the chances were that you were to spend a pretty bit of time in the depot at Rouses Point waiting for the D. & H. to come along and pick you up and carry you south again, this time to Plattsburg and the other places on the easterly edge of the domain. True it was that, after a time, Dr. W. Seward Webb came along and had the audacity to build a railroad right into the heart of the Adirondacks and across the North Country, from Utica, on the main line to Malone and to Montreal, but that was not until the 'nineties. Prior to that sad day the heart of the Adirondacks was an unspoiled paradise—Saranac Lake and Lake Placid and the St. Regis Lakes and the Fulton Chain. Paul Smith and a few folk who had summer camps in the wilderness had to have the courage and the stamina to ride for miles in buckboards or rough stages to reach them.

In the Watertown of the 'eighties we did not ordinarily give much thought to the Adirondack part of the domain. We were content to know of it as the North Woods and to realize that it held millions of acres of fine, standing timber, which gradually was being cut, but which we believed for a full century or more would give us the spruce for the paper mills that lined the lower twenty-five miles of the Black River and gave the Watertown of those days its chief source of income and its first batch of millionaires. The odor of sulphur, from the chemical pulp, hung heavily over the town those days, particularly so when the wind came from the north. When one drove by the paper mills, one could see mountain ranges of cleanly cut and neatly barked pulp wood, which steadily were being robbed for the chewers and beaters of the mills and as steadily being replenished once again, either by train or, more likely, from the drives down the river. The odor from these piles of fresh wood was more pleasant than that which came from the sulphite pulp. Most of these great mills, from which there issued night and day, seven days a week, the satisfying sound of machinery, of unrelenting industry, made newsprint out of wood and sulphite pulp. One mill, however, by the flume in the very heart of Watertown, had used rags ever since it started business in 1808, and it still is using rags. But it makes far better grades of paper than newsprint, and incidentally it is one of the few mills in or about Watertown still engaged in the trade which once made the place famous. Most of the other mills are gone; either they burned or have been torn down or abandoned. The ride down the north bank of the Black River to Dexter, some eight miles distant, used to be through an almost continuous zone of industry. There was a great paper mill every mile or so and a trolley line to connect them all; miles of railroad sidings and the miniature mountains of pulp wood. Now it is almost all gone. The reason is simple. They stripped the North Woods of their spruce, just as long before that they had stripped them of much of their other timber and had failed to replace it, by any sort of intelligent reforesting. Some pulp wood was brought down from Canada, still is being brought, but transportation costs, unfriendly tariffs, and the like have militated heavily against the continuation of the newsprint paper industry in and about Watertown.

Thanks to an aroused public sentiment and reasonably quick action on the part of the state, the more picturesque parts of the Adirondacks were saved before it was too late. And practical attempts are being made toward a continuous commercial reforestation of the whole area. The state conservation commission and the forestry schools of Syracuse and St. Lawrence universities are making intelligent and unceasing efforts to bring this about.

Fortunately for Watertown there have been other industries in the town that have kept it from retrograding, but not all of the North Country has been so fortunate. Industries that once were sizable have disappeared. Oswego once was famous for its iron works and its starch factory, Watertown for its carriage factories and its works for making sewing machines and stationary and traction engines, as well as for its paper mills. These have gone, as went long before them the woolen mills that once upon a time sought out its abundant water power.

The Watertown of fifty years or so ago was so pleasant a town and typical of so many other smaller cities of the state, that I may be permitted a brief description of it. I knew it well. My father for some years kept the chief hotel in the town, and to that ancient hostelry, the Woodruff House, which still is the chief hotel of Watertown and so has remained for eighty-two long years, came most of the more important visitors to the place—the better-known county families, of course; once a week the cheese buyers and sellers (Watertown was an important cheese market); the reverend bishop down from Ogdensburg on his frequent parochial visits; circuit judges and lawyers for the court sessions; important figures in the theatrical and musical and political worlds. Watertown never pretended to be a tourist place in those days. It was the shiretown of a rich and important county and, as has been said, the virtual metropolis of a domain that stretched nearly two hundred miles to the north and east. It boasted five national banks and a savings bank, and that alone spoke volumes for its wealth and its commercial prosperity. It had two excellent daily papers, and several weeklies as well.

It was indeed a pleasant place in which to live, despite the length and the severity of its winters. These actually seemed to harden the health of its inhabitants and to incline them toward longevity. The men who had laid out the town had brought ideas as to planning from their native New England that led them to arrange for two great open squares, or oblongs, placed at right angles to one another. The one became the Public Square and the other, the first two blocks of Washington Street, which, with its double rows of noble elms, ranks with Hillhouse Avenue in New Haven or Washington Street, Hartford, in real beauty. In my boyhood days the Public Square also was filled with fine old trees and grass plots and was a really lovely *platz*. A city administration, hell-bent on making the small town metropolitan, came along and, unannounced, overnight tore out all the trees. The town was infuriated. But that was about all the good that it did it. The trees were gone.

The fine feature of the place, however, was its old houses. There were a good many of these, and the best of them were built of the native limestone in a very simple and effective way. Perhaps the finest of these old gray stone houses was the Sterling residence, built about one hundred and twenty years ago, and standing in a great park filled with lovely trees. Originally there had been a front entrance to this mansion down at the foot of the slope in State Street, but that was long before my time. When I knew it, as a small boy, the State Street frontage had been sold for building lots, and even in the park, itself, there was another house, a curious edifice of Victorian parentage, that faced the stately Sterling residence. The Sterlings still lived in the old house. They were gentle folk, bookish, and the town was proud of them. There were others of these houses of lineage in Watertown, the homes of the Paddocks, the Sewalls, and the Hungerfords in Washington street, still inhabited by the descendants of their original builders; also some over on the north side of the river, which was not fashionable, but where a few of the old families hung on, quite bravely it seemed. And, of course, dozens of younger houses, all of them handsome and dignified, even though there had come a tendency to build them of brick rather than of stone.

The folk who dwelt in these houses, and many, many others, lived a pleasant and unruffled life. Most of them kept carriages and they drove out on pleasant afternoons or on warm summer evenings. There were band concerts down in the Public Square each Saturday evening in the season, and these were well attended. The volunteer fire department paraded on the first Monday evening of each month at seven and generally put up the hook-and-ladder and played the hose, either on the towering Woodruff House or on the American Building. The final parade of the summer was a knockout, with all the apparatus in full force at once, and the chief and his assistants marching nobly in their best uniforms, with huge bouquets tucked in their silver-plated speaking trumpets. There was a good deal of rivalry among the various companies; but every one agreed that there never had been, never would be, another steamer like the *Roswell P. Flower,* named after the most famous man who ever came out of Watertown; and one of the most loved. The F. W. Woolworth, who was to come forth from our place to found the five-and-ten-cent store business, was a pretty big man, but he never stood as high in the public esteem as Roswell P. Flower.

One could, of course, drive out of town, to Sackets Harbor and back—ten miles each way and quite the limit for a one-day drive—to see dress parade at the historic Madison Barracks there; or down the river to Brownville or into the back-country hills or to the Brookside Cemetery, two miles distant and a rather stiff march for the National Guard company each Decoration Day. If the weather was bad there were church meetings and festivals to fall back upon; supper parties (Watertown still ate its dinner in the middle of the day) and cards, decorous whist, and never for money. Even simple prizes had their moral questioners. For other recreations there was church twice a day on Sundays (people still went to church quite conscientiously), an occasional lecture, and the theater. Watertown always loved the theater, and for years it had a plentitude of very good theater.

In my earliest days, Washington Hall was the local temple of the drama. It was a huge and ungainly firetrap which stood at the corner of Washington Street and the Public Square, and on its third floor it held a really sizable hall, with a small but practical stage and some twelve hundred seats. One side of this auditorium was lined with tall windows, in which the blinds were forever closed, alternated with small brackets upon which rested marble busts of heroes of classical fame. That is, I assume they were marble. No one ever came near enough to touch them. The shallow gallery ran around the other two sides of the room, and in front of it was another small bracket, upon which rested a bust of the immortal Washington. It was easy to touch this. Flippant young men who sat in the gallery used to reach forward and place their hats upon the brow of the Father of His Country. A humorless man, named John A. Sherman, had built Washington Hall, very largely as a public monument, and this flippancy used to enrage him. He used to call upon Ed Gates, the manager of the theater, to have Charlie Champlin, the local chief of police, come and put the offenders in the jail down at the foot of Court Street. Gates used to have a good deal of trouble quieting Mr. Sherman.

To this curious old theater came most of the great actors of the 'seventies and the 'eighties—Booth and Barrett and Mary Anderson and Joe Jefferson and William J. Florence and others of their ilk. Also Harrigan and Hart—the *Mulligan Guards* was the first play I ever saw and I remember it to this day—and Joseph Murphy (in the *Kerry Gow*) and Sol Smith Russell, the last, the most beloved of all actors who ever came to Watertown. In it *Pinafore* played twenty-seven nights, and the whole North Country came to see it. There were other Gilbert and Sullivan operas as well.

John A. Sherman died and bequeathed Washington Hall to the Y.M.C.A., and that was pretty nearly the end of play-acting in that place: Watertown caught its breath, dug into its pockets and built a real ground-floor theater, one of the handsomest in the country at that time. To this City Opera House when it opened (almost exactly fifty years ago) came John Drew and Maude Adams and Helena Modjeska and Rhea and Chauncey Olcott and DeWolf Hopper and Francis Wilson, all of these mighty local favorites. The town really was enthusiastic over the drama, spoken or sung. And once when it hankered to hear the first all-star cast in *The Rivals,* it induced the company to break its stand in New York for Christmas Day and come to Watertown by special train and play that evening to a packed house at five dollars a seat.

If one wished for a real surcease from care in the summer he went from Watertown to the Thousand Islands. "Down the river" was the phrase, and despite the fact that the St. Lawrence ran within twenty-five miles of the county-seat of Jefferson, it was not a trip by carriage, but by train. In the 'nineties, the Thousand Islands attained their very pinnacle of popularity. Three presidents had visited them, General Grant and Chester A. Arthur and Grover Cleveland, and had enjoyed the fishing there, and they soon became a mecca for the fashionables from all parts of the East.

There were two main gateways to the region, Cape Vincent, almost at the very point where Lake Ontario debouches into the St. Lawrence, and Clayton, eleven miles further down the stream. In the beginning Cape Vincent was the more important of the two. It boasted two fine hotels, a theater, a newspaper and other evidences of real progress. In and out of its long covered station on the wharf ran many crowded trains; these connected with large steamboats, bound to and from island points; and the historic ferry that ran for a dozen or more miles across the head of the St. Lawrence to the fascinating fortified city of Kingston in Canada. In my boyhood day it was the steamer *Maud* that performed this ferry service most of the time. The *Maud* was Clyde-built and had been brought across the Atlantic in small sections and set up in a Kingston shipyard. She had an extremely complicated engine, and the only man who really understood it had an unfortunate habit of getting in his cups from time to time. On such occasions he invariably was discharged—"for the last time." Invariably he was rehired. The owners of the boat found that they could not run their ferryboat without their engineer. He was indeed invaluable.

Before the *Maud* there had been the *Pierrepont* and before that the *Watertown,* all of them sizable side-wheeled steamboats. Much of the time they either went around the head or the foot of Wolfe

Island, a rather extended and tedious trip; on occasion a disagreeably rough trip. There was a canal straight across Wolfe Island for three miles, and in my boyhood day running through this waterway was a joy, with the white highway bridges opening and shutting as the *Maud* made her dignified progress. Gradually this canal became filled, and for many years now it has been unused. The ferry service between Cape Vincent and Kingston is now performed, quite irregularly, by motor-boats or an occasional small steamboat. The two chief hotels and the theater in Cape Vincent long since burned, the great trainshed on the wharf blew down and killed one or two people in so doing. A "jitney car" upon the railroad makes a single trip each day back and forth to Watertown. Cape Vincent is a sort of ghost town, but has lost little of its charm in the transformation. It has some particularly lovely summer homes.

Clayton, which followed it in popularity, also has slipped from grace. Time was when the large river steamboats ceased coming to Cape Vincent wharf and patronized the Clayton one instead; it was much nearer to the island region and also served by through trains from many parts of the state. Between Clayton and Alexandria Bay, a brief ten miles, were most of the large hotels, the greater part of the cottage life of the Thousand Island region. Many of the island homes were, and still are, pretentious. Huge caravansaries rose above Round Island, above Thousand Island Park, Alexandria Bay, and elsewhere. Most of these are now gone—burned. Those that remain are very old. The Thousand Island district suffers, as Saratoga has suffered, from the lack of really modern hostelries. The season there is too short to operate them profitably, and this last summer, the historic Thousand Island House, landmark of them all, finally ceased to be operated as a hotel, after sixty summers. Its old-time neighbor, the even more historic Crossman House, may yet come to the same fate.

Truth to tell, the whole method of life at the Thousand Islands has changed radically. Cottage life there still is gay and charming;

done much more elaborately than forty or fifty years ago. The motor-boat, in itself a swift and efficient thing, with the motor-car, has in a sense been the ruination of the region. Between them, they first drove the steamboat almost out of existence within the waters of the upper St. Lawrence. About the only steamboats that still operate there are the line boats that come down the river from Toronto and Rochester on Lake Ontario bound to Prescott and Montreal. It is a loss to be genuinely mourned. That there was a charm in riding on these old-fashioned, comfortable craft, with their broad decks, their restaurants, their small orchestras, and their general air of leisure, is not to be denied. The *St. Lawrence* was the queen of this upper river fleet, and long ago she was sunk and dismantled in Kingston harbor. So perish many dynasties. . . . The motor-boats, highspeed and to an extent unregulated and unpoliced, have brought many fatalities in their swift progress through the narrow channels of the Thousand Islands, and so have done their own part toward the destruction of the place as a really democratic and popular resort.

Yet time, and passing fads in transport, can never erase the beauty of the upper river, with its eighteen hundred islands, large and small, tucked closely within the first twenty-five miles of its course. The islands, tree-clad and surmounted with homes in charming taste, still rise abruptly above the narrow channels. Great ships, going through from Chicago or Duluth to Liverpool or Hamburg, still thread these channels on the mightiest inland water trip in all the world. The hoarse whistles of the freighters echo in the wind-blown tree branches of the quiet streets of old Cape Vincent. In the ancient, grass-grown cemetery in Market Street in that little village of the past, you still can find the monument to the twenty or more folk who perished when the *Wisconsin* sank off bleak Grenadier Island, more than eighty long years ago. As long as I live, I shall recall the peculiar note of those whistles as they rounded Tibbetts Point Light, out of the dangerous open reaches of Ontario, into the even more dangerous rock-filled, narrow channels of the upper St. Lawrence. It was a sound to thrill a small boy, supposedly fast asleep in his bed, late at night.

The Watertown of today is not so greatly changed.

There is a golf club or two, a thing unheard of in the earlier days. The motor-car, as everywhere else across the land, has made the carriage a museum piece. Occasional horse shows are held, and there is some cross-country riding, but this is sporadic and kept alive very largely by the near-by Madison Barracks. That important military post and the summer army maneuvers at Pine Plains, fifteen miles up the river, do much to keep Watertown awake, socially. There is no more theater. The people of the town would hardly know what to do if a good strolling troupe of players came their way again. The handsome theater still stands, but, with another house or two, it is dedicated to the trash that comes out of Hollywood. For real theater the Watertonians must go to the Big City.

With a few important exceptions, manufacturing industry is dormant within the town. Despite its abundant water power it is quite too far away from raw material and cheap labor. Yet it has held its population figures astoundingly well. The one industry that remains to it in old-time force is the dairy one; the production of milk and cream and cheese goes on unabatedly in the North Country. That and the fact that Watertown still is—and always will be—its metropolitan center, saves it from going backward. It no longer is the important railroad hub that it was fifty or even twenty-five years ago. The handsome large station that was built two decades ago is now too large. The bulk of the Watertonians travel by motor-car, even when they go sizable distances, as to Buffalo or to the Big City, and even as far as Boston or Washington. That is one thing the colossal improvement of the highroads of New York has done to the railroads—all but ruined them. The motor-car and the bus (this last only to a slight extent) have taken away the passenger traffic; the motor-truck, the cream of the freight.

One feature of the North Country, and it is its most charming feature, is that it changes but slowly. The fine old houses remain. How the greater part of them have escaped the ravages of decay and of flame all these years is both a mystery and a miracle. But there they stand.

To understand how many of these old settlers came into existence, one would have to delve deeply into the history of the North Country. This book makes no pretense of being history. Yet to envisage this terrain the more clearly, let it be understood that the French played no small part in its settlement. In that hour, a century and a half ago, when France was in her greatest travail, many of her landed gentry were glad to take ship and make their way to the little-known America. They knew a little more of the Northern New York country than some of the rest of it, perhaps due to the records of the early French explorers up the St. Lawrence Valley. Joseph Bonaparte was the most distinguished of the earlier *emigrés*. He built for himself a large wooden house on the high bank of the lonely Adirondack lake, about forty miles from Watertown, which still bears his name. Unquestionably he prepared the way for the coming of his great brother. A small house on the bank of the St. Lawrence at Cape Vincent (a village of strong French origin), known because of its curious shape as the Cup and Saucer House, was planned to become the residence of the French Emperor after he had succeeded in making his flight from France or St. Helena to America. How the attempts at flight were intercepted has been told many times. The Cup and Saucer House burned to the ground, Joseph Bonaparte, lonely and homesick, returned to France, and his house also was burned. Fire has done some sad things in the North Country.

A more practical emigrant by far was James Donatien Le Ray de Chaumont. As a boy he had stood by his father's table in Passy and had listened to the distinguished guest of the house, Benjamin Franklin, expatiate upon the glories and the possibilities of the new America. And when France went down into the ashes of humiliation and ruin, young Le Ray took advantage of the minister's kindly offer of a letter to his good friend, Judge William Cooper of New York State, and set forth across the Atlantic. Eventually he came to the young village of Cooperstown and there met the squire, who received him genially. But the Coopers had exhausted the immediate neighborhood, and so Le Ray was sent further north, to Constableville in the Black River Valley, and from William Constable, an important early landowner of the North Country, he purchased many thousands of acres. He made a swift trip to France, and when he returned he set out building himself a country-seat and a village by a small lake, hardly a dozen miles from the great falls of the Black River at the present city of Watertown.

The sweet old house that he built, a miniature Versailles, still stands, in a tolerably good state of preservation. Now, as then, it faces the little lake; the small hamlet of Leraysville is on the far side of the water. A *tapis vert* leads from the rear of the stately manor house to the waterside. Once it was lined with statues, and there was a little house to the roof of which the lord of the manor might ascend and with his spy-glass watch the labors and the antics of his people in the neighboring village. There were distinguished visitors to the manor house, Frenchmen of rank and an early President of the United States, and much entertaining in it and its surrounding grove.

My maternal grandfather was a country doctor, a zealous man and a kind-hearted one. To a great section of the countryside of Jefferson County he was more than doctor or surgeon; he was father confessor, financial advisor, good friend. As a boy I rode frequently with him upon his rounds. The farmhouses opened wide their hospitality to old Doctor Sill. He was their help and their comforter in adversity; the joyous sharer of their happiness.

No house was to be more eagerly anticipated than the old mansion at Leraysville. We drove out to it over ten miles of rocky country road, then plunged by a side road right into a wilderness of second-growth timber. Another mile or two of this, and we suddenly faced, in a clearing and reflecting itself in a small formal pool of water, the lovely yellow-white, pillared manor house. The charming old lady, who was its chatelaine, was a product of other days. She had very black and shiny hair, gay ringlets, and insisted upon speaking French, and nothing else than French. She was the granddaughter of a secretary of the great Le Ray, who within a few years had become afflicted with the nostalgia so common to many Frenchmen and had been glad to take advantage of quiet conditions once again in his native land, and to return to his old home to die. He turned the mansion in the woods over to his secretary, and it still is in the hands of the descendants of that personage. The impress made by Le Ray de Chaumont upon the North Country can never be erased. The names of the townships of Jefferson, Orleans, Cape Vincent, Alexandria, Plessis, Worth, Le Ray, Chaumont, reflect the whim and personality of the old Frenchman. He did much more, however, than merely naming towns; he established (in 1808) one of the earliest agricultural fairs in America, which still flourishes each autumn at Watertown, and he improved the breeds of cattle and of sheep, even to the extent of importing blooded animals from Europe for this purpose. He built dams and mills and powersites. He not only erected his great manor house in the forest, but he built two other stout stone houses in the county of Jefferson, both of which still stand. The smaller of these faces the waters of Chaumont Bay; the other is close to the rim of the blue St. Lawrence, at Cape Vincent. This last is an elaborate and very beautiful home, which evidently Le Ray planned to use as a summer residence. For many years it was occupied by the members of two intermarried French families, the Peugnets and the Beauforts; in fact to this day it is known by the villagers as "the old Beaufort house." Under the intelligent hands of its present owner, a charming woman from Watertown, it has been completely restored and exquisitely furnished in the prevailing French mode of the year of its erection. Its broad casemented windows look directly out upon the waters of the mighty river; there is a fine balcony and delicately curved stairs with iron rails upon this façade of the house. The frontage that it turns to the main street of the village is hardly less lovely.

Another house of fine tradition in our North Country is Constable Hall, situated in the broad Black River Valley, halfway between Utica and Watertown. Until very lately it was rarely seen, being three miles remote from the Great Road down the valley. A few years ago an improved highway was constructed north from Rome, and this passes directly through the ancient village of Constableville, one of the quaintest and least spoiled of all New York State towns. The old tavern which stands by the road (it recently has been restored) has been doing business at that corner since 1796 and still specializes in good North Country cooking. As you drive north from the village you gain a vista of the Hall, facing the countryside, and a little further on, you will pass a lych-gate and a little cemetery. Within that plat once stood the first Episcopalian church west of the Hudson River.

It is the Hall that charms and fascinates. Here was to be the pride and the glory of William Constable, erstwhile merchant of the city of New York, and in 1791 purchaser, with John Jacob Astor's former partner, Alexander Macomb, of nearly two million acres of North Country land. And yet the William Constable that made this giant purchase was doomed never to see this house. His son built it, of the native gray stone, so characteristic of the North Country, and fashioned it after the manner of the country-seat of the Constable family, outside Dublin. He took three years to build it and finished it in 1822; but never lived in it. On the day of its completion, while handling a heavy flagstone, he slipped and fell, broke his back and died soon after.

His widow continued on at the place. For the last fourteen years of her life she lived in it the entire year round. Despite the hard winters and the remote location, much of the time she was alone, except for her servants. She lived regally. Each morning at seven-thirty, dressed in somber black, she descended to the main floor of the house, her many keys hanging from her reticule, and gave instructions for the day's program. That done, she retired to her own rooms, until the formal two o'clock dinner, and spent the morning reading, writing, sewing, mending—what she willed. Downstairs the work of the house went on in accustomed rote and form. It did its own spinning and its own weaving. It was a self-contained community, independent of the outer world. The lady of the house had little to do with the folk in the village. Only the rector, she recognized as social equal; he also was the tutor of her children, when they were small. His was the only house to which she ever went.

When she became an old lady, Mrs. William Constable realized that the end was not many months away. So she went into Utica, engaged an entire floor in Baggs Hotel and for a memorable Christmas fortnight there entertained forty-two members of the family. Utica did not soon forget that party. For it she even brought the older sons back from their school in Switzerland (the Constables were never, never educated in America). It was a very successful party. And when it all was over, Mrs. William Constable turned over in her bed and died.

Constable Hall has all the charm of good taste and the attractiveness of historic importance. A daughter of its first occupant married William C. Pierrepont, of Brooklyn, who established his own country-seat, also still standing, at Pierrepont Manor, in the southern part of Jefferson County. William C. Pierrepont was the second president of the Rome & Watertown Railroad, and it was his fancy to take sun time by his sextant on pleasant days and then walk down to the depot to adjust the clocks and watches of the road.

For many years Constable Hall was definitely closed territory; even the inhabitants of the little village that it faces were sternly forbidden to trespass upon its acres. The gilded wooden eagle over its broad front door gazed down upon the lonely little splashing fountain in the front and over the broad sweep of gentle country to the sharp profiles of the distant Adirondacks, nearly eighty miles distant. Over the rear door was a buffalo head, and this looked out upon the broad verandah and the outbuildings, ranged into a hollow square, after the fashion of foreign country homes of rank. Inside that rear door still hangs the leather coat, with wampum, that the chieftain of the Oneidas gave to the builder of the house, in token of enduring friendship.

These houses, the small group of them in Watertown, a few up in St. Lawrence County and in Franklin and Clinton and one or two in Martinsburgh and elsewhere along the old Great Road through the Black River Valley, are about all that remain of the earliest days of the North Country. One of the finest of them all is nearly gone. This was the stately residence that John Lafarge built in the north part of Jefferson County. It had its own distinction in becoming the first home of one of the earliest Catholic colleges, in America, St. Johns, founded by Bishop Hughes and some years later removed to Fordham, in New York City, where it has since become a very strong and vibrant institution of learning. The Lafarges, of Lafargeville, had several distinctions. Lafarge's son and grandson became eminent painters and architects. But of the old house only a single wing remains, fast falling into utter ruin, yet a definite indication of the splendor of the one-time mansion and its entertainments.

Two or three other fine old houses, two of them of red brick in best accepted Southern tradition, face the lake at Sackets Harbor and give hint of the time when that small village was a port of importance. Reference already has been made to Sackets Harbor (originally the place was spelled Sacketts Harbor, after a distinguished North Country family, but time and an unsentimental Postoffice Department have done strange things to some of these old names). In 1814 it was the locale of a battle, of which apparently the least said the better. Both the seasoned British forces and the unseasoned volunteers from the surrounding country seemed to be a bit afraid of one another; and the skirmish ended in a rout, in which each side felt it had been thoroughly defeated. Yet the fact remains that the British withdrew, having completely failed to sack the town and post.

Sackets Harbor has remained a military post, but nothing much of importance has happened in the village since the day of the battle, save possibly a devastating fire or two, which only increased the penury of the little village. Once the blue of its small harbor was dotted with the white sails of brigs and schooners, trading up the lake. Steamboats, too, made it a port of call; in fact the first steamboat ever to be built on Lake Ontario was made in a shipyard there, back in 1816.

Until but a few years ago the village was the possessor of the smallest Navy Yard in the United States; and I am old enough to remember clearly the gaunt frame of the battleship *New Orleans,* which was fabricated in the long point at the end of the Yard to go forth into the Second War; but the War ended before the *New Orleans* could be finished, and there she stood for some seventy years until they tore her old bones apart and carved them into canes and window-seats and what-nots for the whole North Country. And the timber proved to be as sweet and sound and good as the day when it first had felt the blow of the adze in its call to glory.

General Grant once was stationed at ancient Madison Barracks at the Harbor, and so was General Pershing; the roster of the brilliant young men from West Point who did their turn of duty at the historic post reads like a roll of honor of the Army, itself. General Zebulon M. Pike, mighty traveler and explorer of the Far West, is buried in the small graveyard attached to the post. Half a mile beyond that, up the Watertown road, is a small brick house, in which chloroform was first invented, by Dr. Ossian M. Guthrie.

Oh, Sackets Harbor has had its day. All that now remains of that day are the old houses, with the French pictured paper upon their walls; Christ Church, one of the neatest bits of colonial architecture in all York State; the crumbling Navy Yard, with the gun carriages for the *New Orleans* that have rested in the old sheds for one hundred and twenty long years; and the thriving Post, with a full regiment in station and a lively band to whip up things on dull afternoons. In my boyhood days there were two attractive small hotels in the village, and frequent trains back and forth between the village and Watertown. Now the hotels are both gone; and so are the trains. A new era; and sometimes it is a little hard to think of it as a better one. It was rather pleasant, driving a smart pair down to Sackets from Watertown of a summer's afternoon, listening to the band and watching the maneuvers of the blue-coated

Ninth Infantry, having a good fish dinner at one of the hotels, and then returning to Watertown over the hard, straight road in the moonlight.

In its historic lore and tradition, St. Lawrence County is hardly second to Jefferson. Actually it is a little larger, a shade more populous. It has no town quite as large as Watertown, but it has a string of sizable places such as Gouverneur (named after Gouverneur Morris of New York, who had his own manor house near by); Canton (the county-seat); Potsdam (ancestral home of the Clarksons); Massena (the seat of great aluminum works and the chief industrial town of the county); and the city of Ogdensburg, situated at the confluence of the Oswegatchie and St. Lawrence rivers (the most populous of all and by far the most historic).

We begin with Ogdensburg. For here it was that St. Lawrence County, much of the whole North Country in fact, had its beginnings.

He lives in an old house in an old garden by the side of a very old river. On the river sail many ships, and in his fine mind there must sail other ships, the argosies that so often float through the mind of a man of three score and ten. This is the reverend bishop of Ogdensburg. His domain is the souls of men and women over a great diocese that covers one-quarter of the area of the state of New York. I am not of his religious faith; as he discovered one night as we rode toward New York in the sleeping-car.

"Has your one-time church ever done anything to bring you back into its fold?" he inquired gently.

"Not that I have ever discovered."

He cleared his throat.

"If I knew a single soul in my diocese that tonight was struggling for faith," said he quietly, "I would arise in the middle of the night and go to it, no matter what the weather, what the hour, what the distance."

And he would. Bishop Conroy is the only bishop that I ever have known who looks as I think a bishop should look. Gentle, spiritual, he sits, a majestic figure in his purple and black vestments, in a great room back of a great desk, and there he deals love and authority and advice and judgment, all in good measure and all well admixed. His cathedral, not a very large affair, of a gray stone and vineclad, is attractively set in a side street of Ogdensburg. The altar lamp of its faith has glimmered with some intermission for nearly two hundred years. Prior to 1759 the French were at Ogdensburg; building a fort for the protection of their bodies and a church for the protection of their souls. Fort Presentation disappeared long years ago, but the little church, grown to be the cathedral church of a far-flung diocese, lives. It was from Fort Presentation that two successive expeditions set out for the relief of Fort Duquesne (now Pittsburgh), a journey of terrific distance. But those early Frenchmen seemed to think nothing at all of such marches.

After the French finally had been driven out of their beloved valley of the upper St. Lawrence, Fort Presentation fell into sad ruins, and the little village at the mouth of the Oswegatchie all but died. It was not until 1796 that it took hope once again and began to be a thriving river port. These were the days of a new prosperity. Two important men, William B. Ogden, of New Jersey, from whom the town drew its new name, and the well-famed David Parish, son of the English consul at Hamburg and later of Philadelphia, became the overlords of the place. Paris furnished Northern New York with one of the fine romances of its history. He built for himself a large house of red brick in Ogdensburg (it still stands as the Frederic Remington Museum, named after a famous son of the town and holding many of his wonderful pictures of the West) and around it built a high brick wall. The Philadelphia banker, having thus assured himself of comfort and of privacy, brought to the quiet little river town an exquisite mistress from far-off Italy, and in so doing shocked it immeasurably. He also brought a billiard table from Philadelphia to his new house; and secured an artisan to come up the river from Montreal to install it properly.

Below Ogdensburg on the bank of the river are the very old towns of Waddington and Louisville, sleeping the sleep of long years, and the comparatively new one of Massena; while directly across the St. Lawrence, on the Canadian shore is Prescott, with a fascinating ancient blockhouse and fort; and the famous lighthouse at Windmill Point, fashioned from a lofty stone mill. More fighting has raged around this landmark than might easily be recorded within these pages. For the history of this section of the St. Lawrence is that of much fighting; the French and Indian War; the Second War with England, with a battle in the streets of Ogdensburg; and the absurd and tragic little Patriots' War of 1837.

St. Lawrence County has broad green acres, with black and white cattle grazing in them; swift and powerful rivers, brown-black; comfortable, serene, tree-shaded towns, towns of culture and refinement. Potsdam has its Clarkson School of Technology and its huge Normal School; and Canton, that excellent and thriving rural institution, St. Lawrence University. But just to show that St. Lawrence is not too rural, permit me to remark that its campus contains, in its chapel, what I know is the handsomest building in Northern New York; certainly one of the handsomest in the entire state. There also is a men's dormitory, very good-looking and very appropriate in its design; this last borrowed from that of the old North Country houses. The other buildings on the campus are not so fortunate, in their design or in their placing. But the campus itself is lovely; and I think that I never like it better than on a clear crisp winter day, when the thermometer is somewhere sub-zero and you stand in the hard, glistening snowy pathways and look across long miles to distant Adirondack peaks, outlined sharply by the eternal greenery of their conifers. Such a setting, such a school, breeds fine young men and young women. St. Lawrence University is full proof of this statement.

The casual visitor to St. Lawrence County is apt to miss one of its most charming features, the historic Black Lake and its vicinage. The railroads and the trunk highways leading through the North Country seem to succeed in avoiding it completely, as well as the little ghost towns of Rossie and Oxbow, just adjacent.

Black Lake, more than twenty miles in length, runs rather closely parallel to the St. Lawrence, and so wide is it that one not knowing the territory and coming upon it unexpectedly might easily mistake it for the great river, itself. Close to its head stands ancient Rossie, where the enterprising David Parish once had extensive iron mines and a huge woolen mill. The stone walls of this really large structure still stand stoutly by a swift-running mill-race, although it is more than ninety years since the mill was abandoned and left to fall into ruin.

Oxbow, for me, has interesting recollections. I can recall, while still a small boy, driving there many years ago with grandfather Sill and meeting an old gentleman who, with his knee breeches, his immaculate ruffled shirt and his three-cornered hat, made a distinct impression upon childish eyes.

"That, my boy," said my grandfather, as we left, "is a man to remember. That is Major Benton and he married the daughter of the King of Spain." The story of Joseph Bonaparte's infatuation and morganatic marriage with Annette Savage of Utica still is part of the saga of the North Country. Their daughter, wife of that selfsame dignified Major Benton, lies buried in the little neglected cemetery at Oxbow, a place of pilgrimage for many North Country folk sentimentally inclined.

Franklin County and Clinton and Essex, possibly Oswego also, are, it will be remembered, geographically part of the North Country. But because they sentimentally attach themselves to certain other portions of the state which are treated in other chapters of this book, they will not enter this one. Jefferson and Lewis and St. Lawrence are far more closely knit together, politically and by tradition of nearly every sort. They are a clean open great space in great New York, a sort of lungs as it were, for the more congested portions of the state. In their period, vivid Americanism, they rather resist incoming immigration and the new ideas and fervors that come with it; standing stoutly still for old days, old traditions, old ideals.

CHAPTER XI

The Lady of the Snows

AFTER all, it is the dead of winter, perhaps, that, best of all, typifies our North Country. There is something about the silence of a January night up there, when the little villages and the houses have all gone to sleep, that is almost awesome.

Winter comes early each year to our North Country; and lingers late. There is a fairly short summer and (usually) a hot one; little spring and not too much autumn; but a bounteous supply of winter, if you wish to put it that way. Yet the North Country really likes it. And in recent years it has begun to learn how to capitalize it, particularly in the Adirondack region, reaching a very high spot in 1932, when the winter Olympic games were held at Lake Placid, for the first time.

Long before 1932 the Adirondacks had begun to prepare themselves. The folk who have been going up into the Big Woods during the winter for the past fifty years or more, long since had rendered themselves pretty expert as to all of this; beginning, quite naturally, with tobogganing and bob-sledding, snow-shoeing and skating; then, in time, taking up ice hockey. Skiing is a more recent sport, and imported. But within the past three or four years it has taken such a warm hold upon the affections of athletic America, of all ages and of all conditions, that it now bids fair to become a sort of winter golf, in popularity at any rate. Incidentally it has become a sort of life-saver for some of our Eastern railroads. For the past two winters they have used it as a method of upbuilding a sizable excursion business, special trains and all the rest of it. But it was the Olympic games, there in February 1932, with skiing and bob-sledding as dominant features, that made Lake Placid, the whole Adirondack country, in fact, first known to the entire world. On one night over three thousand people journeyed all the way up from New York for them; while there was a total "gate" of between thirteen and fourteen thousand persons—pretty good for a town of less than three thousand residents.

Lake Placid had, of course, been known to many, many people long before 1932. There is the danger, particularly in the minds of its residents, that it now may become too much regarded as a purely winter resort and not enough as an outstanding summer one, one for all the year round in fact. Its greatest hostel, the Club, remains open the year round. The greater part of its visitors, by far, come to it in the hot months of midsummer, when it is, itself, not the least bit hot. Its nearly two thousand feet of altitude insures against that.

The town is on the historic Northwest Bay road, that was put through the North Country wilderness from Westport (once Northwest Bay), on the west bank of Lake Champlain, to Canton, the county-seat of St. Lawrence, and Ogdensburg, its chief city and port, more than a century and a quarter ago. A rough, hard road it was, but it carried much traffic. Folk succeeded in making their slow way upon it. One of these was a pioneer who became guide and trapper. His name was Paul Smith, and it will be remembered almost as long as the Adirondacks are remembered. His log hut became an inn, in time a small hotel, and then a sizable one. Its very inaccessibility, there in the depths of the great forests, made it all the more attractive to people. Some time in the 'eighties, John Hurd built his lumber railroad south from Moira, on the old Ogdensburg & Lake Champlain (now the Rutland), south nearly a hundred miles into Tupper Lake, and then it became somewhat easier (none too easy) to reach Paul Smith's, on the Upper Saranac, even though you had to go by rail away around almost to the Canadian line to do it. But many people did it. Paul Smith had a knack of making friendships; of bringing important men up to the North Woods, men who could and would help in the proper development of it as a vast refuge for the health and physical development of man. And pretty soon another railroad or two were knocking for admission to the heart of that hitherto all-but-inaccessible area. A little narrow-gauge, the Chateaugay Railroad, found its way south and west from Plattsburg, past the lonely and the dreary great prison on the hillside at Dannemora, and up the valley of the Saranac, as far as the present thriving village of Saranac Lake. There it was, for a time, estopped. A feeling was beginning to develop across the state against the growing invasion of the Adirondack domain; not only by railroads, but by other forms of commercial and industrial enterprises. And, as we shall see in a moment, this was to lead to the creation of the great Adirondack Park and elaborate plans for the protection and the conservation of all its natural resources. So the group of men who obtained a charter for an extension of the Chateaugay Railroad into the village of Lake Placid (the very heart of the Adirondacks; but ten miles distant from Saranac Lake) worked with a good deal of swift precision and hush at Albany. Nor did they particularly advertise the fact that their valuable charter permitted them to charge as much as ten cents a mile for the Saranac Lake—Lake Placid haul. This actually was charged for a number of years.

Before the lid finally was clamped down upon the Adirondacks, and clamped down hard, one other railroad gained admission to the sacred domain. This was a Vanderbilt enterprise. Dr. W. Seward Webb, an Adirondack enthusiast and landowner, who had married into the family, felt that the region should be made accessible to the many (this of course was long before the reign of the motor-car and the paved highway). It might turn out to be a good business enterprise as well. Accordingly he bought another small narrow-gauge, running from Herkimer up along the West Canada Creek to a point not far from Trenton Falls. This he speedily made into a standard-gauge line, which, known as the Mohawk & Malone, he at once put through the entire Adirondack country; in fact, finally brought it right into Montreal, itself, and, by buying and extending the Hurd railroad, across the St. Lawrence and into Ottawa as well. A brilliant plan it was, although never a financially successful one.

A short branch line led from this road into Saranac Lake village, and soon negotiations were under way for a joint use of the line into Lake Placid, which already had been acquired by the Delaware & Hudson Company. There was a good deal of maneuvering; no small contest. But the thing was accomplished, and the Central, having done the obvious thing and purchased the Seward Webb road, soon had its sleeping- and parlor-cars running from New York right into Saranac Lake and Lake Placid villages, and no longer could any one complain that they were inaccessible. They were as easily reached from the Grand Central as Boston or Buffalo; and with frequent service of through trains.

In the meantime the Adirondacks were gaining great reputation for themselves. Charles Dudley Warner and others had written much about them. Poor old Robert Louis Stevenson, forever battling against the inevitable, took a cottage for a winter or two at Saranac Lake, and then the world knew about Saranac Lake. A brilliant New York doctor, Trudeau, had heard of it, even before Stevenson. He suffered from the same terrible disease as the author, although in nowhere near as advanced a form. To Saranac Lake he therefore had gone, and Saranac had saved his life; or at least prolonged it, for many years. Trudeau already had dedicated that life to fellow sufferers from the same dread disease. In his years of work and achievement on the hill back of the village he had not only created the first of a group of great sanitariums, but led in research work combating the white plague. His record is a monumental one.

The railroads that had pierced their way into the heart of the Adirondack domain justified the hopes of their promoters in bringing in the people. Hotels, large and small, began to spring up. Choice sites for "camps" were snapped up and some of these were elaborate affairs, indeed, with huge houses and hundreds and even thousands of acres. They might have log-cabin exteriors, but there was little of log-cabin simplicity in their interiors. Henry van Hoovenberg built his Adirondack Lodge at Heart Lake (a dozen miles south of Lake Placid and right under the very shadow of lordly Mount Marcy), three stories high, and fabricated of giant spruce logs, two feet or more in diameter, and knew that he had built the largest log structure in all the world. That was in 1878, and Adirondack Lodge grew more and more famous all the while, until a June night in 1903 when a terrible forest fire, always the scourge of the Adirondack domain, swept the region and laughed at Adirondack Lodge and smacked its lips over the fine morsel of fine, dry spruce timbers, like a glutton over a thick steak. Poor old Henry van Hoovenberg nearly went crazy, in the insanity of despair and defeat.

Fire is one of the evil gods of the Adirondack country. Fortunes are spent to anticipate it and to combat it, and the careless flick of a cigarette may cause a catastrophe. That is the evil genius of the fire god, always. Woods and camps and hotels and whole towns go quickly once his bitter tongue begins to lick upon them.

But no one thought much of fire in those days. Paul Smith, encouraged by success and adulation, built at last his newest and biggest hotel. George Stevens put up another, equally large, at Lake Placid. Upper Saranac Lake had the great Ampersan, and the Lower, Hough's Saranac Inn. There were many others. The Adirondacks were "made." At least, so it seemed. All the way from the Sacandaga and Lake George in the south up through the Keene Valley in the east, the Fulton Chain and Big Moose in the southwest to Loon Lake and within shooting distance of Canton and Potsdam and Malone, came the big "development."

And then it lagged. The fire god caught some of the larger hotels;

more important, the summer habits of America were changing; slowly but surely. Young men and young women began to scorn big summer hotels and "dressing up" and sitting on verandahs. It was, like billiards and croquet, outmoded. More vigorous vacations were demanded. The summer hotels in the Adirondacks awaited the same dire fate as their brethren in the not-distant Thousand Islands. Only the camps, and the tuberculosis sanitariums, seemed able to survive the blight of time and change. Of the sanitariums the Adirondacks seemed to have an uncanny monopoly, or near monopoly. Would the lungs of the great state of New York be lungs—in medical sense—and nothing more? It now looks as if that dire possibility has been passed, completely. The domain of the North Woods in the day of King Motor-Car and Queen Highway is enjoying a fat, new reign once more, while the Dowager Queen—the railroad—enjoys at least her share of the prosperity.

Melvil Dewey was afflicted with nothing as tragic as tuberculosis. His ailment, a fairly common one here in America, a comparatively trifling one, but annoying—hay fever—sends many of us each year to the higher altitudes and the thinner air of the forests and the mountains. Himself a distinguished educator and a leader in advanced library methods, he gave no small study to this perplexing personal problem. For fifteen years, Dr. Dewey and his wife traveled all over the country, seeking to find some place that would serve as a permanent summer haven against his besetting affliction. They found it at Lake Placid, upon the rim of the tiny Mirror Lake that nestles close to the larger one, as a fawn does against the side of the mother doe. And there Melvil Dewey set out to bring his great plan into being.

For the man had ideas far beyond the mere bringing of comfort to himself for a few short weeks of midsummer. His years of searching had evolved an idea within him, that finally took firm root at Lake Placid. He was seeking to create there a center for intelligent and cultivated and companionable people. Not a hotel, not a country club, not a "camp," in the occasionally glorified

Adirondack sense of evening dinners and evening clothes and butlers and all that with them goes—just a different sort of hostel.

I wonder how many men have ever dreamed that sort of dream? I have dreamed it myself, many times. The quiet simple inn, with its low ceilings, its open fires, its good meals, its comfortable beds, and, above all, its abundant good fellowship, the sort of thing that one takes out in dreams. Only Melvil Dewey's fortune was different. It really came to pass. And the funny little obscure New York State village to which the railroad had pushed its way by 1893, became the theater of a great achievement.

No longer can you call Lake Placid either "funny" or "obscure." Even before the coming of the Motor Era, the Coolidge prosperity and the mad excitement of the Olympics, it stood firmly upon its feet. And Melvil Dewey's dream had become its most conspicuous institution. He called it the Lake Placid Club. In an extremely simple and unostentatious house on a five-acre lot, where some thirty men and women of congenial tastes and occupations had been drawn together, to pay a dollar a meal and such other moderate costs as were necessary to their mutual comfort.

At first no one paid very much attention to the club, but it began to grow and grow, and presently Dewey was resigning his job as secretary of the State Board of Regents, down at Albany, and was giving all his time to it, save what he held for his remarkable scheme for the simplification of the spelling of the English language. Gradually the club came to be an institution, with a building as big as three or four ordinarily big hotels, and sometimes it housed as many as sixteen hundred guests of a single night, with a staff of upwards of seven hundred employees to look after their wants, a ten-thousand-acre site, four golf-courses, two toboggan slides and a bob-run (winter sports continue mighty popular at Lake Placid), hockey fields, five hundred cows in its own fine dairy—these statistics could run on forever. But enough have been given to show that it is a sizable institution. The clubhouse remains open the year round, and that is one of the reasons why winter sports have been developed to such a high degree at Placid. Dr.

Dewey is gone, these several years now, but his memory is kept green by those who carry on after him, and who manage the four million dollar property; and continue to give a meed of attention to the simplified spelling.

The Lake Placid Club is a *club* in the fullest sense of the word. That word is used quite often these days by resort hotels, seeking to avoid a state law which tries to remove racial restrictions among those whom they may accept as guests. But the Lake Placid Club never has been anything else. It is as fussy and as pernickity about whom it elects to take in as members, as the Union Club, or the Somerset. And it is a bit rigid as well as to what its members may do with themselves, once they have been admitted to its portals. The enactment of the Eighteenth Amendment and its subsequent repeal meant nothing whatsoever to the Lake Placid Club. It never has countenanced liquor, either as a public practice or a private joy. It doesn't particularly like girls smoking cigarettes around the premises, or sloppy dancing, or "shorts" or "halter blouses." It even forbids evening dress at dinner; and then puts dinner in the middle of the day, so there shall be no question about it.

You might get the idea from all of this that the Lake Placid Club is a rather priggish or a smug, sanctimonious place, like a sanatarium or a religious "retreat." It is nothing of the sort. The folk who go to the Lake Placid Club, literally by the thousands each year, bankers, merchants, professional men, even a few manufacturers, who still have the price of its rather moderate charges, love the place because they can be so informal in it. It is so changeless, so restful. All of which might be set down as a sure-fire recipe for resort hotel success.

It is but a step (actually less than two miles) from the gayety and life of Lake Placid to the silence of North Elba; and it is at North Elba that John Brown is buried, close beside a giant Adirondack boulder. Seemingly it is one of the loneliest places in the world, a treeless, windswept plateau top, empty save for the burial plot and the near-by unpainted farmhouse. But, roundabout, is the awesome beauty of the Adirondacks everywhere, with great peaks rising in every direction, as if to proclaim the eternal glory of a man who died upon the hangman's scaffold, defeated and friendless. There is no more profoundly impressive place in all New York State than this; few more so anywhere. I find it more compelling even than Washington's grave upon the soft bank of the Potomac; vastly more so than the dramatic and the tawdry Parisian tomb of Napoleon. Every tree-top in the whole North Woods sings and mourns for old John Brown. And in the dead of Adirondack winter, when there are no motorists to come to the spot, and the stillness becomes more unearthly than at any other time of year, our Lady of the Snow blankets his grave with a soft, deep robe of immaculate white that rests undefiled until the coming of another year of warmth and sunshine and greenery.

It was that other distinguished citizen of upstate New York of sixty or seventy years ago—one Gerrit Smith, abolitionist—who really was responsible for Brown's coming to the Adirondack country. Smith, a wealthy man, had had a fantastic idea of making a great refuge for fugitive slaves in its inaccessible heart, and for this purpose he set aside thousands of his acres in the town of North Elba. John Brown went there to prepare the way. The scheme was wildly impractical, hopeless. But Brown loved impractical and hopeless things. For some years he lived on at North Elba; even after he had gone out into Kansas, he left his family there in the North Country wilderness. He felt that they would be quite safe from molestation.

Too poor to afford a tombstone of his own of even the simplest form, John Brown shares the headstone of his grandfather on the farm at North Elba. Recently a very effective statue has been erected of the tall, gaunt figure of the Abolitionist, with his arm resting protectingly across the shoulders of a negro boy. This heroic bronze, by Pollia, is a gift of the colored people, which makes its beauty the more poignant. The state (through its conservation department) has made a simple sort of a memorial park of the whole place—the old farmhouse and the burial plot; with the grave shared by John

Brown and his grandfather; that of his son, Watson, and the unmarked grave of the twelve men who died beside him in the beleaguered engine house in that memorable day at Harpers Ferry.

The state's remarkably successful conservation department does all these things well. It may be either a minor or a major extravagance, but it is one decidedly worth while, broad in its scope and intelligent in its management. We already have seen the state at Niagara Falls half a century ago ending the rapaciousness and greed of those who preyed upon tourists. There was no state park or conservation commission then, but that job alone would have justified one's existence, let alone anything else.

But conservation has done very much more. Its name indicates much of its functions. As you drive around the thirty-five thousand miles of paved road that form the New York highway system of today, you will see from time to time various small areas, carefully set aside, kept immaculately in order: shelters, camps, cabins, picnic tables, outdoor fireplaces, swimming beaches, almost everything for the joy or the comfort of the lover of the outdoors. There are seventy of the small parks alone.

New York is the pioneer state of the Union in the preservation of its natural beauties as well as its bountiful resources of forest, water and wild life. The gods indeed were good to New York; and New York is trying these days to show her appreciation of their beneficence. In 1885, when the work began in this state, no other commonwealth, not even the federal government, had taken steps to conserve natural resources or beauties; and, as a matter of fact, there was no great enthusiasm in New York over the idea. It took a lot of persistent pounding to educate the body politic to it. To many folk, it all seemed like a very definite invasion of personal rights and liberties. Rugged individualism opposed it. Already there was a law which prohibited individuals or private corporations from cutting timber on state-owned lands, but this statute apparently was regarded by many folk up in the North Country as something cut from Joe Miller's Jokebook. At any rate, they stole timber right and left, and bragged of it. In the few cases where they were apprehended and prosecuted, they expressed great indignation; and frequently they succeeded in dodging punishment.

There are over two million acres of state-owned lands in the Adirondacks. Which, in turn, comprise about half of the great area, within the so-called "Blue Line," which extends from Lake Champlain west to the Black River Valley; and from within twenty to thirty miles of the Mohawk up to within thirty of the Canada line. This is known, officially, as the Adirondack Preserve. There is much private property within the Blue Line, whole sizable towns, such as Saranac Lake, for instance, with eight thousand inhabitants; there are plenty of vast camps and private preserves. Yet always there will be those two millions of acres of woodland that belong to the people of the state; that are protected for them by the provisions of their constitution. There can be no more railroads, and few more highways. There are now quite enough of both to insure the region perfect accessibility, from every direction.

One highway, which may be the final one, was completed in the summer of 1935, after three years of most arduous labor, up to the summit of Whiteface Mountain. This road already bids fair to become one of the outstanding motoring attractions of all America. Starting at the foot of the Wilmington Gorge of the Ausable River, in eight brief miles it ascends some thirty-five hundred feet to within a few hundred feet of the summit of the mountain, 4872 feet above the surface of the sea. No mean peak is it.

Whiteface differs from most of the Adirondack peaks, including old Mount Marcy, the doyen of the flock (its original Indian name of Tahawus really should be restored to it), in that it stands sentinel, almost like the volcanic peaks of the North Pacific coast. Its steep sides descend abruptly from its summit in every direction and form splendid incentive for real mountain-climbing. Those who have no ambitions of this sort can now go to the top in their motorcars; if they are throttle expert and the car is a good one, without shifting gear out of high. For the grade is kept almost uniformly at eight per cent—never exceeds ten. The engineers were told that they must build the great, wide road, in less than nine miles of length and ten per cent of ascent. They kept well under both limitations and have produced a mountain road without an equal anywhere else in the world, not even in Switzerland.

The road leads to within but a few hundred feet of the summit and a superb view. On a clear day you see not only Lake Placid (as you cannot possibly see it from that village), the Saranacs, the St. Regis, many miles of the sweep of broad Lake Champlain; even glimpses of the St. Lawrence, of Ogdensburg, of Montreal and its guardian mountain. Eventually it is planned to build a resthouse at the summit (the scheme for a War Memorial monument there fortunately was quashed), but this is at the moment of writing a matter of some agitation between the state's highway and conservation departments. A question of authority is concerned.

I hold no brief for either. The state highway department has done splendid work (except for its decimation of shade trees and covered bridges), and the conservation department is quite without a parallel elsewhere, not only in the upbuilding of the many, many parks, large and small, across the state, from the wonderful Jones Beach on the south shore of Long Island to the Alleghany and Niagara Falls parks at the extreme western end, but in the preservation of fish and game, with which New York is richly stocked indeed. It is difficult business in these days of the paved road to maintain these reserves of wild life. The state is trying to offset the increased accessibility of its wooded and mountainous districts by the establishment of twenty-six fish hatcheries and five game farms. These have a little more than compensated. New York never has sacrificed her position as a splendid state for hunting and fishing. Incidentally, this is one feature of her paternalism that does not cost the average taxpayer one blessed penny. The license fees (together with a small amount from fines and penalties) completely support this division of the work; and yet these fees in New York are lower than those of any other state in the Union, save Vermont.

As a matter of fact, unless you own Adirondack property, or are a member of one of the numerous clubs which have their own private preserves or have a friend with a generous camp of his own, it is not very easy to do much hunting or fishing up there these days. The entire countryside has become canny about sportsmen, not properly introduced. "Posted" signs abound, and their warnings are sharply enforced. The public grounds are apt to be crowded. It all is a part of the rapidly changing trend of the times everywhere. There still are guides, and excellent ones they are, but high-priced.

Not long ago the Syracuse *Post-Standard* dug out, at a barbecue at Lake Meachem, one of the older guides of the region, one George Debar. George was feeling depressed. His feelings got the better of him. Finally he delivered himself to the reporter after this fashion:

"This makes me right sad," he mourned. "They're having a good time and I am glad to see them happy, but it makes me think of the days when Lake Meachem was something. Everything around here looked so different then. . . . Right over there was the best runway I ever sot eyes on. This was most woods, 'cept the hotel did have a little clearing. And the fishin', say there never was a time when we couldn't go right out and get a meal of lakes or a bucket of brook trout.

"Conservation's all right," he mourned, "but we didn't need it then and I kinda hanker for them days that'll never come again."

A good many older folk will agree with George, even though it does not take long to realize that it would be a pretty sad sort of an Adirondacks today without a conservation organization to hold rapaciousness in check.

Customs may change—barbecues and picnics may come to Lake Meachem and Fourth Lake and Big Moose and all the rest of them —but the Adirondacks themselves are changeless. They are the oldest mountains in all the world, and possess the dignity and serenity that Mother Nature always gives to great age, together with the purity of the vast forests that blanket them so completely. It is only at the very peak of mountains such as Whiteface and Marcy that one comes to timber line, and the fact that, there, century-old pines are a bare thirty inches in height, may be ascribed to exposure and Laurentian rock as much as to mere altitude. The Adirondacks never have preened themselves upon mere altitude. They leave that to the far-distant Rockies. They have not the jagged outlines of western mountain peaks and ranges. They are softly molded. I always think of our New York State mountains as like the folds of a giant green blanket, with shaggy nap, that some god has thrown down hastily and carelessly upon the rough face of the earth, with streams that rush madly toward the great Hudson or the greater St. Lawrence, night and day, the entire year round. None of your *arroyos sec* for our New York, if you please.

That "Blue Line," so sharply defining the Adirondack Preserve, runs for miles along the rim of Lake Champlain and so makes that lovely sheet of water, 108 miles long and in places from ten to twelve in width, its eastern border. The rider upon its waters is intoxicated by the scenery that is presented upon its banks—on the one hand, the Green Mountains of old Vermont and upon the other the quiet strength and reserve of the unforgettable Adirondacks. There are few lovelier steamboat rides in all the world than that from Plattsburg and Burlington (Vermont) to Crown Point and Ticonderoga, where one changes to a still lovelier lake voyage, through the French Lake Sacrament (for the past two centuries, Lake George, after a king who was not particularly popular here in America for a long time). Lake George is sometimes called the American Como, but having gazed upon the real Como, I should be more inclined to style it the Italian Lake Sacrament.

Nowadays one has to say that one of the loveliest steamboat rides *was* on Lake Champlain, for the steamboats upon that lake (as well as Lake George) have had hard sledding—if one may break metaphor in that fashion. A small steamboat still plies George, but the comfortable *Horicon* has been reduced to being a show boat, which is like putting a famous opera star in "three-a-day" vaudeville. But the tragedy is even greater upon Champlain. Until the summer of 1934, the Champlain Transportation Company had

THE LADY OF THE SNOWS 281

navigated that sheet of water for 108 summers, without interruption and without serious accident of any sort. And now it is almost completely out of business.

To look out upon the lake any fine day from the terrace at Essex or the veranda of the fine inn at Westport and not see the *Vermont* making her queenly way up or down to and from Plattsburg, is just like not seeing Lake Champlain at all. The oldest inhabitant along the rim cannot remember when there was no *Vermont* (of one generation or another) to ply upon the lake, and brighten its midday somnolence with mighty whistle toots and the noisy splashing of her paddles. You used to take an evening train out of Montreal down to Plattsburg and there go upon the *Vermont* in the late evening, have a wonderful sleep as she rested, tethered to her pier, and by the time you were fully awake, and ready for coffee and ham and eggs and cakes or pie, the *Vermont* was paddling ahead serenely with Plattsburg far astern and Burlington looming up on the quarter bow. (Mr. William McFee will be sure to set me straight if a sidewheel steamboat has no quarter bow.)

Changing tastes and changing habits once again. The motor-car is a marvelous addition to our American life, but it will be a pity if it has to rob us of *all* our riding on fine steamboats down the wonderful lakes and rivers that the gods gave us ever and ever so long ago. It is pleasant still to get over to Switzerland and see the *Wilhelm Tell* and the *Stadt Luzern* noisily splashing in their own lakes, but to some of us it would be far pleasanter if the *Horicon* could be a real steamboat once again, and the *Vermont* again set to work upon the waters of her beloved Champlain.

For really to see that lovely lake, which is to the northeastern border of the state as the broad Lake Erie to the far western one, one must go out upon its waters. Nothing else will do. Then it is that you perceive not merely the splendid border of the Green Mountains upon the one side, but the equally superb Adirondacks upon the other. And if you are out there at end of day, you will observe Marcy and McIntyre and Whiteface emerge in silhouette against the setting sun, in all their finest sublimity. While if your mind is properly imaginative you will find yourself enacting in fancy the conflicts that long ago waged upon its now somnolent waters and shores.

For Lake Champlain, like the valleys of the Mohawk and the Hudson, also is pathway of empire. It is a sort of secondary pathway, to be sure, branching off from the Hudson stem at Fort Edward and Whitehall for more than two centuries past, but an important one nevertheless. For this pathway was (still is) the direct route from the chief city of the United States, New York, to the chief city of Canada, Montreal. As such it long ago not only attained historic commercial importance, but a surpassing military one, as well. In times of peace, portage (gradually superseded by canal) for twenty miles between Fort Edward (at an elbow of the Hudson) and Whitehall (at the foot of Champlain) helped to make this a busy pathway of industry; in times of war, soldiery. There has not been one war in which this country has battled against invading foes that it has not been right in the very thick of the fighting. It was so in the French and Indian conflicts of the middle of the eighteenth century and in the far greater war of the American Revolution. It was so again, with a vengeance, in the second war with England. This is not a history, and the details of the fighting in Northeastern New York would fill many chapters, but they are easily accessible and should be read by any one who ever visits, or intends to visit, Lakes George and Champlain.

For what else mean these gaunt ruins of gray stone that line the western rim of old Champlain? Fort Frederick and Fort Crown Point (close to one another) and Fort Ticonderoga (ten miles further south) each has a saga of its own to sing. And what sagas! Fighting, and no end of it. When you studied your history in the grade schools you read every word, every syllable about Ethan Allen and the Green Mountain Boys, and never forgot one single line of it, and today you can go to Ticonderoga and stand in the very doorway into which Allen strode one hard night, more than 160 years ago. Affection, plus good taste, and intelligence have created sort of a twentieth-century miracle at Fort Ticonderoga. Two of the three barracks of the fortification have been carefully restored, actually rebuilt, and the Pell family, who own the place, plan to build the third, when opportunity offers. All the bastions and battery are now as they originally were. With hundreds of guns mounted, the ancient fortress presents a bristling and a military appearance, indeed.

It began its career in 1755, under the French flag. Yet, almost a full century and a half before that, intrepid Samuel de Champlain had seen the spot. He had been led to it by a party of friendly Hurons and Algonquins, and close to the site of the present fort they had gone into victorious conflict with their traditional enemies, the Iroquois. Later that loyal servant of the French king, the Marquis de Vaudreuil, began the construction of the fort there at the most strategic point upon Lake Champlain. A mighty task it was. It took two thousand men nearly three years to build the fortress, staunchly, with thick walls of the native stone. Vaudreuil called it Fort Carillon. But the French were to be fated not to hold it more than one single year. Sir Jeffrey Amherst, loyal servant of the British king, took it, after three days of hard fighting, raised his flag above and began its immediate reconstruction. The French, leaving rather hastily, wrecked it at their going.

From 1759 to 1780 it was a British fortress, and an important one. Yet once in that time the ensign of a new-born nation flew valiantly over it. That was the time (May 10, 1775) that Ethan Allen and Benedict Arnold and the Green Mountain Boys made their unforgettable and successful sortie against it and in so doing acquired immortality. The fact that the British were able, two years later, to recapture it did not soil the glamor of their victory, particularly as it was to be short-lived victory indeed for the soldiers of the English king. After an unsuccessful attempt by the Americans to recover it, the British garrison finally marched out. Thereafter it never again was a military post. The British took away all guns and munitions, stripped it thoroughly. The years swept past and the proud old fort fell into ruin. Fire attacked it and burned away its roofs and other wooden parts. Even the thick stone walls could not stand inviolate against marauders who found it easier to steal than to cut new stones for their needs. Then, a quarter of a century ago, the restored fort blossomed forth again, with President William H. Taft, Governors Hughes of New York and Prouty of Vermont and the French and British ambassadors present to assist at its formal reincarnation.

Forts Frederick and Crown Point (the former a French fortress and preceding its British successor by about a quarter of a century) have had no fairy godfathers to bring them slowly back to pristine glory. But the British fortification at Crown Point (even larger than Ticonderoga) has had its ruins carefully manicured and at least put into decent order; while it now is planned to restore the French Fort Frederick (a timber fortification). Their grounds form still another state park and are freely open at all times; even camping facilities are attached. Half a dollar is charged for admission to Fort Ticonderoga, and it is well worth it; if for nothing else than to stand upon its ancient ramparts and gaze down the sweep of Samuel Champlain's lake toward the south and the mountains that there rise so sharply up from its waters. If you seriously object to that fifty-cent expenditure, you can go into the handsome house of the New York State Historical Association in the near-by village of Ticonderoga and there get your fill of history. But you had better spend that half-dollar over at the fort. That is only about the price of a "movie," and no movie has ever been compounded with one-half the interest.

Of the entire eastern district of the North Country, as you go up into it from Troy or Albany, the three outstanding towns are Glens Falls, Plattsburg and Saratoga Springs. Let us consider the first two of these for a brief moment. They have very little to yield in charm or beauty to towns in any other portion of the state.

If you drive north from Troy or Albany, it is at Glens Falls that first you begin to get the real feeling of the North Country. . . . Northern trees . . . pine and cedar and tamarack intermingling with the maple . . . elms shading town streets . . . swift-flowing, coffee-colored rivers . . . the scent of fresh-cut wood. In Glens Falls the girls in the hotel have black hair and eyes, dark complexions. They betray their French-Canadian blood.

This becomes more marked when you get to neat old Plattsburg, twenty-five miles from the Canada line. There and roundabout are many so-called "French churches," Catholic in faith and generally bearing some French title of distinction; Our Lady of Victory seems to be a favorite one. Formerly these churches were French in fact as well as in name; very French indeed, with most of their services held in that language. In recent years the situation has reversed itself. Few of them now have more than one Mass a Sunday in French. Most of the children speak English. Even the older folk understand English. Immigration from Canada has been shut off pretty tightly of late, but the French-Canadians are a prolific folk, and despite this legal restriction, their congregations show a continuous, steady growth.

There has been little change in Plattsburg (county-seat of Clinton) in recent years, save the erection of the splendid battle monument, as well as one to Samuel de Champlain, and the completion of a fine City Hall. Glens Falls, on the contrary, has changed, mightily, within the past quarter century. The Glens Falls that I knew, rather intimately, some thirty years ago still was dominated by the men (or their sons) who had made their money out of the forests, either through lumbering, wood-working, pulp or paper. A good deal of money had been made that way. The town showed it. There were big, handsome houses, set in broad lawns, plenty of fine horses, good clothes, good living. I recall one handsome woman, wife of one of the richest and finest of the paper mill men, who dressed herself in gay pink décolletté and drove a team of glossy blacks hitched to one of the yellow buckboards which were made in Glens Falls and of which the town was exceedingly proud. The lady had a pink ribbon on the handle of her whip. She was born of the North Country, and to no small extent was she quite typical of it.

The paper mill industry has hung on rather better at Glens Falls than at Watertown. It exists on timber brought from far-off Russia, by ocean and river to Albany and canal to Glens Falls.

A more distinctive industry, by far, of the easterly edge of the North Country is that of iron. It is more than 130 years since first they began taking ore out of Essex County, melting it into pig iron, in crude stone furnaces, most of which still remain—many in ruins. That was 1803 and the initial place was the Cheever Mine, near Port Henry. There was an early mine and furnace at John Brown's, North Elba. Terrible transport over unspeakable roads doomed it. Port Henry, being on the very rim of Lake Champlain, had good transport, and soon it became the chief center of the industry in New York. It has had, at one time or another, not less than eight blast furnaces, twenty forges, three rolling-mills and two foundries. Its ore went down to Troy to make the plates for John Ericsson's *Monitor* in the Civil War and the first steel rails in the United States. Production was at its height in the 'sixties. Lake Champlain's black magnetic ore was in Pittsburgh long before the Lake Superior red ore, which by reasons of its cheap methods of mining was to vanquish it; yet never completely. The New York ore is known to the metallurgical world as the finest iron ever developed, and the most adaptable, and in recent prosperous years the Port Henry furnaces have turned out not less than two hundred and fifty thousand tons of it annually. Even in these duller ones they still are used, for a portion of the year at least, and continuous employment is being resumed in the near-by mines. Moreover the increasing cost of production out at the Messaba Range now is benefitting the New York State ores. They are beginning to come into their own once again. There can be no industrial strength for any territory to be compared with the development of its own resources. It has taken some of our York State towns quite a time to discover this simple fact.

And after all of this, Saratoga.

No one knows when men first began to go to the springs. Certain it is that the Indians discovered them, many years before the first white man came, and reveled in their curative properties.

There are several hundred springs, all within a short radius, and apparently they are the only natural carbonic springs east of the Rockies. This, and their variety, have tended to add greatly to their popularity. The white man was not slow in adapting their beneficial properties to himself. Before the Revolution was entirely over, one Norton had an "inn"—more of a log hut it was—in which he entertained travelers, at remarkably low cost. Fifty years later Saratoga had emblazoned itself as one of the great tourist centers of the land. From every corner, folk flocked to it. Large hotels (fine hotels for that day and generation) sprang up. Almost the earliest railroad in New York State found its way to it. Saratoga was the rage.

There is plenty of record of the popularity of the place. The guide-books of that earlier day paid much attention to it. In 1841 Faxon & Read, of Buffalo, printed a handbook for travelers, written by S. de Veaux, which gives much space to a suggested "Jaunt to Saratoga." De Veaux is rather meticulous with his details. At the very outset he writes:

In selecting a house it is better to depend upon the advertisement of the proprietor in the columns of some respectable newspaper, than the irresponsible recommendation of runners or of anonymous bills thrust into cars and stages. These things should never be depended upon. . . .

Having brought his traveler thus into the fascinating spa, de Veaux suggests that after ablutions, dressing, refreshments and the like, "if in health" they go to the fountains at once. Generally Congress Spring is chosen first of all. He adds:

. . . A lad is usually in waiting at the spring—with a staff, at the end of which is a small metallic frame which hold three half-pint tumblers; he dips in the fountain and raises the sparkling waters, and presents them round to those who come to drink. No pay is asked, though a slight acknowledgment is customary. . . .

De Veaux explains the various springs and the curative properties of each at length, with many analyses, and even is generous enough to include the waters of the near-by village of Ballston Spa within his small volume. He then devotes himself to the village of Saratoga; and says that "it is, for its situation, suitably laid out; a part is compactly built; and many handsome buildings and seats are observed around"—an observation which is even more true today than when Saratoga Springs first was incorporated, more than a century ago.

De Veaux does not neglect the amusements of the town, of which there were many and varied. The Recreative Garden had three bowling alleys, one of them "reserved for the exclusive use of the ladies." Covent Garden had rustic huts and summer houses and shady bowers, also platforms of flying horses, upon which riders were "whirled around" quite rapidly. But de Veaux reserved his greatest approbation for the Circular Railroad. This line, in Congress Park, was one-eighth of a mile in circumference, double-tracked and provided with two cars, each resembling the body of a light gig, one seat for a lady, the other for a gentleman. The gentleman's legs enacted the rôle of locomotive.

. . . With much ease the gentlemen gives power to the movement, and when both cars are flying round with the velocity of the wind, and passing each other as feathered arrows, a thousand fashionable promenaders, chatting and laughing, fill up the ground: the scene is truly joyous and animating. . . .

Three years before de Veaux, William Bartlett had written of Saratoga and its hotels in his *American Scenery,* saying:

Congress Hall has for years held the palm of fashion among the rival hotels of Saratoga. It is an immense wooden caravanserai, with no pretensions to architecture. . . . The traveler passes from the magnificent promise of the outside to a chamber, ten feet by four, situated in a remote gallery, visited once a day by the "boots" and the chambermaid. His bed, chair and washstand resemble those articles as seen in penitentiaries. A bell rings at half past seven in the morning, at which every one who intends to breakfast must get up; another bell at eight to the call of which if he prefers hot omelette to cold, he must be punctual. Dinner and tea exact the same promptitude. . . . Tea is at six or half-

New York state is dotted with points of historical interest. The De Winot House, upper left, was one of Washington's headquarters; the Mabie Home, next to it, is the oldest residence in the Mohawk Valley (1680); below it is the Delaney Home at Plattsburgh, left center the Van Alstyn home at Canajoharie; the country house, lower left, is on John Brown's former farm at North Elba; next to it is the old church at Stone Arabia.

Nothing suggests the rich traditions of New York state more readily than its old houses. The old home near Claverack, in the upper left, the sumptuous one at Peermont, the Putnam County Court House at Carmel, pictured below it, or the Garret Smith residence at Peterboro are enduring examples of good taste. The Leeds Bridge near Catskill was built before the Revolution, as was the ancient house on the road to Albany, shown next to it.

past, and consists of cold meats, hot rolls, Indian cakes, all other kinds of cakes, all kinds of berries, pies, sweet-meats and jellies, coffee and tea. This is not a matter to be slighted after a fast of four hours; and home hurry beaux and belles from their abbreviated drives, with a loss of sentiment and sunset, and with profit to the keepers of stables who let their horses "by the afternoon." . . .

This, in 1838. Saratoga began growing more and more elegant, more and more sumptuous all the while, the hotels bigger, with more food and more drink upon their menu cards, the negro head-waiters more pompous all the while. . . . Great was Saratoga! Of course folk began to forget a bit about the springs, but no one seemed to worry about that. They were not the chief source of the town's profit. Dress and food and drink and amusement decidedly were. The little yellow trains staggered into the trainshed of that old depot, back of the United States Hotel, each baggage car a magnified Saratoga trunk, holding in turn hundreds of those homely hump-backed containers.

Folk came from far and near. Sharon and Richfield and Schooleys and Lebanon were forgotten; even that haughty Newport over on the Rhode Island shore was outdistanced. Southerners, in particular, loved Saratoga. . . . Then they ceased coming at all. There were rumors of war, war far to the south, and old friends lined up against the boys of Saratoga Springs arrayed in soldier blue. The war ended, but the Southerners did not come back. They were wounded —in body, in purse and in pride. But Saratoga took no account of that. A great fire or two raced down her Broadway, and she only laughed at the smoking ruins and built in their place the greatest hotels that the world ever had seen—huge affairs they were, with mansard roofs and vast piazzas, with pillars three stories in height along the fronts and, within, great courtyards with the elm trees that the bigger houses boasted. They had "cottages" four stories high, with great chandeliers, and a retinue of servants for each of them. That was the Saratoga of the 'seventies.

John Morrissey came along and built his gambling house, within a stone's throw of the pure waters of the Congress Spring; he also built the present Saratoga racetrack, which for sheer beauty never has been exceeded anywhere. The 'seventies gave way to the 'eighties and the 'eighties to the 'nineties, and Saratoga only increased in popularity. Long Branch lived—and died—and other competitors of earlier days became paralyzed or moribund. Not Saratoga—she laughed and grew fat.

John Morrissey became old and passed out of the picture. And Richard Canfield came to replace him, at the casino. Canfield made it a pretentious and magnificent place, beside which Morrissey's was as nothing. He had taste, that man Canfield. He had manners, affability; he was an ideal man to run a gambling house in Saratoga—or anywhere else. He scoured Europe for good paintings and good sculptures. He employed many architects and decorators and landscape gardeners. And the result was a modern fairyland. He tore down Morrissey's old kitchen and replaced it with a restaurant such as America had not seen before. For the gambling room, he had woven a great carpet-rug, in one piece, thirty-two feet by sixty-seven.

You still can see that lofty room with its carpets, its mirrors and its chandeliers, low-hung to better light the faro tables in the center. But the faro tables, the croupiers and the players are all gone. The sweet old room is like an ancient belle, bending archly to wave her faded fan toward you. They came of a night thirty years ago and closed the place and smashed its gambling devices and ruined Canfield. But you never can tell about men of that sort. They are not easily licked. Politics is a curious thing; and when politics and reform begin to go hand-in-hand you have a skittish and generally unmanageable team.

Ambitious plans are afoot for the future of Saratoga Springs. The state, which has helped about everything else in sight, finally has come to the aid of the resort, which was getting in a bad way. Its wave of virtue a quarter of a century ago did it no commercial good. Moreover the precious natural carbonic gases of its many natural springs were being taken away in all directions, for the manufacture of "soda-pop" and other vicious drinks. Saratoga was being robbed, right and left, and to no good purposes.

So it was that in a great park just to the south of the village the state began buying the springs and setting up new bath houses and therapeutical establishments of wide variety. Commissions went to Europe and studied the great spas over there. And finally, a huge single unit, carefully planned in all its details, was devised, and this it was that was opened to the public in the past summer. In all, some eight millions of dollars have been expended in the reincarnation of the Saratoga Springs. Started as one of the state's minor extravagances it now bids fair to become a major one; but perhaps there is none more worth while.

Up until this latest development, the state of New York, which has done many things in the name of the public weal, had not before ventured into the hotel business. Yet here *was* a problem. The projectors of the newest development of the spa faced the fact that while they were creating one of the most wonderful bathing establishments in all the world, Saratoga still had its seventy-year-old hotels. These houses, generally very well run, but terribly handicapped by their venerability, are, the larger of them, only open from six to eight weeks out of the year—a real handicap for a place seeking to be a genuine "cure." In August of each year, Saratoga still puts on its best clothes and its best manners. That is the month for racing, and Union Avenue, which leads from the village out to the handsome track, then has again more than a semblance of the gayety of other years, with sleek and shiny motors replacing the smart traps and victorias of the earlier era. The village becomes genuinely aristocratic. Bar Harbor and Newport and Southampton are dull in comparison, and smart folk are glad to get away from them and hie themselves for a few weeks to a place where there is not only the best that racing has to offer, but plenty of other diversions, such as the Brook Club, which is to Saratoga as the Beach Club is to Palm Beach.

The problem now is to bring folk to Saratoga the other eleven months of the year. Until it develops at least one or two large modern hotels, it cannot hope for this desideratum, despite the attested medical value of its cure. The state's new hotel, the *Gideon Putnam* (named after an early Saratoga tavern-keeper, who kept an inn on the site of the present Grand Union Hotel) is beautifully designed and located, well furnished, and very charming in every way. But it is comparatively small and designed primarily for the accommodation of those who are seeking to take the cure in a thorough and orderly way. It is in the center of the new development, a mile away from the heart of the town. Around it are the truly magnificent group of modern structures for the treatment and recreation of those who come to Saratoga, as well as a model bottling works. All this is set in a great and gardenlike park that is a mile square. There are pools; golf links, skillfully adjusted for the use of folk with weakish hearts; and a variety of bathing arrangements, some of these very fine and decidedly *de luxe;* with a great *kurhaus* or drinking hall as the central feature of it all.

In the side of this great hall is set a small gallery for the musicians. Concerts at various times of day are to be a feature of the new arrangement. Saratoga, like Carlsbad or Weisbaden, must have really superb orchestras, drama, operas and perhaps open casinos as well to achieve a complete success. Here comes the rub. The state which found it rather difficult to enter the hotel business would find it even more difficult to go into the opera and casino ones. There is the crux of the Saratoga problem. And until it is solved, the lovely spa will have to continue at its present pace.

Troy, to me, is the least bit reminiscent of Elmira, except for its closely built streets, as against the open lawns of the Southern Tier city. Troy is also a bit of a Cinderella. Always she has sat in the shadow of Albany, six miles away, and has been quite overshadowed. Yet her own beginnings are in the best tradition of the Hudson River Dutch. When they progressed, Troy progressed. At the extreme head of natural navigation upon the Big River, she finally succeeded in bridging it, some years before Albany. But she has never held any aspirations to becoming an ocean port. There was a time, in the 'seventies, when she did hold high hopes of becoming a great railroad center. They finally succeeded in boring the Hoosac Tunnel, a few miles to the east of her, and Troy found herself the west terminus of a considerably shorter route to Boston and one of easier grades, than the historic railroad from Albany. But the Boston & Albany intersected many important towns, industrially and otherwise, as it made its way across Massachusetts, while the Fitchburg had very few indeed. And, some years later, the Fitchburg (now a part of the Boston & Maine) was extended through to important western connections at Rotterdam Junction, in the valley of the Mohawk, so that Troy ceased to be of very much importance to it.

I well remember the old Troy depot. A busy place it was, and an imposing one, with its great vaulted trainshed and, running alongside, the passenger house with the tall clock tower. Trains ran out from it in all directions—through ones up from New York and off to Saratoga and Vermont and Montreal; trains to Williamstown and Boston; lots of local trains for Schenectady and for near-by Albany; these last ran every thirty minutes, on each side of the river. The trains came out of the tunnel and threaded themselves right through the heart of Troy in every direction—a busy and confusing affair it was.

Now it is about all gone. The picturesque old Troy depot has disappeared, replaced long since by a far handsomer modern one. A good many of the through trains seem to have forgotten Troy by this time; there are none of any sort to Schenectady any more, and only a few locals down the river to Albany. Even the fine system of interurban electrics that formerly reached out from Troy in every direction is now entirely gone.

Troy once held high hopes industrially as well. She started in, chest out, head high, to be a center for the manufacture of iron and steel products. The first Bessemer steel to be rolled in America came out of her forges. Already we have referred to Henry Burden, that canny Scot, who came to this country more than a century ago to make a fortune, and made it. Burden arrived first at Albany, but not long after he went over to Troy and there got a job in the old Troy Iron & Nail Factory. Within twenty years he owned the plant; and he had made it the largest of its sort in all the world. He was inventor as well as manufacturer, and Henry Burden & Sons (as the iron and nail works had been renamed) was a dominant affair. Troy was well on her way toward becoming a Pittsburgh; the upper waters of the navigable Hudson would rival the upper Ohio in smoke and murkiness.

But somehow Troy failed to be a Pittsburgh. She was too far from raw iron supply; more important, much too far from cheap fuel. The balance between westbound bituminous and eastbound red ore—that made transportation upon the upper Great Lakes the most efficient and cheapest in the world and, incidentally, made the modern Pittsburgh what she is—was denied Troy. And so the Burden Iron Works, after nearly a century of achievement finally gave up. But the smart Irishmen that they brought over to work within those works remained in Troy; their descendants still remain, and dominate its life.

There stands one vivid souvenir of Henry Burden—the mammoth waterwheel.

If you ask the modern Trojan the way to the Burden waterwheel, you are apt to find him just the least bit perplexed. It is the older folk of the town to whom it is sharp memory, who can direct you to it, or at least to what is left of it. Yet the day was, and it was not so very long ago, when folk came from a long distance to see Troy and Henry Burden's great mechanical achievement.

He had set his works down in that deep gully leading into the Hudson, known as Wynant Kill. He had a seventy-foot head of water, very plentiful it was, and five swiftly turning wheels to furnish his power, when the idea of the "Niagara of Waterwheels" (as Troy used to love to call it) first came to him. As was his way always, he suited action to thought, and in 1838 he built the big wheel—sixty feet in diameter and twelve feet in width—and it was all fabricated of wood, save the 264 iron rods which acted as its spokes. It turned at a furious rate and generated about twelve hundred horsepower. For forty-five long years Henry Burden's "Niagara" continued to spin its efficient way (with the exception of a few months in 1851, when he took it down and completely rebuilt it), and then its work was done. There was a new plant down by the very edge of the river, and it was steam-driven. The old wheel then was retained, solely as a curiosity. The Burdens were proud of it and for years they kept it, as a sort of memorial to the first of the clan. In recent years it has fallen into disrepair, but it is hoped that some day some one will restore it. Of late, far less interesting things in York State have been restored.

With its steel-making hopes extinguished, Troy still had one very important industry left to it. For a good many years now, it has been making men's shirts and collars. This last device was invented there. According to an authenticated tradition, the collar was devised in a rather humble house in old Troy; the man of the house had complained that he must change his shirt too often, merely because its collar became soiled. His smart wife caught the idea, took some linen and an old shirt and—presto!—the collar was invented and Troy given still another status, and one bound to be long-lived in the industrial world. The detachable collar has become a veritable symbol of its prosperity. Troy makes four-fifths of those worn in America and a good proportion of those worn in other lands as well. One of the factories boasts a museum in which one may see collars once worn (and autographed) by Theodore Roosevelt, Ramsay MacDonald, Woodrow Wilson and Clemenceau. The town is adept in the manufacture of shirts, although in recent years this particular industry has lapped over into Glens Falls and other surrounding places.

Where Troy is more reminiscent of Elmira than in any other way is in the fact that she, too, has made monumental contributions to education in America. Elmira had the first woman's college (incidentally, opened for a short time in Auburn) but Troy had the first school for girls; and that great woman, Emma Willard, ran it and ran it well. It still carries on in a group of splendid new buildings on a hilltop, overlooking the city. The former buildings of the Emma Willard school down in the heart of the town, now form the Russell Sage College, devoted to the slightly higher education of women and already attaining the rank of a college.

But Troy's larger contribution to the cause of education was an even greater thing than the work of Emma Willard—a thing to be ranked with the foundation of Harvard College, itself. This was the real beginning, more than a century ago in one of her older houses, of technical education in the United States. The Rensselaer Polytechnic Institute was founded in 1824, and it has given Troy an even greater worldwide fame than ever her collars gave—and that is saying much.

If you had moved around New York State anywhere during the first third of the past century, you hardly could have avoided running into Stephen Van Rensselaer, the last of the great patroons of Albany; and the greatest. Like Alexander Hamilton, he also married one of the daughters of the famous Philip Schuyler, of Albany. Those Schuyler girls were as famed in their day as were the Langhorne sisters, of Virginia, about a hundred years later. The man who got one of them was much envied. But Stephen Van Rensselaer was a bit fêted and courted himself. Born in 1769, he was educated at Albany schools and the old Kingston Academy. Then he went to Princeton, but was removed from it hurriedly—because the British troops were unpleasantly near and he was deemed too rich a prize of war—and sent to Harvard. He returned to Albany and looked after all his properties, with great vigor and effectiveness. We saw him in the war of 1812 upon the Niagara Frontier, and even if his career there was not entirely covered with glory, he had a good alibi in the fact that the troops he commanded were raw militia and inclined to be a bit finicky in raising the point that their enlistment papers did not specifically state that they would have to fight on foreign territory. He rode on the *Seneca Chief* on its trip which inaugurated the Erie Canal in 1827, and four years later he was a passenger in the first railroad train in the state, hauled by the diminutive *De Witt Clinton,* from Albany to Schenectady.

You really would have been astonished if Stephen Van Rensselaer had permitted himself to miss any of these history-making events. No President of the United States in later years ever traveled more persistently—or effectively—than the last of the Albany patroons.

Such a man might have been expected to look with kindly eye upon the beginning efforts of education in a still-new country, to give it such assistance as he could. At any rate he decided upon starting a school for boys—"a practical school" was the way he phrased it—and for some reason he seized upon Troy, which was not as well-provided with schools as his native Albany, as the locale for the experiment.

Remember how Ezra Cornell and Andrew D. White worked hand in hand, in later years, in the establishment of the immensely successful university at Ithaca; Cornell, the financier, and White, the dreamer? The same thing happened at Troy, forty years earlier. Stephen Van Rensselaer was handy and generous with the finances, and Amos Eaton was the dreamer.

Amos Eaton has been dead over ninety years now, and still his spirit hovers over Rensselaer Polytechnic Institute. They speak of him, almost as if he were about to step out of the nearest classroom door, as if that was his hat or coat upon the peg. Eaton was a student, a scientist and an author—well-famed in all of these. But, better than all else, he had the God-given ability to translate his knowledge to the benefit of others; to make himself a successful and an effective teacher; to give the vital spark of life to a struggling young institution and make it of far greater importance and value than its founders had ever even imagined possible. That was the thing that Amos Eaton did.

After all, Rensselaer Polytechnic—they merely called it Rensselaer School at the beginning—had started upon a rather vague idea of Stephen Van Rensselaer's. He had wanted taught "practical science" (whatever that might really mean) for the benefit of boys upon the farms or in the factories that just then were beginning to spring up across America. He had brought in Amos Eaton (already in the fiftieth year of his life) to work out the plan, as head of the faculty; (a Presbyterian minister from over in Lansingburgh was the first president of the new school). Eaton gave his task hard study. There were no precedents to follow. The previous year a school had been established down in Gardiner, Maine, to give instruction "in the chemistry of agriculture and the arts," but apparently its purpose had not been well defined or carried out, for within the decade it was dead.

Eaton ignored it. With twenty-five boys enrolling themselves at the outset, the future course of Renesselaer School had to be carefully charted. Gradually some things were eliminated (chiefly the agricultural ones; apparently times were not ripe for colleges of scientific agriculture), and the school began to gain force, to develop ideas. In 1827 Eaton put one of his ideas into practice. He liked laboratories, and under his guidance, the Rensselaer School was the first in all America to install them for the use of each individual student. A real innovation, this was; and soon to be followed with another—of far different sort:

With Van Rensselaer's active help, Eaton organized a class of a dozen or more young men of the school and despatched them upon an entire "flotilla" of canalboats, the entire length of the Erie, and back, with stops at Trenton Falls and Niagara and Lockport—an educational jaunt. The trip was a good deal of a success. The idea is being used pretty much by American schools right up to this day.

In 1829, just five years after it had started, something else happened to Stephen Van Rensselaer's unusual school for boys in Old Bank Place, Troy. It had a new president; none other than our old friend, Dr. Eliphalet Nott, of Union College, Schenectady—yes, that same Eliphalet Nott, who always was getting into things and getting out of them, generally with overwhelming success. Dr. Nott came over from Schenectady to Troy (just fourteen miles) each week, and just as a side-job, he ran the Rensselaer School, and ran it successfully. He stood by it as president for sixteen years, until he had seen it well upon its way. He found a new home for it and increased its size and its scope and, after the death of its founders, carried on with it. The Civil War burst upon the land, and because of that, Rensselaer Polytechnic (as it now was called) had a hard time of it. Moreover its home had been burned to the ground in the great fire that nearly wiped Troy out of existence (in 1862), and gave the town for years afterwards one of the best volunteer fire departments in all the land. Yet before that war was over, Rensselaer Polytechnic Institute—almost every one knows it now as R.P.I.—was housed in a much finer building, which lasted for exactly forty years, when it, too, was destroyed by fire.

If you will look up almost any one of the closely built crosstown streets of downtown Troy, you will see R.P.I. standing above you on the high crest of the hill. Only you probably will mistake the cluster of high spires of the neighboring Catholic convent for the technical school, which has no religious pretenses whatsoever. It houses and feeds the sixteen hundred young men who come to it from every part of the country (from almost every corner of the world, in fact), but aside from that it is little more than a giant workshop, with a library and classrooms as mere accessories. Yet the list of R.P.I. graduates is a truly astounding one. Its development started in a day when there were canals but hardly a mile of railroad track in the United States, and not one locomotive, no bridges of iron or steel, no electric lights or dynamos or motors, no internal-combustion engines, no photographic cameras, no telegraph, no telephone—when the automobile, the airplane, the wireless were all dreams of a vague and a fantastic future. Within its busy lifetime, Rensselaer Polytechnic has seen all these marvels of applied science, and many others, come into practical and popular use. More than this, it more than once has led the way in their development and perfection. Stephen Van Rensselaer, the last patroon of Albany, and Amos Eaton, the educator, wrought better than they ever were to know.

It seemed rather hard to go by the old building of the Troy *Times* just the other day and to realize that no longer was smart Editor Francis alive to guide its destinies; that no longer was there any

Troy *Times* in fact. It went out of existence within the past year or so. There has been for a quarter of a century or more a heavy death list in upstate journalism, as well as in that of metropolitan New York. I remember when it began, more than forty years ago; the late James J. Belden of Syracuse bought the historic old *Standard* and *Courier* of that town, and the new morning *Post,* and merged them into the present *Post-Standard,* which has had marked success and with much thoroughness each morning covers all Central and Northern New York. It was at about that time that another historic paper, the Utica *Morning Herald,* snuffed out the candle that had burned brightly for so many years. The Albany *Argus* once was a dominating paper in its field. It, too, is now gone. And so is the Binghamton morning *Republican.* The Buffalo *Express* and *Courier* merged into the *Courier-Express* some years ago; and upon the death of its brilliant editor, Louis M. Antisdale, a decade past, the Rochester *Herald* disappeared. Before it, had gone one of the best edited evening papers of the state, the Rochester *Post-Express.* Joseph O'Connor made the *Post-Express* famous, the whole state over.

The tremendous growth of the powerful morning newspapers of New York City, which now are able to reach even Buffalo for breakfast with their "bulldog" editions, is largely responsible for the heavy decimation among the upstate papers, particularly the morning ones.

The evening prints have hung on pretty well. The Kingston *Freeman* long ago changed from morning to evening publication. A goodly number of them are in one chain, with its headquarters in Rochester, and the proprietor of that chain, Frank E. Gannett, is a man of idealism and generally liberal ideas, so their prosperity is a deserved one. The further one gets away from the metropolis, the stronger the individual newspapers; as, for instance, the Watertown *Daily Times,* which has the remarkable distinction of having an evening circulation equal to the population of the sizable town in which it is printed. (The only other newspapers that I know that can claim such distinction are those of Des Moines, Iowa and

Josephus Daniels' *Observer,* down in Raleigh, North Carolina.) The Watertown *Times* has come out each evening for three-quarters of a century now, and it is a recognized and powerful institution all through the North Country. The *Times* covers world news, as well as merely local and national, with a remarkable precision for a newspaper in so small a city, and every Watertownian is excessively proud of it. There are other good newspapers across the state—very good papers. The Ithaca *Journal* is one hundred and twenty years old. Another historic sheet is the Oswego *Palladium,* whose editor, the late Clark Morrison, stuck to that job for over sixty years. The Syracuse *Herald* is not a very old paper, but its editor, John B. Howe, has been for forty years an outstanding force in upstate journalism. The weekly journalism of the state never has been permitted to die. Small weekly papers such as the Dansville *Advertiser,* the Lyons *Republican,* the Cape Vincent *Eagle* and the Canton *Commercial Advertiser* have subscribers who have been carried upon their books for upwards of half a century. We New Yorkers do not, ordinarily, die young.

CHAPTER XII

The Long Island

LONG ISLAND is like a cocktail; one part sour, two parts sweet, three parts strong. The sour part is, pretty nearly all of it, west of Jamaica. East of that point, the Long Island is pretty sweet; and almost always strong enough, at any time or place. It is a curious sort of a terrain, this 110-mile-long appendage to the state of empire—an island, supplemented by a group of islands which reach far out into the Atlantic. The big island is anywhere from ten to fifteen miles in width. Its north shore is deeply indented, hilly, rises somewhat abruptly from the waters of Long Island Sound. Some of the hills are rather steep and one of them rises more than four hundred feet above sea level. The rest of Long Island is flat, save for the picturesque Shinnecock Hills toward the extreme end of its south fork. The south shore, especially, is monotonously level, most of it bordered by the Great South Bay and its tributaries. And outside the Great South Bay is that sandy, treeless spit of land, which, with a few interruptions and openings, runs, under one name or another, all the way from Rockaway Point at the west to Southampton, nearly a hundred miles away, at the east.

The interior of the island—east of Farmingdale, at least—is sandy land with scrub trees and with few villages—thinly populated—

and is still a refuge for a quantity of small game. Both the shores are well populated, however; the south more thickly than the north; while the extreme westerly end of the island becomes the Big City—Brooklyn and Queens between them making the two most populous boroughs of Greater New York. There also is density of population all through Nassau County. The single railroad system, which with its main stems and branches serves Long Island from one end to the other, is a very busy railroad. It carries more than forty million passengers in and out of Manhattan each year. In the summer months more than eight hundred trains a day pass in and out of its busiest interchange station, at Jamaica.

There are few rivers on Long Island and hardly any lakes—the islanders like to designate these last as "ponds." But there is plenty of water almost everywhere. For sailing or bathing or fishing there are great bays and the Sound—to say nothing of the open ocean itself—and for potable water, innumerable springs bubbling up almost everywhere in the sandy soil, making the entire terrain arable and livable. It has been said that Long Island's remarkable supply of pure water really comes through the solid rock for miles under the Sound, all the way from Connecticut, to find its way up and out through the sand of the island itself; a sort of mighty filter, it is. Things grow easily upon the Long Island. Where the soil is not too sandy, and there are many places where it is not, there are fine trees, in vast variety. And everywhere there are flowers. England in May is not more luxuriantly floral than the south and east parts of our island the entire summer long. Nowhere else on the Atlantic seaboard do climbing roses grow as they grow in the Hamptons.

Let us see the island for ourselves. We choose to do it, rather intimately. For that reason we decline to use the red trains of the Long Island Railroad, which whisk you the whole length of the island in almost no time at all, and decide to use *Dolly Varden* once again upon the highroad.

Dolly Varden is the small, powerful car that, in the spring and early summer of 1935, carried me over nine thousand miles of the pathway of empire, for the making of this book. Perhaps as a railroad man—one whose affection for the Iron Horse was born with him and which has never deserted him—I should not have made this confession. But the fact remains that while, for me, no other method of transport can ever quite supersede the railroad, it is impossible nowadays to make an intensive study of New York or any other state, save by some form of motor transportation. Many of the side lines now are being abandoned, and the passenger trains on the rest generally are few and far between. . . . So *Dolly Varden* becomes my Five-Fifteen. She is a dependable little train and she generally starts and stops just when and where I want her to. Which is more than trains do.

We decided—*Dolly* and I—to make a thorough job of this exploration of Long Island. She had never been out upon it, and I, not east of Port Jefferson (and that is hardly halfway) for nearly twenty years. We dug ourselves into road-maps, guide-books and histories. And after a deal of cogitation decided upon the North Shore for the outgoing trip; in slight preference to the South. It does possess a little more of the romantic interest, and the scenic. The hard, straight roads through the center of the Island are hopeless, unless you are speed-mad and hell-bent to be in Riverhead for lunch. *Dolly* and I had no such ambitions. We wanted what we had had upstate, narrow roads and twisting roads, with little traffic and no signs and hot-dog stands; just trees and occasional vistas of open waters, with the sunlight dancing on them and white-sailed boats maneuvering in a stiffish wind. And we found them.

In almost every other direction egress is easier from the Big City than toward Long Island. When they built the great Queensborough Bridge (a little over twenty years ago), they wondered if ever there would be enough highway traffic really to justify it. So they put a lot of railroad tracks (for rapid transit service) upon its two decks. Since then they have taken up some of the tracks to make additional roadways, and even now there are not nearly enough.

One of the finest gothic churches in America is the Protestant Episcopal Cathedral of the Incarnation at Garden City, Long Island.

The stone lighthouse at Montauk Point is strategically located to guide ships in trouble. Its light, 168 feet above sea-level, is visible for nineteen miles.

Long Island's Jones Beach is only a few years old but it is internationally known as the largest and most attractive beach in the world. The buildings on the beach, which include restaurants, lounging

It is quite a trick to handle traffic on Queensborough Bridge. There are three other highway bridges across the East River (and another one—the Triborough—is being built), but they all land you in Brooklyn, which has charms of its own but certainly offers little to a motorist trying to hasten out upon Long Island. The Borough of Queens is bad enough. Queens has some attractive corners, and they are very attractive, such as Flushing and Forest Hills, for instance. But most of it is pretty dreary. After you have managed to disentangle yourself from the mighty traffic of the great bridge, you drive for miles over a broad boulevard, magnificent in scope, but lacking much in realization, and in pavement. Everything seems so unfinished. Perhaps some fine day they will get around to finishing it; and there will then be better entrances to the island of Manhattan, both by way of that new Triborough Bridge and the Midtown Tunnel, that is to slip, like the one for the railroad tracks, far, far under the East River.

Suddenly, you make a turn to the left (if you have properly studied your road-maps) and swing into a broad parkway of real beauty, with trim lawns and abundant foliage. It is called the Grand Central Parkway, which is a pretty grandiloquent sort of a name, and it leads, at the city border, into the Northern State Parkway. Then it is that you begin to study the road-signs.

Roslyn.

Here it is. . . . Roslyn, 4 miles. . . . Roslyn, 3 miles. . . . Roslyn, 2 miles. . . . *Dolly* turns sharply upon her precious heels, and off we go from the pretentious highway into a side road of narrow girth and dubious riding quality. But it brings us to Roslyn; which is one of the centers of the social life of Long Island. For remember that the island for its entire length and at almost any time of year is a sort of haven for smart social New York; more so, of course, in summer. Locust Valley and Old Westbury and Glen Cove and Oyster Bay are, all of them, high spots for this sort of life. For its details you will have to look to any of the ultra-publications which specialize in this sort of thing. This expedition has little to do with any of it.

Dolly and I prefer to think of Roslyn as a sweet old waterside town, with memories of one William Cullen Bryant hanging rather heavily over it and a swell lunching place to be returned to at some future time—an ancient mill, hanging itself over the brackish waters of the inlet, and restored to a new phase of life, as a restaurant and tea-room. It was built in 1701, and you still can see the mill-stones, the grain-hoppers and the great wheel, the soundness of its heavy timber construction. And in a near-by park is a restoration of an old paper mill, said to have been the first built in New York State.

Roslyn is one of the string of fascinating old North Shore towns, which begins with Flushing (and its ancient Quaker meeting-house) and Port Washington and continues on through Oyster Bay and Huntington and Setauket, all the way to Southold and Greenport. Each of these has its own charms—Oyster Bay with Theodore Roosevelt's grave set high in its small local cemetery, a place of pious pilgrimage for thousands each year; Huntington, with its ancient church, white-spired, raising itself high above the town. Centerport, famed for its shore dinners; Smithtown and St. James, with racing and horsey traditions of almost every sort. Setauket has not one, but two, very old churches. The Presbyterian meeting-house is old enough, God knows, with more than a century behind its stout fabric, but it is a mere child when you compare it with the little chapel of Episcopalian faith, across the village green. That is the Caroline Church, and it has stood there, little changed, since first it opened its doors, in 1730. But Setauket that day already was three-quarters of a century old.

There is, perhaps, something of a sameness about these North Shore waterside towns. Most of them are situated at the heads of deep high-banked coves or inlets from the Sound, and theirs are rather busy local harbors, with fishing as their chief business excuse. Formerly there were steamboats from almost all of them right into New York, but now these are gone and only the well-patronized long-distance ferries across the Sound to Connecticut remain.

Beyond Port Jefferson the terrain becomes less rugged, and so less picturesque. The narrow, twisting North Country Road bends away from the shore and down toward Riverhead, joins the direct Jericho Turnpike, running down the backbone of the island, and together they come into the brisk county-seat of old Suffolk, which has been doing business as a county for two hundred and fifty years. Prior to that time Colonial Long Island was roughly split into several "ridings," a very loose form of government. But in 1683 all Long Island was divided into three counties—Kings and Queens and Suffolk. Of these, the last covered about half the total area. Kings County still exists as Brooklyn, and Queens as all the rest of Greater New York upon Long Island. Between the line of the Big City and old Suffolk is the comparatively new Nassau County (that part of Queens which was not taken into Greater New York), with its county-seat at Mineola—already well populated and very rich indeed.

If you take only a passing glance at your map of Long Island you will see at once that it bears a certain likeness to a great fish, whose head is close to Manhattan and the East River and whose mighty tail is divided into two huge fins, with the Great and Little Peconic Bays in between. Forks, the Long Islanders call these fins. The shorter and the least important is the north one, with Greenport almost at its end, although it continues another ten or twelve miles to Orient Point and the historic Plum Gut, passageway for vessels, ever since vessels first appeared in this part of the world.

The south fork, much longer, has at least three of the Hamptons, Montauk Point, and dozens of ancient windmills. And having a love for windmills only second to our thirst for covered bridges, *Dolly* and I decided that we would concentrate a bit upon it. There is a fine paved road from Riverhead to the South Country (or Merrick) Road, right to the Hampton Bays and Southampton, but we both decided *against* that. Too uninteresting. Then, too, we wanted at least a quick and passing glimpse at the north fork. And so we turned our noses from Riverhead out toward Jamesport and Mattituck and Cutchogue. There is a sort of melody in these old Long Island names, such as Amagansett and Quogue and Patchogue and Moriches and even little Yaphank. Ronkonkoma suggests something rollicking (it really is an uninteresting little inland lake upon which Maude Adams had a summer place for years). And as for Speonk, some years ago some fresh real estaters decided that Speonk was no name at all for a town, especially if you were going to try and sell lots and houses in it to unimaginative New Yorkers. And they moved the Post Office Department down at Washington to change the name to Remsenhurst, or something of that sort. This brought down upon them the everlasting wrath of the Long Islanders, who are rather sot in their ways and touchy upon things of this sort. The Postmaster-General was scared at the wrath of the Speonkers, and they had their old name back and have hugged it carefully to their bosoms ever since.

They think a good deal of their old-fashioned names, these Long Islanders. They just revel in such monnickers as Bread and Cheese Hollow, Divinity Hill, Fire Place, Good Ground, Hither Plains, Promised Land, Scuttle Hole and Wreck Lead. All of these are as distinctive in their way as the Indian ones—and more thought-provoking.

Greenport once aspired to a considerable distinction as a traffic hub. When the aspiring Long Island Railroad had been completed through to it (in 1844), it at once sought to make itself part of a direct through route between New York and Boston. The railroads on the north side of the Sound were having a hard time getting through Connecticut—the broad estuaries of the Thames and the Connecticut were not easy to bridge. But Norwich and then Stonington were comparatively simple to reach by the new railroad already completed down from Boston. It was not a great distance by steamboat across from Stonington to Greenport, then the link over the new railroad down the middle of Long Island to New York (or rather, Long Island City, just across the East River) and there you were! New York to Boston in ten hours, instead of eighteen.

But after three or four years the all-rail route between New York and Boston finally came into being, and the one down Long Island was abandoned, for through traffic at least. Greenport sank back into being a sleepy little harbor once again, with a small ferry across to the mainland, the occasional departure of a Sunday excursion for more distant Providence or Newport, and the busy little ferry across the channel to near-by Shelter Island.

It was to Shelter Island that *Dolly* and I turned our noses. It is a fairish expensive trip—not the lowest ferry tolls in the world— but a worth-while one. If you would like to know the island by its original name, try and remember Manhansack—ahagusha-wamock, which, being translated, reads, "Island sheltered by other islands." It brings you quickly into a distant past. For no part of the pathway of empire is more remote, either in its time or its geography, from the rest of the busy state than this at the eastern end of the Long Island. There is a group of little islands at the tail of the big one. And because Shelter Island is nearest at hand, we come to it the more readily.

Once, long years ago, it was known as Sylvesters Island; and that was when (in 1652) one Nathaniel Sylvester, member of a royalist family of England and expatriated, came to it with his bride, Grissell Brinley, and began to build a manor house on the water-surrounded tract that he had purchased, with his brother, for "sixteen hundred pounds of good Muscovada sugar." There the Sylvesters, generation after generation of them, lived through the long years. They were a kindly and hospitable folk, and when men and women of a strange new sect, the Quakers, were driven out of rigorous Massachusetts, they found refuge on the island of the Sylvesters. And that is one of the reasons why all of Long Island became so identified with the Quaker faith.

For the Quaker tinge of Long Island is a strong tinge indeed. It perhaps reached its height in the person of one Elias Hicks, born in Hempstead but a resident of Jericho from the time of his marriage until his death (in 1830, at the age of 81). Hicks became a preacher in the quiet, old-fashioned faith, and he was a powerful one. It is related of him that he traveled more than ten thousand miles in the United States and Canada, not only making many converts, but bringing about much reform in the life of ordinary folk. The Hicksites, as they were often called, continued to be a force in Long Island for many years thereafter. And there still are Quaker meeting houses left upon the Island.

To return for a final moment to the Sylvesters. In the course of a number of years they all died off. The first manor house long since had become entirely too small, and in 1737 Sylvester Brinley had built the second, which still stands, its broad front door guarded by two small brass cannon. The family of Sylvester became the family of Horsford, and the island took its present name. It still is largely the property of the Horsford family, who own the two ferries that link it to the "forks" of the larger island, and maintain a guiding hand in its affairs.

Gardiners Island is not nearly so easily reached; in fact you do not ordinarily go to it unless you are bidden. Lying a little way out to sea, it is a highly private principality, every one of whose acres has been in the possession of the Gardiner family almost since the white man first established himself in North America, and that, as far as Gardiners Island is concerned, was just three hundred years ago. The Jonathan Gardiner who died at East Hampton in August 1933, was the fourteenth successive owner of the estate; a record of unbroken ownership such as rarely is found in America, save perhaps in Mexico or in Peru. Its roomy manor house is not the original one, but it is two years older than the nation and is in a splendid state of preservation.

The entire island is but seven miles long, and from one to two in width (about three thousand acres all told), a rich preserve with fine dense woods and open rolling downs of green, and some sixty folk resident upon it, all of whom, save the keeper of the lighthouse at the north end of the island and his family, are servants or tenants of the proprietor, or members of his family. It is a world remote. Other worlds do not seem to trouble or to molest it these days. It stands alone. Its sovereignty is as absolute as that of some of the remarkable little islands off the southwest of England, miles away from the mainland but speaking the same language and adhering to many of the same customs.

Yet its past is filled with romance.

Lion Gardiner, a name to be reckoned with, was the first of its proprietors. He was a fighting man and of fighting blood. And in the days of his youth he crossed the Channel from his native England to fight in Holland for King Charles. In Holland he met and married a young woman, Mary Willemsen, of Waerden, and became, in his own words, "engineer and master of works of fortification in the legions of the Prince of Orange, in the Low Countries."

But Gardiner was not to be content to remain the rest of his days in peaceful Holland; that was not the way of fighting men. He became fired with tales of the New World far across the Western Ocean, and in 1635 he leaped at the opportunity to go to the new plantation of Connecticut and there, under the guidance of John Winthrop, the younger, to take root for himself. Under Governor Winthrop's direction, Lion Gardiner's skill built a "strong fort of hewn timber" at the mouth of the Connecticut River. This he called Saybrooke, and it was the first stronghold erected in New England outside of Boston.

Lion Gardiner had all the fighting those days that he wanted. He became skilled in Indian warfare, and after he had had his own large part in the vanquishing of the doughty Pequots he purchased from the Paumanocs, for "ten coats of trading cloath" their island of Manchonake, sixteen miles off at sea and three or four distant from the Long Island, or Nassau, as it was then known. This domain he at once christened Isle of Wight, after his own birthplace, but it was his own name that was destined to stick to the island. Gardiners Island it soon became, and Gardiners Island it has since remained.

Its remote position may have left it a world alone, but that was not always to be reckoned as an advantage. Isolation had its perils, particularly when pirates came along. In the days of the third lord of the manor, John Gardiner, this form of brigandage had come to large popularity. Twice pirate craft came to Gardiners Island, ransacked and sacked the place, and once they beat up the proprietor.

But that was as nothing compared with the renowned Captain William Kidd. In 1699, at the end of the three-year-cruise, when the English government had put a price upon his head, this renegade mariner sailed his sturdy sloop—six guns mounted—into John Gardiner's private harbor. Lord John went out in a small boat and called upon him. Kidd received him courteously but suggested a tribute of six sheep and a barrel of cider. Gardiner acceded to the demand. When it was all delivered, the boss pirate showed his pleasure by sending Bengal muslin to Mrs. Gardiner and giving pieces of gold to Gardiner's men. Then he sailed away, in the direction of Block Island, and the Gardiner family wished him a longish cruise.

But that was not the last of Captain Kidd.

In a little while he was back again, this time leaving a heavy metal chest and other property behind. John Gardiner was warned that Kidd would return for all of it, and if any of it were missing, his life and his son's would be demanded in payment. But Kidd never came back for his booty. He finally was captured, and the King's governor over at Boston was the man who demanded the treasure, which turned out to be a very considerable quantity of gold and precious stones and other goods of high value. The Gardiner family breathed more easily after Captain Kidd had been hanged in grim old Execution Dock, in London. There are endless tales of pirate treasure buried upon the quiet old island, but none of it ever has turned up. The most exciting thing that happened there after the Kidd episode was nearly eighty years later, when a British fleet came by and helped itself to food and other supplies accumulated there. But that was warfare, or what passed for it, and the Gardiners of that generation, loyal to the new nation, accepted it as such.

The Indians having been subjugated, and the first Lion Gardiner having gained their respect, and even friendship, he set about to live the life of a man of peace, establishing an off-shore fishery. In those days there were many whales roundabout, and Lion Gardiner made a prosperous business of it. But he also owned much land upon Long Island, and in his later years he was prone to return to that land more and more; in old East Hampton he now lived, and there in 1663, he died, at the age of sixty-four. He is supposed to be buried in the town's older cemetery, but no one seems to know exactly where. There are many other Gardiners buried in that ancient place; still more of them upon the Island. It is hardly more than half a dozen miles away from East Hampton, itself. You drive from the village down to a point, yclept Fire Place (in olden days they built fires there to summon the boat from the island), and that is where you embark for the short four-mile sail across to the ancient principality.

Sag Harbor is three or four miles from the Shelter Island ferry dock on the south fork of Long Island. In other days it was a brave, gay port, with its fine harbor dotted with whalers, its main street busy with their captains and their crews, three hundred men working at the docks, all the business of an enterprising and successful industry. Think of it, over a million dollars invested in it (in 1840); a million dollars worth of sperm and oil coming in, in a single season; over six thousand tons of fine whaling craft belonging to the port and sailing out from it, along with other water-borne traffic. Sag Harbor used to dream of the days when it might rival Providence, or even New York or Boston, in the magnitude of its tonnage.

It is well to dream dreams while the dreaming is good. If Sag Harbor ever had pleasure in that sort of thing, that pleasure now is gone; and so are the fine square-rigged ships. The last whaler was sold over twenty years ago. All that remains are the old houses, the curious white church of Egyptian architecture whose lofty spire looks for miles out to sea, its clock, long since stilled and dead, and the lazy, idle main street. That is the epic of Sag Harbor.

East Hampton is beautiful, very beautiful.

In these long pages I have written again and again of the beauties of the upstate New York towns—Cooperstown and Ithaca and Geneva, in particular. Each of these towns has the charm of site that combines the quality of deep lakes and high hills adjoining. There are no high hills at East Hampton, no lake, but the pounding Atlantic less than a mile distant, makes good substitute. And there is no main street in all York State quite comparable with the elm-shaded main street of this old Long Island town. For what other one possesses a small and delightful freshwater pond between the two ways of a single street, and an old-fashioned buryingground as well? And what other one is lined by three fine windmills?

For this is the windmill country of America. There must be several dozens of them still left, both on this tip of Long Island and on Gardiners and Shelter. Few of them are still doing duty, pumping or flouring. The sails are ripped off most of them, in some cases the wooden frames upon which the canvas was wont to be hung. But here they stand, vigorous reminders of a vigorous yesterday.

East Hampton and with her sisters, Southampton, Westhampton and the less conspicuous Bridgehampton, were for many years practically isolated from the rest of the island, the rest of the state, of the nation. When the railroad finally was put through to the tip of the south fork, they began to come into their own, to acquire a peculiar social prominence which never has been dimmed. Of the four, Southampton is the queen, socially at least. It never can have quite the beauty or the charm of the east village, but it long since established itself as one of the chief social centers of the entire land.

Southampton never has gone in for splurge or display. It prefers to leave that to Newport. It is serene, confident, in its established position in the proper order of things. It has the prestige of antiquity. Job Lane and all its other important thoroughfares bear upon their street-signs the years of their establishment, and they are all just after the middle of the seventeenth century. If a particular relic is sought, any townsman will direct you—any hackman drive you —straight to the old Sayre House, built in 1648, and for ten long generations handed down from father to son; or the old Pelletreau house, which Lord Erskine occupied as headquarters during the British occupation of the seaport town, in 1779. But Southampton, as I have just hinted, has never gone in heavily for things historical. It lives in the present, for things temporal, rather than in the past and things more nearly spiritual. And after all it has no shrine quite comparable with East Hampton's little cottage, with its attendant windmill, where once lived in boyhood John Howard Payne, and which is supposed to have been the inspiration of his "Home, Sweet Home." Now that is a shrine worth establishing.

But Southampton is a bit careless about shrines, too. I really think that she prefers her handsome estates, with shingled houses; her close-clipped lawns; her trim and verdant hedges; her abundant growing flowers; her general look of smartness; her main street lined, not with windmills, but with the branch shops of New York's aristocratic and exclusive stores. Her demesne reaches to Water Mill and Good Ground and Westhampton; each of these only the least bit less social and elegant.

Never before had I been beyond East Hampton on the island. On my last visit there, nearly twenty years ago, the road from Amagansett east was a miserable sort of straggling sandy lane, sometimes passable for good motor-cars, but never appealing, even to the most hardened motorist.

Now the picture is a different one: There is a fine concrete highway right up to the very tip of the island. After you have passed Amagansett, last of the historic villages, you drive for miles along a steadily narrowing neck of land, with the open water beginning to show itself upon either side. Much of it is now state park; officially the Hither Hills State Park, and a place of popular resort. Its beauty should make it such. You see more of the ocean than of the bay, and that is well. At one place you come to a high point of observation, draw up your car and look backward; there is mile upon mile of white sandy beach and rolling surf behind you. With the low treeless land around about it, it is reminiscent of stretches of the drive along the shore from Los Angeles down to San Diego.

And the town of Montauk, itself, is reminiscent of Southern California—in some of its less pleasant phases.

Poor old Montauk. It, too, has been a dreamer—and not a particularly successful one. Years ago when one Austin Corbin was in command of the fortunes of the then struggling Long Island Railroad, he did some dreaming on his own account. He drove out (horse and carriage) toward Montauk Point, and there—some five miles short of the extreme tip of Long Island—he found Fort Pond Bay, a small fishing village and a superb natural harbor.

Ergo, thought Corbin, here will be a future great passenger terminal for the city of New York. Another Liverpool or (English) Southampton, or Le Havre; more likely another Fishguard, such as was attempted in Great Britain just before the war and did not succeed very well. The great transatlantic ships, dreamed Corbin, will come to dock here at Montauk, and then my fast trains will carry their passengers right to the city of New York. Time and trouble—particularly time—will be saved. And he at once put his railroad through to the shore of the deep water harbor of Fort Pond Bay. But somehow the big ships never came to meet his trains. They seemed to be quite content with their New York piers. After all, if they were to stop at any point short of the Big City and tranship their passengers and mail to rail, why not Boston or Portland? These were still nearer Europe and already possessed of excellent port facilities. So the dream went the way of far too many dreams.

Another dreamer came, and he revived the idea, plus one of a superb resort city on the shores of Fort Pond Bay. Perhaps if Depression had not hit the land quite as hard as it did and at just that time, he might have made a success of it. As it is, there is an uncanny souvenir of the least lovely phase of Southern California out there, close to the far tip of the Empire State—skyscrapers, perish the thought, standing isolated and uncomfortable; a large theater (unused); an inn (closed); a number of very handsome dwellings, which appear to be very much in use; and a really lovely hotel, standing high upon an eminence and looking—in clear weather—out to sea.

We drove up to the hotel. There was little view that July afternoon. Back in the Big City, hardly more than a hundred miles away, it was stifling hot, folk were collapsing in the sun-baked streets; out here at Montauk, it was bleak and cold and foggy and uncomfortable, and the wood fires burning in the great lounge of the hotel were a welcome sight. A charming house, perhaps, but all we seemed to see were bellhops, bellhops in neat maroon uniforms, and seemingly no guests. This is not the day, not the year of the big hotel. Long Island never has had very many of them. Formerly there were some huge houses, practically all of them upon her south rim, facing the sea. Fire or the wreckers have done away with most of them now. But the Island has many smaller hostels, and charming houses they are apt to be; as a rule set in lawns and surrounded by broad verandahs. *Dolly* and I found such an inn that July evening back at East Hampton. It was a remodeled village house, and while Dolly was permitted to forage overnight in the yard, I was led to a huge old-fashioned room, filled with comfortable old-fashioned furniture; like the bedroom of a farmhouse, but with "genuine New Orleans gin-fizzes" and other accompaniments of modern civilization close at hand.

It is five final miles from Montauk town and Fort Pond Bay to Montauk Light—the beginning and the end of all things New Yorkish. In between there is a large bay—Great Pond—almost like an inland lake, which serves as an admirable seaplane base; and then—the Light.

You see it from a long way off, standing like a sentinel against the eastern sky. And when you come close to it, it seems to rise abruptly right out of the old Atlantic. Around it there is a half-abandoned wooden inn, a fine windmill, a turning point for the concrete road, a generous parking place—nothing else. The Light rises dominant over land and sea alike. You can see it from many miles away. From the ocean it must be an impressive sight.

The beginning and the end of things; the beginning of the state of empire, or the end—just as you may choose to put it. Once, a few years ago, I was at Lands End in Cornwall. A guide directed me atop of a slender, precipitous rock.

"Now you are the first man in England," said he.

"Oh, let's give the King a break," I replied. "Let him be the first man in England; I am quite content to be the last."

It is all in the way you look at things.

It must be tremendous to be at Montauk of a stormy winter day and see the great waves come breaking up over that abrupt promontory; to know that the sea is wily and uncertain and that mother earth is stable and a refuge always; to have the thick fog come in about you and the strong light atop of the tall tower become faint and almost impotent. It is at a place like Montauk that the forces of nature become elemental, that one sees at close range the eternal contest waged between land and sea; and gives full credit to the inherent strength and force of both.

If you drive down the Island on the North Shore you will be almost sure to return upon the South, so different in its character. Once you have passed the Shinnecock Hills, still inhabited by the descendants of the tribe—although it is quite a number of years since a full-blooded Shinnecock has been known to exist—you will find the country pretty level. And the towns along the main highway are almost continuous after the Hamptons: Quogue, the Moriches, Bellport, Patchogue, Sayville, Islip, Bay Shore, Babylon, Amityville—all the way through to Freeport, which is a considerable town and an eternal refuge for old-time actors, especially of the vaudeville fraternity.

You will see fascinating side roads going off all the way toward the near-by sea, and you will be tempted to take every one of them. At Tangier is a highway (marked "Private") that leads to Smith Point, at the east end of the Great South Bay, and if you were to take it you would come in a few miles to one of the few unchanged parts of the south shore of Long Island. Here, for a little more than two hundred years, a certain distinguished family of Smith has held to its homestead. The present house (built 1810) is the third of the line and is a comfortable and generous old-fashioned residence. In front of it there used to be a huge iron caldron, used for trying out blubbers when whales came very close to Long Island.

The genealogy of all the Long Island Smiths is a rather complicated thing. You see there is one branch—up on the North Shore near Smithtown Branch—and these are all Bull Smiths, descendants of a redoubtable ancestor who was reputed to use a bull instead of a horse on his farm and moreover to ride it fearlessly upon occasion; hence the nickname that stuck all the years. And when you get to the South Shore here are the Tangier Smiths, descended from one William Smith, who once was English governor of Tangier in Africa, or something of that sort. And these, in case you wish to know, were the beginnings of the important Smith clan of the Long Island.

Many miles it is before you come to Freeport, on the South Country Road, more generally known now as the Merrick Road, which became so crowded with traffic that it was necessary, some years since, to give it relief, by creating a parallel thoroughfare—Sunrise Highway—alongside it. But if you are really interested in seeing the South Shore you will stick to the old road. It passes through the hearts of the villages and the larger towns and gives you at least a fair glimpse of their life and activities. And, before you come to Freeport, you make a sharp turn to the left and you are driving over the marshes straight out to Jones Beach.

In other days, when first I came to live in the Big City, we used to think a good deal of going down to Manhattan Beach or Brighton or even Coney Island. The nicest way to go down to the sea from Brooklyn in those pleasant days of a quarter of a century or more ago was on the small trains of the Brighton Line. It had begun as a steam railroad with trains in and out of the Flatbush Avenue terminal of the Long Island. In my day this had been changed and the Brighton line had been made electric, with trains from Brooklyn Bridge and even from Park Row, Manhattan. One other route shared its aristocratic prestige. This was the Manhattan Beach branch of the Long Island, whose larger steam trains departed from the old Long Island City terminal close to the East 34th Street Ferry. This was even more swanky than the Brighton route. Some of its trains had parlor-cars, and on racing days the elect were pretty well-dressed as they rode aboard them.

Manhattan Beach was (as its name might indicate) chiefly for Manhattanites, while Brighton Beach was the ocean paradise for Brooklyn folk. The only way you went from one to the other was to ride for a few hundred feet on the Marine Railway, a transportation freak which charged ten cents to ride one way on its trains —and got it. The alternative was to climb over a high fence with barbed wire, and probably get arrested into the bargain.

Brighton had a fine hotel and a fine racetrack, but Manhattan Beach certainly was the more elegant. It had two splendid hotels, one for the crowd and the other, the Oriental, for the elect. You ate, sumptuously, on the piazza of the Manhattan Beach Hotel and listened to Gilmore's Band in the near-by pavilion, but if you went on to the piazza of the Oriental a blue-coated policeman would ask you as to your business there. It was that exclusive. It turned up its nose at mere transients.

Somewhere between the two was the tiny beach and the bathing pavilion (more admissions), and squarely in front of the Manhattan Beach Hotel, the pavilion where Gilmore played—and Anton Seidl too. Sometimes they also had light opera there. But one best recalls the concerts. When Patrick Gilmore played the *1812 Overture* trained gunners at the far end of the beach brought in the cannon fire—at just the right moment. It all was quite wonderful. Lillian Russell used to enjoy it, and so did Pete Dailey, Diamond Jim Brady, and Mayor Gaynor, and Big Tim and Little Tim Sullivan, and a lot of other celebrities of those days.

And Coney Island—then as now—was Coney Island, far less expensive and far less elegant. It had its own assortment of small railroads, and if you wished to go down for a nickel you could ride on the new Coney Island & Brooklyn trolleys—the Smith Street cars, with the bright red dashboards; not very quickly, but if you were in good company what was the hurry, anyway? A good many people seemed to feel that way about it. On pleasant summer days the Smith Street trolleys were almost always overcrowded.

At the one end of this spit of ocean beach was the exclusive cottage colony of Sea Gate, and at the other end, the perennially popular Sheepshead Bay, with its own fine racetrack. In the five brief miles between them, everything else in the world. Coney has changed a bit. I recall as a boy the great wooden elephant which rose, seven stories high, like a Trojan horse, above all else and had fleeting ambitions to be a hotel; and I was well-grown when Fred Thompson and Skip Dundy, flushed with their success with *A Trip to the Moon* at the Buffalo exposition, went down there and made a great killing with their Luna Park. But it did not seem as if Sheepshead Bay would ever change, with its fine lawns and its shore dinners. They tell me that its successor, Belmont Park, is a more beautiful place, but that seems hard to believe.

All this, as prelude to Jones Beach.

Jones Beach is vast, Jones Beach is modern, Jones Beach is magnificent. Good architects and landscape gardeners have done their best to make it what it is and have made a grand success of all of it. . . . The distances are tremendous. There is no crowding. Gone are the stuffy little trains with sweating human beings pressed into their narrow aisles, the open trolley-cars with men hanging on to their running boards. Truth to tell there is no railroad whatsoever at Jones Beach, not even a trolley line. Laugh that off, if you can. There is a branch of the Long Island over at the adjoining Long Beach, a place which has had its ups and downs; mostly downs. But to Jones Beach you ride on hard paved roads, pay a modest toll for admission for your car, and another for its parking. There are plenty of charges and many regulations. But the charges are not high, and the regulations are reasonable—and probably necessary for the safeguarding of so many people.

Ten or twelve years ago, there was no Jones Beach—just that long sandy spit that runs east and west so many, many miles and separates the Great South Bay from the open ocean. There were occasional colonies upon it, relying for their connection with the mainland on crude little ferries, and at Fire Island (where there is a particularly famous lighthouse) there once was a large and barnlike summer hotel, which my distinguished fellow townsman, the late Rosewell P. Flower, governor of the state, brought to public attention during a serious smallpox scare when he commandeered it and turned it into an isolation hospital. But on the entire length of the long spit in those days, there was nothing modern, nothing fine, nothing more than barely reachable.

Perhaps with our Jones Beaches we do progress after all, even though memories of the old Brighton and the old Manhattan beaches persist; and we still have Coney Island; the one place that we might most easily have spared of all.

No chronicle of Long Island, no matter how brief, may omit mention of a group of communities rather closely gathered in its heart.

Of these the oldest, by many years, is Hempstead. Formerly it stood upon a great and arid plain—its own heath, as it were, which ran nearly all the way across the island, from the one shore to the other. This broad flat terrain across the island, always has been a sort of communal property, held in fee by the town, which possesses many curious charter rights. Hempstead is a very old town. This is shown by its chief lion—old St. George's Church, at Front and Greenwich streets, first built in 1704. The parish's charter was granted by King George II, and its most prized possession is the silver communion service presented to it by Queen Anne and now shown only at Christmas and at Easter.

Hempstead closely adjoins Garden City, and Garden City, in its inception at least, was a product of the imagination of another dreamer, that shrewd and never-too-happy Scotch merchant of the New York of three-quarters of a century ago—Alexander T. Stewart.

Stewart, once his several merchandising enterprises had come into fruition and were pouring money into his pockets, began to dream of many things—factories, hotels, even a model hotel for working girls (this last he built, in lower Park Avenue, New York, and it continued as a hotel until but a few years ago, although *not* for working girls), finally a whole model community for working people. This was Garden City, modeled after similar communities in England. For its site he purchased a large sector of the Hempstead Plain, and there he presently began the erection of a town. There was to be a great church (possibly a cathedral), shops, a fine hotel, schools of reputation, pleasant homes of every sort. To make the place more accessible he decided to build his own railroad from New York to the new town. At that moment there were several competing rail lines upon Long Island, and Stewart took advantage of this and tied himself with the North Shore, which took over the operation of his road and eventually extended it through to Bethpage and to Babylon upon the South Shore of the Island. There was nothing miserly about the vision of Alexander T. Stewart.

But he did not live to see this dream come true. When he died (in 1876) the Garden City project was less than half finished. The railroad was running, there were streets and houses and two fine boarding-schools, one for boys and one for girls. But no working people. The place was as ill-adapted for them as was his magnificent Park Avenue Hotel. The Garden City hotel was uncompleted, and there was no sign of any future cathedral. It all looked pretty hopeless.

Yet the project did not die. Stewart's widow made it her life work to build and finish the cathedral. It took seven years and over three million dollars to do the job. But it was a thorough and a beautiful one. The Protestant Episcopal Cathedral of the Incarnation, standing in its own immaculate grounds, is one of the most beautiful Gothic churches in America. It is a cathedral in miniature, and yet not so very miniature. It is 170 feet long, and the tip of its slender spire rises 207 feet above the Hempstead Plain and surveys the countryside for miles around. The man who dreamed the dream lies buried in the crypt; beside him, the woman who made the dream come true. At least A. T. Stewart is *supposed* to be buried in the crypt. His body was once stolen, from its first resting-place in the burying ground of old St. Mark's Church in New York City. Some incredulous folk still refuse to believe that it ever was recovered. But whether or not, Stewart's soul and Stewart's vision triumphed—and that is always vastly more important.

Other men came along and finished the hotel, upon a magnificent scale; made it a superb and stately structure, of which you can see only a vestige of the original—and then only upon the closest examination. Houses came a-plenty, smart shops and many of them, a great publishing house built its workshops there. . . . Garden City came into its own, with a vengeance.

And as Garden City has come into its own, so has Long Island. Geographically a part of New York State, physically rather completely separated from it, living to no small extent a life of her own, her traditions, her stolid conservatism, New England rather than upstate, she is, none the less, pretty firmly bound to the rest of the commonwealth by the powerful single link of the metropolitan city of New York.

Year upon year, metropolitan New York spreads more definitely, more distinctly, out over the Island. It has, seemingly, room for millions more; homes of every sort, large or small, simple or elaborate, to greet them all. It is practically metropolitan city all the way now to the east boundary of Nassau County, further still along the two main rims of the Island. Eventually it may be city well through Suffolk. The thing is not impossible, not unthinkable. All the while new pathways are being cut across it, off toward the east; and traffic crowds upon these almost as soon as they are open and ready for it.

Yet it will be a long time indeed before the Big City comes to swallow up completely the quiet life and the long-established traditions of eastern Long Island—the slumbering shores of the Peconics. For years, generations, centuries to come, Montauk Light will continue to rise upon the treeless, wind-swept plateau, majestic in its very loneliness; upon the one side the waste of the open sea, upon the other, the waste of the open land . . . the far-eastern sentinel of the pathway of empire, the beacon that points distinctly toward its strength and vastness and eternal progress. That's the imperial state of New York.